PRAISE FOR LOUISE J. KAPLAN

On *The Domesday Dictionary*

"A dictionary pertinent to the times. A work to be read with hypnotizing shock."—*Newsweek*

"Excellent encyclopedia of the folklore of the Atomic Age . . . A factual, terrifying and very funny book."—*Washington Star*

"Measured and brilliant handling of the tragic irony which in itself would make the book a delight and perhaps even a weapon the Great Lost Cause which the definition of the human imagination and of human anything appears to have become."—W. S. Merwin

"*The Domesday Dictionary* is an imaginative work. It integrates paradox with infuriatingly true characterizations in a surprising and original manner."—Theodor Reik

"One of the season's most interesting books . . . A striking critique of 20th century life and thought."—*Wilmington Delaware Journal*

"A brilliantly done job."—William Styron

"A sleeper in more ways than one. In format and style it is unusual. The authors do a fascinating job on contemporary civilization."—*New Haven Register*

On *The Family Romance of the Impostor Poet Thomas Chatterton*

"Clinical psychologist Louise Kaplan combines meticulous scholarship with shrewd and mostly jargon-free insights into the dynamics of imposture."—Dennis Drabelle, *Washington Post Book World*

"Fascinating and often highly illuminating . . . Louise J. Kaplan approaches this remarkable story as a psychoanalyst with a special interest in the problems of adolescence . . . The book is well worth reading. Chatterton was an extraordinary individual, and he turns out to be even more extraordinary in realistic close-up than in romantic legend."—John Gross, *The New York Times*

"What raises Kaplan's biography above the norm is her study of Chatterton as a precocious and neurotic adolescent . . . Her presentation of a highly talented fatherless boy surrounded by adoring female family is very convincing."—Anstiss Drake, *Chicago Tribune*

"Louise Kaplan has the gift of bringing to life any person or subject of interest to her."—Judith Rossner

"At last, a psycho-biography that works . . . a rich and illuminating mix of biography, history and psychoanalytic theory."—Vicki Goldberg

"A kind of psychoanalytic detective story with many of the trappings of a picaresque novel . . . a thoroughly unusual and enjoyable piece of work."—Morris Dickstein

On *Adolescence*

"Kaplan has blended poetry, scholarship, and sensitive psychological insight to produce a major contribution to the literature of human development."—Aaron Esman, M.D.

"A groundbreaking book that redefines the meaning of adolescence."—*Publishers Weekly*

"Kaplan gives a fresh interpretation of that phase of human existence about which nobody agrees . . . a naturally lyrical style enables the author to do what adolescents do: to weave past, present and future on a thread of imagination and create new possibilities."—*Contemporary Psychology*

"The author's magisterial style and psychological insight combine to make this book a watershed in the study of adolescence."—*Cultural Information Service*

"Kaplan's understanding of these traumatic years is a milestone in the literature of child development."—*Tulsa Daily World*

"Parents will embrace this professional's eloquent understanding, and Kaplan's colleagues will surely benefit from her empathy and insight."—*The Boston Sunday Globe*

"At last, adolescence is treated with the respect and understanding that has long been its due . . . Dazzling scholarship, warm sympathy, original insights and brilliant interpretation make it a must for anyone who is puzzled by the behavior of adolescents."—Bel Kaufman

"Brilliant, original, fascinating, poetical, beautiful, vibrant, spontaneous, clear, compassionate, eloquent, dazzling, insightful, warm, sympathetic, sensitive, deep, and aesthetically pleasurable. When so much jargon is lavished on adolescence, it is refreshing to obtain an original portrait of this enigmatic age."—E. James Anthony, M.D.

On *Oneness and Separateness*

"Sound, knowledgeable and powerfully written . . . unified by Dr. Kaplan's unblinking focus on real human babies and how they act and by her own clear and lyrical voice."—*The Boston Globe*

"An eloquent and beautiful book . . . a stunning interpretive drama of the mother-child relationship that reaches into the very mind of the baby."—Molly Haskell

"Here is a book I would give to every mother- and father-to-be . . . Kaplan makes the first years of life come alive in such a tactile, empathetic way that the reader not only feels with the infant, but for the child who lives on in himself."—Nancy Friday

On *No Voice is Ever Wholly Lost*

"Scholarly and poetic, *No Voice is Ever Wholly Lost* speaks to both the intellect and the heart, offering profound and healing insights into loss, grief, and reconnection."—Judith Viorst, author of *Necessary Losses*

"With all the self-help junk passing for books, it's a pleasure to read a work with depth, vision and scholarship on a subject that merits these strengths."—Betty Rollin, author of *Last Wish* and *First You Cry*

"A lovely, deeply comforting meditation on loss, grief, and the triumphs of human survival."—Martha Lear, author of *Heartsounds*

On *Female Perversions*

"This masterful study breaks new ground in our understanding of sexuality, gender roles and the way modern society trivializes erotic expression."—*Publishers Weekly*

"A great discovery, a new lens focused on the female condition."—Fay Weldon, *Allure*

"A fascinating and ambitious new study."—*The New York Times Sunday Book Review*

"Lucid, provocative, and tremendously literate."—*Voice Literary Supplement*

"Kaplan has done that rare thing—to write a book for a general audience that can also interest the more narrow technical audience of psychoanalysts. This book is that almost lost phenomena in the contemporary corporate publishing world: an intellectually accomplished book accessible to a general readership."—*Psychoanalytic Psychology*

"Written with a sense of moral courage, breaking new ground in various ways about gender and society, cultural and political supports that enhance but also diminish who we are as infants, children, adolescents, and adults."—*Psychoanalytic Books*

CULTURES OF FETISHISM

By Louise J. Kaplan

The Domesday Dictionary (with Donald M. Kaplan and Armand Schwerner)

Oneness and Separateness: From Infant to Individual

Adolescence: The Farewell to Childhood

The Family Romance of the Impostor-Poet Thomas Chatterton

Female Perversions: The Temptations of Emma Bovary

No Voice Is Ever Wholly Lost

CULTURES OF FETISHISM

Louise J. Kaplan

CULTURES OF FETISHISM

© Louise J. Kaplan, 2006.

First published in 2006 by
PALGRAVE MACMILLAN™
175 Fifth Avenue, New York, N.Y. 10010 and
Houndmills, Basingstoke, Hampshire, England RG21 6XS
Companies and representatives throughout the world.

PALGRAVE MACMILLAN is the global academic imprint of the Palgrave
Macmillan division of St. Martin's Press, LLC and of Palgrave Macmillan Ltd.
Macmillan® is a registered trademark in the United States, United Kingdom
and other countries. Palgrave is a registered trademark in the European
Union and other countries.

ISBN-13: 978–1–4039–6968–2
ISBN-10: 1–4039–6968–X

Library of Congress Cataloging-in-Publication Data

Kaplan, Louise J.
    Cultures of fetishism / Louise J. Kaplan
        p. cm.
    Includes bibliographical references and index.
    ISBN-10: 1–4039–6968–X (alk. paper)
        1. Psychoanalysis and culture. 2. Social sciences and psychoanalysis.
    3. Fetishism. I. Title.

BF175.4.C84K37 2006
150.19'5—dc22   2006043197

A catalogue record for this book is available from the British Library.

Design by Newgen Imaging Systems (P) Ltd., Chennai, India.

First edition: October 2006

10 9 8 7 6 5 4 3 2 1

Printed in the United States of America.

For Ariel and Marae

CONTENTS

PERMISSIONS

The author gratefully acknowledges permission to quote:

From *Writing Lives, Principia Biographia* by Leon Edel, copyright © by Leon Edel, 1984, 1959. Used by permission of W.W. Norton and Company, New York.

From *Robots*, by Daniel Ichbiah, translated from *Genese d'un peuple artificiel* by Ken Kincaid. Published by Harry N. Abrams, Inc. New York. All rights reserved.

From "Full Pockets, Empty Lives" by Paul L. Wachtel, copyright by Paul L. Wachtel, 1999.

The author also gratefully acknowledges:

Peter Rudnysky, editor of *American Imago*. The introductory pages of chapter four, "The Body of a Woman: Making Films." are derived from a paper I delivered at the spring meeting of Division 39 on April 14, 1993, and subsequently published in *American Imago* Winter, 1993, Vol. 50, published by Johns Hopkins University Press. Chapter Four is a much expanded version of some of the ideas in "Fits and Misfits."

Howard Levy's classic *Chinese Footbinding: The History of a Curious Erotic Custom*. Levy's extensive research helped to inform the details of the imposturous memoir in chapter three, "My Beloved and Terrible Lotus," purportedly written by A Hsui. I also thank Brian McMahon, the permissions editor at Prometheus Books, for granting permission for this use of Levy's research.

ONE

FETISHISM AND THE
FETISHISM STRATEGY

This book is about *the fetishism strategy* and the cultures that breed and nurture that strategy. You will not find "the fetishism strategy" in your dictionary, listed among the "extravagant, irrational devotions to some material object, idea or practice"[1] that define the word "Fetishism."

The irrational devotions you might find listed in a standard dictionary are:

1. The belief and use of magical fetishes; natural objects such as feathers, or artificial objects such as wooden carvings which are believed to have the power to protect its owner because of animation of the spirit embodied in the object.
2. The displacement of erotic interest onto an object, such as a shoe or a part of the body, such as a foot.
3. A devotion to a religion or to religious and cultural practices marked by the use of magical fetishes.

Most people do not consult dictionaries to tell them what fetishism means. They assume that the word "fetishism" has something to do with bizarre sexual practices of one kind or another. In the course of reading this book, you will come to appreciate that the need to transform something unfamiliar and intangible into something familiar and tangible is one of the major principles of the fetishism strategy. In that sense, an appreciation of the ingenuities of the strategy can help to make sense of the power of sexual fetishism, where some people need to employ a familiar tangible object, like a shoe, a whip, or a garter belt to ease their way into that otherwise frightening activity of sexual intercourse.

The fetishism strategy is a strange and unfamiliar term. Unlike fetishism, the sexual perversion that usually heads up a diagnostic inventory of bizarre sexual practices, the fetishism strategy is not even mentioned as a phenomena that might help to explain the power of the irrational devotion to fetishism. Outside the realms of social criticism, philosophy, and psychoanalysis, very few people have ever thought about it.

It is hard to dispel the commonplace notion that the strategy of fetishism must be somehow similar to sexual fetishism, or perhaps something akin to the shoes and whips and garter belts that usually accompany the practice of sexual fetishism. Compared to the strategy of fetishism, sexual fetishism, bizarre as it sometimes can be, is a relatively friendly and familiar term. Unfamiliar terms, like the fetishism strategy, are off-putting. You can't quite pin it down with a handy definition. Until you understand what it means, it is intangible and ambiguous, and therefore a little frightening. Familiar terms, like fetishism, even when they represent acts that are irrational and perverse, are reassuring.

The fetish object, the shoe or the whip or the garter belt, is a tangible thing; something that can be seen and felt. It reassures the person who sees or holds it that he need not fear that he is entering into unfamiliar, dangerous territories. It calms the anxieties that can sometimes arise in connection with the uncertain vitalities of the living, breathing human body.

It takes courage to allow yourself to enter a realm of something so unfamiliar and enigmatic as the fetishism strategy. Therefore, let us embark on our explorations by standing for a few moments on firmer ground.

Let us begin in the world of the familiar, with a few popular associations to the more ordinary term, fetishism. These associations will be our fetishes, the props and tangible objects we will use to reassure ourselves about exploring the mysteries of the fetishism strategy. Holding on to something familiar is a good way to approach the unfamiliar, and when you don't need the props anymore you can let go of them. Little children do this with their security blankets, and when they are ready to move on to a new stage of development, they get rid of them—or maybe hang on to a little shred as a reminder of feeling safe. As we shall be seeing, social critics, philosophers, and psychoanalysts also hold on to their props of safe, familiar ideas, especially when they are about to embark on some new and as yet unknown formulation or theory. At various turns in our journey, it will be useful to fall back on these more familiar versions of fetishism. However, in the end, in order to move on to a new way of participating in the world around us, we will be safer and more true to ourselves when we keep in touch with the elusive meanings of the fetishism strategy. The more familiar forms of fetishism cannot be trusted. They are imbued with falsehood. This should not surprise us.

The word fetish came to the English language via the Portuguese *feitiço*, meaning false or false values.[2] *Feitiço* was used to describe the veneration and worship of seemingly useless objects that the Portuguese explorers had discovered in African religions. Furthermore, like many words deriving from the Latin *factitious*, fetish or *feitiço* suggests mask, masquerade, disguise, fake. In turn, fetish is derived from the French *factice*, fictitious, false, or artificial. Another derivative from the French is *feint*, feigned or simulated.

In general, fetishism refers to the practice of worshipping. Fetishist refers to the person doing the worshipping. Fetish refers to the object being worshipped. And, as I suggested at the outset, what usually comes to mind first and foremost are the bizarre sexual practices of fetishism, and the sort of person who is irrationally devoted to these practices, the fetishist. The fetishist is thought of as some sort of weirdo who desperately worships his fetish, perhaps a pair of stiletto shoes or boots (which either he or his sexual partner may wear), which he employs to enable and enhance his sexual escapades. Aside from the infamous stilettos, the fetish objects that come most readily to mind are the garments worn by prostitutes, porn stars, movie starlets, and just plain ordinary teenagers, mothers, and grandmothers who want to look sexy: black stockings, preferably with seams up the back, tightly-laced corsets, lacy lingerie, garter belts, panties, bustiers and bras, or, as in recent years, some kind of underwear as outerwear.

In a *Fashions of The Times* article, "Rubber Maids," William Norwich described what was then the very latest word in fetish fashions; rubber and latex dresses, pants and other articles of clothing designed to feel and look like a second skin. "Its no stretch to suggest that fashion is becoming kinky . . . The line between fashion and fetish is blurred."[3]

A few years later these obvious forms of fashion fetishism had all but disappeared from the runways and been replaced by a return to the respectabilities of the days of yore: flowing chiffon, organdy, crushed velvet, puffed sleeves, lace inlays, and embroidered collars. Despite their innocent surface, these fashions from grandma's attic exuded sexual innuendo. After all, white stockings, lace and velvet are standard fetish items. Childlike purity is as much a sexual turn-on as latex and rubber pants or stilettos.

Of course, there are other fetish garments and fetishistic practices that do not derive their attraction and desirability from sexual innuendo. For example, there is the altogether everyday, seemingly rational devotions to purchasing, owning, and wearing the latest designer outfits produced by Versace, Dolce and Gabbana, Prada, Hermes, Marc Jacobs, and Chanel tweeds à la the new "Mama" Madonna, who, temporarily at least, traded in her career as an underwear-as-outerwear pop icon for motherhood and authoring books for children. These usually high-priced designer label garments are respectable and fit to be seen in the best places. Those who are attracted to these fashions sense there is something vaguely fetishistic about the fashion advertisements that bombard them from billboards, television, newspapers, and magazines. However, they don't usually think that their needs to possess these objects might be reflections of their personal irrational devotions or a worship of false values.

But they are wrong. Material objects that are regarded with extravagant reverence and sought after with a compelling, "I've got to have it," are fetishes. Such items could be almost anything—chiffon scarves or Manolo Blahnik stiletto sandals, or Prada handbags or Chanel jackets, or Gucci sneakers, or Perla bras. Or, to leave the world of fashion, there are kitchen utensils, or cell phone attachments, iPods or the latest SUV or Moto Guzzi, or a hot new Baby Einstein CD that we've been told will transform our babies and toddlers into geniuses. The person afflicted with this form of fetishism might even concede, "I have a fetish for kitchen gadgets." "I have a fetish for Manolo Blahniks."

If we persist in exploring the varied associations to the word fetishism, we discover that any excessive activity or heightened devotion could be referred to as a fetish. Bertrand Russell once described the German military as "a goose stepping army that makes a fetish of discipline."[4] Any false belief that is widely held by a group of people could be called a fetish, such as Theodore Dreiser's "the fetish that birth and station presuppose superiority."[5] Any activity or practice that is engaged in with a sense of urgency and necessity might be regarded as fetishistic. "She suffers from a fetish of weekly housecleaning." "He has a fetish for tying his left shoelace before tying his right one."

In recent years, contemporary social and literary critics have taken to using "fetishism" in a manner that suggests they are aware, consciously or unconsciously, of the implicit duplicity, falsehood, and fakery that is inherent in the term.

In a *New Yorker* essay on Diane Arbus' photographs, Judith Thurman protests that even though Arbus' subjects;—the freaks, female impersonators, gangsters, dwarfs, groupies, nudists, widows, fetishists, diaper-derby contestants and ethnic beauties—may have been objects of her ardent lust, "she never fetishized them."[6] Aside from the fact that she is using the term pejoratively, Thurman's "fetishized" is ambiguous. Does she mean Arbus never eroticized her subjects? Never falsified them? Never portrayed them as objects of worship? Most likely she used the word loosely to express an easy-going amalgam of the three possibilities.

Harold Bloom opens his Preface to *Genius* with a dismissal of those Groupthink representatives of the Age of Information, "who have dismissed genius merely as an eighteenth-century fetish."[7] Bloom is claiming that these misguided academic hacks were deceived when they regarded genius as an idea or object of false worship.

Fetishism is imbued with falsehood. Therefore, even honesty can become a fetish—especially in times of deceit. A *New York Times* editorial column by David Brooks entitled "A Fetish of Candor" demonstrates the several ways that the Bush administration, having become addicted to a "slippery" form of honesty, is now "facing an insincerity crisis."[8] The administration "seems to be drunk on truth serum."[9] Thus rather than taking out Saddam and pretending to abide by the rules, Bush scandalized the world "by announcing what he was going to do before doing it." ". . . The administration has taken to honesty like a drunken sailor. It has made a fetish of candor and forthrightness. Things are wildly out of control."[10]

In certain instances, dictionary terms and their commonplace associations are the same or similar. As I indicated, the derivation of the word "fetishism" is usually traced back to the fetish objects that are worshiped by "primitive" or "savage" peoples. Without even knowing about the derivation, many people nevertheless do associate the term "fetishism" with the worship of these "primitive" fetish objects. And, as we arrive at this shared understanding between the dictionary definitions and the commonplace associations to these "primitive" fetish objects, we begin to approach the essential spirit of the fetishism strategy. The "primitive" worship of fetish objects embodies one of the prime principles of the strategy that informs *Cultures of Fetishism*. We have already come across this principle, which entails the substitution of something tangible for something that is otherwise ephemeral and enigmatic.

In the "primitive" cultures, the fetish is typically a natural or artificial object such as a tiger tooth, or crow feather or wood carving of a bear, that is imbued with the power to protect its owner. The fetish object is believed to be inhabited by a god or spirit that can determine the fate of its worshipper.

Here are some questions about the worship of fetish objects. Why not worship the god or spirit directly? Why is there a need, instead, for a tangible object that represents the spirit? Why do human beings get so emotionally invested in objects that are concrete and tangible? In contrast to the god or spirit who is ephemeral and intangible, the fetish exists within the realm of the real and actual world. A fetish can be held, seen, smelled, even heard if it is shaken, and most importantly it can be manipulated at the will of the fetishist.

In this manner, some essentially unknown, intangible, spiritual, and ambiguous "someone" or "something" that seems to have a will and energy of its own, is transformed into something tangible and concretely real and therefore capable of being controlled and manipulated. However, the belief that the gods and spirits, who we cannot touch or see or hear, can be controlled through the possession and manipulation of a fetish is misleading and duplicitous. It is a false belief. And that false belief underlies the principles of the fetishism strategy.

PRINCIPLES OF THE FETISHISM STRATEGY

As I list the five basic principles of the fetishism strategy, one by one, and separate them into neat and orderly categories, it should soon become apparent that they are not entirely distinct. They are shades and reflections of one another. They overlap. They usually operate in tandem.

1. *Fetishism is a mental strategy or defense that enables a human being to transform something or someone with its own enigmatic energy and immaterial essence into something or someone that is material and tangibly real, a form of being that makes the something or someone controllable.* This first principle of the fetishism strategy comes in many guises. It applies to the religious fetish as well as to the sexual fetish.

We will also encounter this first principle in the several ways in which cultures transform human beings into dehumanized commodities. For example, the culture of "Reality TV" depends for its effects and its enormous profits on the commodification of human beings. In contrast to a human being with his or her human energies and vitalities, a commodity is a nonliving thing with no life of its own. However, in the process of submitting to the exploitations of Reality TV, otherwise ordinary human beings are dehumanized and transformed into mechanical, stereotyped representations of actual human beings. They become commodities.

In "The Working Day," the tenth chapter of *Capital*, Karl Marx reveals the "secret" of commodity fetishism. He tells us that a central driving force of Capital is "to absorb the greatest amount of surplus labor."[11] He then explains how this is accomplished. "Capital is dead labour, which vampire-like, lives only by sucking living labour and lives the more, the more labour it sucks."[12] Thus, Marx's theory of *surplus labor* turns out to be nearly identical with the first principle of the fetishism strategy—*a human being transforms other human beings, with their own enigmatic energies and vitalities, into things that are material and tangibly real. Through the process of providing surplus labor value for the capitalist, the worker is transmogrified into a commodity.* Though Marx wrote in the mid nineteenth-century about the transformation of working-class human beings into commodities, what he said then has relevance today in many twenty first-century cultural phenomenon. In a speech, written ten years before the publication of *Capital*, he warned, "All our inventions and progress seem to result in endowing material forces with intellectual life and stultifying human life with a material force."[13]

2. The second principle of the fetishism strategy is a subtle variation of the first one. *Fetishism transforms ambiguity and uncertainty into something knowable and certain and in doing so snuffs out any sparks of creativity that might ignite the fires of rebellion.* The material object, the fetish, is employed to still and silence, bind and dominate, smother and squelch the frighteningly uncontrollable and unknowable energies of someone or something that might otherwise express its own ambiguous vitalities. The unknowable and the ambiguous are experienced as dangerous. The fetish reassures.

3. *Fetishism brings certain details into the foreground of experience in order to mask and disguise other features that are thus cast into the shadows and margins and background.* For example, the fetishism strategy employs sexuality and sexual behaviors to mask an entire range of desires, motives, and defenses. The all-too-apparent, one could say glitteringly present, right-before-our-eyes sexual behaviors command our attention, hampering our capacity to see anything that might lie beneath the surface. *The powerful presence of the erotic surface disguises and covers over the absences that would otherwise remind us of something traumatic.* The dramatic and vivid visibility of the fetish object serves to dazzle and confuse, blinding the viewer from other, potentially more troubling implications that are thus cast into the shadows. The surface layer, the images that captivate the visual field, the words that clamor to be heard, are masquerades.

So, to get beyond the masquerades that pose as erotic turn-ons to something more challenging and meaningful, we have only to look over an official inventory of the various sexual perversions. As our eyes go down the inventory, from top to bottom, we cannot help noticing the vast discrepancy between the relatively commonplace and relatively innocent-sounding *fetishism* that typically heads up the inventory and the seemingly more horrifying and bizarre perversion that is usually placed at the foot, *necrophilia*,[14] the need to have sexual intercourse with a dead body.

Unlike *fetishism* which can be understood as a homey preference or an occasional enthusiasm, *necrophilia* is more blatantly *outré* and dangerously unfamiliar. However, after many years of thinking about the encompassing nature of fetishism, which has long been recognized as the ruling and guiding perversion that plays a role in all perversions, I have come to believe that necrophilia isn't so far away from fetishism as I had originally thought. Necrophilia, it turns out, is the key to a less obvious but, in certain crucial respects, more essential meaning of fetishism.

In *necrophilia*, sexual arousal, erection, and orgasm are possible only with a corpse or a dismembered, dying body. Usually, for the male fetishist at least, a female corpse is the preferred enthusiasm, but for some male necrophiliacs, the dead or dying body of a male, a child, or an animal does the trick. Necrophilia, so far as we know the rarest of all the perversions, nevertheless expresses succinctly a facet of the fetishism strategy that is common to all the perversions. In its larger, more encompassing meaning, fetishism is about the deadening and dehumanization of otherwise alive and therefore threateningly dangerous, unpredictable desires.

Therefore, though zoophilia, bestiality, and necrophilia seem a far cry from the comparatively normal sounding fetishism, with which our catalogs of perversion usually begin, the household pets and dying or dead humans and animals are as much fetishistic objects as are the already lifeless and inanimate leather boot, lace garter belt, corset, stiletto shoe, rubberized mackintosh, or blue velvet bathrobe.

And this transformation of living, animate substance into something dead or deadening is the fourth principle of the fetishism strategy. We might even call it the necrophilic principle.

4. *The more dangerous and unpredictable the threat of desire, the more deadened or distanced from human experience the fetish object must be.* By virtue of its fantasized or actual isolation from the woman's (or man's) breathing, responding, sensing, pulsating, experiencing body, the fetish object, unlike the sexual partner, can be controlled and manipulated. A sexual fetish, for example, is significantly more reliable than a living person. It expects neither commitment nor emotional engagement. *When the full identity of the sexual object is alive, with all manner of threateningly, dangerously unpredictable vitalities, the desire he or she arouses must be invested in an object that is knowable and predictable.* Unlike a fully alive, human being with dangerous, unpredictable desires who must be wooed and courted, fetish objects are relatively safe, easily available, and undemanding of reciprocity.

And this leads us to the fifth and final principle of the fetishism strategy, a corollary to the necrophilic principle, an extension of it that exposes the death drive hidden in the folds of the erotic object. This fifth principle, so intimately involved with aggression and destruction, is the one that seems furthest removed from ordinary life and ordinary fetishism. Yet, as I shall be showing in future chapters, it is the key to the strategy of fetishism.

The philosophers who understand the fetishism strategy don't necessarily transform the fifth principle into something more ordinary and accessible. However, sometimes their dense impenetrabilities do yield a measure of understanding about these very complicated matters. With a little bit of patience and courage, we enter into their unfamiliar worlds and are rewarded with a glow of transparency that feels just right. And even if we don't get to a full understanding of their words right off the bat, they ring of some truths that are accessible.

I have found that the French philosopher Jacques Derrida, who is notorious for ambiguity and impenetrability, is worth the effort, particularly when I am trying to solve a problem in my own work. His *Archive Fever* is a reference point for several of the chapters that follow. In this challenging monograph, he spoke of the death drive, the *anarchivic, archiviolithic* drive that disguises or paints or tints itself in an erotic color. He says:

> This impression of erogenous color draws a mask right on the skin. In other words the archiviolithic drive is never present in person, neither in itself nor in its effects. It leaves no monument, it bequeaths no document of its own. As inheritance, it leaves only its erotic simulacrum, its pseudonym in painting, its sexual idols, its masks of seduction: lovely impressions. These impressions are perhaps the very origins of what is so obscurely called the beauty of the beautiful. Memories of death.[15]

Derrida's way of giving voice and substance to an ambiguous, intangible force like the death drive helped me to formulate the fifth principle of the fetishism strategy.

5. *The death drive tints itself in erotic color. The impression of erogenous color draws a mask right on the skin.* As I shall be demonstrating in several chapters, this tint of erotic color can make deadly practices invisible to the naked eye. But if we learn how to detect the skin that lies beneath the mask, we also learn how to protect it from deadly practices. The chapter "The Body of a Woman: Making Films" concludes with films about the deadly practice of skin cutting, a suddenly popular perversion that inspired a rash of skin-cutting films during the past two decades. By the time we come to that chapter and "Writing on the Skin," the chapter that follows it, we will have encountered many other instances of the fifth principle of the fetishism strategy. The glow of transparency in Derrida's dense rumination will shine through.

Each of the chapters that follow will illustrate one or several principles of the fetishism strategy. It is impossible to capture this defensive strategy in all its guises, all at once. Nevertheless, at each confrontation with each succeeding illustration of one or another principle of the strategy, there will be some new light shed on the entire, fuller meaning of the fetishism strategy. The dissimulations that we will encounter are not outright and blatant lies. As with the Bush administration's fetish of candor, they may even employ surface truths to disguise and mask falsehood.

The second chapter takes a new look at Freud's six-page paper, "Fetishism." In that paper, Freud introduces seven characters to illustrate a few of his ideas about the psychological attributes of some typical fetish objects. However, the most important character turns out to be the eighth character, Freud himself, as he unconsciously and unknowingly becomes a victim of the fetishism strategy.

If it weren't an oversimplification that overlooks the way in which the principles of fetishism operate in tandem, it might be concluded that Freud's paper "Fetishism" best illustrates principle five: *The death drive that tints itself in erotic color. The impression of erogenous color drawing a mask right on the skin.*

Freud starts out his essay "Fetishism" referring to the erotic advantages of the fetish employed in sexual fetishism. He concludes his paper with a disparagement of the female genitals and a description of the Chinese custom of mutilating the woman's foot. In the beginning of the paper the erotic tint successfully covers over the destructive aggression that finally gets expressed at the conclusion.

One of the things that fascinated me about this essay was the way that Freud sets out to describe the psychological components of the sexual fetishism and, in the process of accomplishing his conscious mission, falls under the spell of the fetishism strategy. Side-by-side, almost simultaneously, fetishism, the sexual perversion and fetishism, the defensive strategy that is the subject of this book, are expressed. Unintentionally, Freud's "Fetishism" turns out to illustrate the differences between the two forms of fetishism.

Finally, I became captivated by Freud's off-putting way of understanding the ancient practice of binding and mutilating the feet of Chinese women. After some frequent reading and re-reading of Freud's bizarre interpretation of this bizarre cultural practice, after a while, I felt compelled to ask, "What did footbinding feel like to a woman subjected to this practice.?" How would such a woman regard the practice, which was usually inflicted on her by her mother and grandmother?" Thus Freud's paper inspired me to become an impostor-poet.

The memoir presented in the third chapter, which pretends to be written by a woman named A-Hsui, has actually been written by me. I justify my imposture by claiming that I am giving a voice to a woman who would otherwise be unable to speak. In the concluding chapter, I look back on my rationalization and question it.

Each new exploration,—Freud's "Fetishism" paper, footbinding, the making of films, writing on the skin, the writing of biographies, the training of psychoanalysts, the fetishism of commodities, the designing of robots—opens up a new dimension or layer of the fetishism strategy, until finally the idea that we are surrounded by various cultures of fetishism will not seem as strange as it does now at the outset.

We will be looking into the fantasies of the men and women engaged in the engineering and construction of robots, those creatures that exist somewhere in the twilight zone between living and nonliving matter—mechanical "creatures" that are created to seem alive and human, tinted by their creators in the erotic simulations Derrida speaks of. They are designed to deceive us into believing that they are as lifelike as we are—perhaps even more so.

Our daily lives are permeated by the cultures of fetishism that substitute material objects for spiritual values, that captivate our attention with glittery foregrounds in order to push more troubling and potentially traumatic meanings into the background, shadows, and margins, where we can barely detect them, where they can haunt us invisibly and silently. My aim in writing this book is to bring these troubles into the foreground so that we may recognize them.

By the time you arrive at the concluding chapter, "Cultures of Fetishism," you will have been apprised of the many ways that human beings, usually unknowingly and unconsciously, employ the fetishism strategy in their desperate attempts to alleviate anxiety, depression, and the other so-called mental illnesses.

Diagnostic categories of so-called mental illnesses, such as depression and anxiety, and acts of violence and homicide, are usually based on easily observable, surface behaviors. In this sense of substituting symptom for inner psychological meaning, they could be interpreted as examples of the fetishism strategy. The dramatic and vivid symptom of perversion, for example, presents itself as an attraction toward some kinky sexual behavior and invites our full attention to that behavior, distracting us from the manifold underlying meanings expressed in the sexual acts considered perverse. The fetishism strategy enables these latent meanings to remain hidden; an entire history is enabled to masquerade as a detail, anxiety to masquerade as freedom, depression to masquerade as elation, and hatred to masquerade as love.

These confounding masquerades, where masks of death paint themselves in erotic colors, are not the reserved property of esoteric French philosophers. In the spring of 2004, *The New York Times* weekly *Television* section opened with a feature story evaluating the departing TV series *Sex and the City*. The author, Dinitia Smith, interviewed several well-known feminist theorists who, by and large, went along with the obvious surface message of the alleged sexual freedom exemplified by the show. Fortunately, one of the feminists, Elaine Showalter, caught on to the fetishism strategy and how it had infiltrated the depictions of the lives of the four fictional heroines. For example, Showalter claimed that the heroines' desperate need to purchase and possess Manolo Blahnik and Jimmy Choo stiletto shoes and high fashion, high status pocketbooks and "sexy" underwear, and suggestively seductive outerwear, was not in the service of a liberation of their sexuality. Rather than liberation, these purchases expressed the heroines' responses to their unconscious anxieties about their potentially anarchic, chaotic, unregulated sexuality. According to Showalter,[16] the high status fetish objects served the purpose of anchoring these women in an otherwise frightening "anything goes" social environment. In a social context where sexuality of any kind with anybody, anywhere is permitted and ostensibly celebrated, these status objects do act as fetishes; but, not as fetishes in the conventional notion of that term. Although the fashion fetishes were consciously used by the heroines to enliven and enhance their sexuality, unconsciously they were used to control, bind, and regulate what might otherwise have been experienced as an anxiety-provoking, unruly sexuality.

The fashion fetishes in *Sex in the City* are examples of principle 2 of the fetishism strategy. "The material object, the fetish, is employed to still and silence, bind and dominate, smother and squelch the frighteningly uncontrollable and unknowable energies of someone or something that might otherwise express its own ambiguous vitalities." Moreover, the second principle is operating in tandem with principle 5. "*The death drive tints itself in erotic color. The impression of erogenous color draws a mask right on the skin.*"

This is often the case with fashions that have an obvious erotic surface. The perennial stiletto shoe, which these days boasts the newly fashionable "toe cleavage," is responsible for the deformation and mutilation of women's feet. While some doctors complain about the irreparable damage done to women's feet by stilettos, other doctors, one cannot assess how many, amass a huge fortune by slicing off those parts of a woman's foot that would interfere with her being able to fit into these crippling shoes.

In the 2004 publication *Stiletto*, a handsomely produced, glossy, glittery extravaganza of alluring legs poised on many variations of stilettos, the author tries to be even-handed in her evaluations of the shoes that adorn the pages of her book.[17] But, obviously she has fallen under the spell of the stilettos and would not dream of criticizing them. She dismisses the idea that these steely heels might act as shackles that hobble women's body movements. At one point, she equates the recent furor over stilettos with the uproar that greeted the bobbed hair of the 1920s. As with today's stilettos, the major objections in "the roaring twenties" to women's bobbed hair came from the male medical profession. The doctors were fond of advising women that an excessive cutting of their hair would sap their energies. More horrifying was the medical warning that the shorn hair was likely to grow back on a woman's chin. But none of these warnings succeeded in stopping the fashionistas of those days from bobbing their hair.

As accurate as the author's analogies are in some respects, her comparison of today's stiletto with yesterday's hair bobbing is not convincing. Medical warnings about the stilted gait created by stilettos and the crippling of the foot that results from prolonged wearing of them, are based less on the fantasies of conservative male doctors than on some plainly visible facts. The feet that emerge from prolonged and constant wearing of stilettos *are* crippled. The compensatory tilted posture that is invoked as an effort to maintain balance, generates all manner of aches and pains in the knees and thighs, pelvis and abdomen, and in muscles and joints throughout the body, and may eventually create internal bodily ailments as well. Yet, even knowing all this and experiencing, more or less acutely, the bodily distresses the doctors caution about, many women, young and old, find the appeal of these shoes irresistible. They must have them. They worship them.

Much of the appeal and attraction of the stiletto heel probably has to do with the long-legged illusion it creates. In this regard, the physical appearance of the stiletto-heeled leg bears an uncanny resemblance to descriptions of the bound feet of ancient Chinese women:

> When the foot is forced to arch like a bow, it gives the illusion of being part of the leg. Thus, with the help of high heeled [lotus] shoes, what remains of the original foot becomes the extension of the erect leg. It is quite similar to the effect created by high-heeled shoes. Those stilt-like shoes and boots with heels as high as five to seven inches raise the body dramatically, creating the illusion of lengthened and thinned legs as well as shortened feet. More important, the raised heel alters the sudden break of the line of the leg, making the body appear taller and straighter, away from the dirt, from gravity.[18]

And it must be said that women are the ones who pass these traditions of foot-binding and stiletto fashions on to their female children. Men may be the foot fetishists who fall in love with these shoes and the leggy legs they adorn. However, it is the women who have an irresistible urge to spend a week's salary on the purchase of shoes that bind their feet into distorted shapes.

Are footbinding and the worshipping of foot-crippling shoes the outcomes of being born into a culture of fetishism?

Since *Cultures of Fetishism* could be misconstrued as an exploration of the pathology of social communities, I want to insist that a transfer of terminology from individual psychology to social psychology is not appropriate and is, in fact, misleading. A society cannot have a psychological disorder. A society can, however, encourage and sponsor actions and activities that keep the citizens of that social order enslaved to falsehoods and deceptions. Societies do evolve and they construct cultural strategies that serve to perpetuate themselves. It is characteristic of organized societies that they try to discourage any vitalities and energies that might disrupt or challenge the authority that upholds the social order as it is.

The cultures of fetishism I am addressing in this book are much like the prepared culture in a petri dish that incubates, nourishes, and breeds bacteria, and other living organisms, encouraging them to flourish and proliferate. The only difference—and this difference is crucial,—is that the cultures of fetishism discussed in this book incubate and breed materials that are potentially deadly.

The fetishism strategy aims to silence rebellion and perpetuate conformity. And while there have been other attempts by social critics, philosophers, and psychologists to address the idea of fetishism as a strategic form of cultural discourse, the fundamental premise of most of these writings was to focus attention on the sexual perversion, fetishism. There have been notable exceptions, however, that manage to get away from the sex manual definitions of fetishism.

An enlightening example of this more salient approach is Hal Foster's essay on Dutch still life paintings during the middle of the seventeenth-century. Foster captures exactly the spirit of the cultures of fetishism I will be addressing. Foster discusses the "pronk"[19] (*pronken* means to show off) paintings that depict lavish displays of objects like long clay pipes, gold chalices, fine porcelain platters, and extravagant food like oysters and crystal goblets filled with dark wine; all coated in a luxurious glaze of shellac that captures and "lubricates" the viewer's gaze: "Often in Dutch still life, the inert seems animate, the familiar becomes estranged, and the insignificant seems humanly, even preternaturally significant . . . animate and inanimate states are confused, things are consumed by representations, once homey images return as *unheimlich* (uncanny), a whiff or whisper of death hangs over the scene."[20]

The fetishistic quality of these pronk paintings are even expressed in their official nomenclature, "still life" (*still leven*), "nature morte."[21] But, as Foster reminds us, not every still life is fetishistic, or nearly as fetishistic as the pronk paintings of the seventeenth-century Dutch.

During the seventeenth-century, the Dutch Protestant social order opposed the idea that any material object could have a spiritual value. They rejected what they called the *Fetissos* of the Africans and the crosses and icons of Catholicism as "ridiculous ceremonies."[22] However, "As religious fetishism was suppressed, a commercial fetishism, a fetishism of the commodity was released; the Dutch denounced one overvaluation of objects, only to produce another of their own."[23] Furthermore in this displaced fetishism of the pronk still lifes, the glazed objects appear caught between two worlds: "not alive, not dead, not useful, not useless, as if lost between the tangibility of the common thing and the visibility of the distanced commodity. And the pictorial effect is often one of deathly suspension or, of eerie animation with the objects at once chilled *and* charged by the speculative gaze fixed upon them."[24]

Finally, having exhausted the anthropological and commodity fetishisms of the pronk paintings, Foster suggests that these Dutch still lifes are also fetishisms in the Freudian sense. They are structures that express both sides of an ambivalence. For example, the "Reaganomics"[25] that Foster cites (and even more so, I would imagine, the Bushomics of the early twenty-first century), represented the ambivalent structures of fundamentalism and greed, moral restraint, and economic expenditure. With skilled craft controlling and regulating the destructive excess depicted in the paintings, the pronk still life, at the same time, could assuage anxieties about affluence, expenditure, and economic speculation.[26]

Like the Freudian fetish, which both assuages castration anxiety by posing as a substitute penis, and yet also remains as a memorial to castration, in the pronk still life, "a ghost of a lack hangs over its very abundance."[27] Moreover, "the luminous shine on these still lifes is more faultily fetishistic: it recalls our lack even as it distracts us from it."[28]

In the next chapter, on Freud's "Fetishism," as in all the succeeding chapters, although they depict very different cultures of fetishism and an immense variety of fetishistic arts and artifacts, we will be observing myriad reflections of Foster's meditation on the fetishisms of seventeenth-century Dutch still life painting.

Unfortunately, Foster's rich appreciation of the fetishism strategy is not typical of most efforts to grapple with the notion that fetishism is a form of cultural discourse. Since the *strategy* (or discourse) of fetishism has eluded many of the investigators who tackled the subject, the basic notion underlying these attempts has been to propose the several ways in which the *perversion* of fetishism could be enlisted to disrupt and challenge cultural norms.

In contrast, I am arguing that the fetishism strategy aims to keep human beings enslaved to cultural norms. Fetishism, as a strategy or item of cultural discourse, is a servant of authoritarianism. The fetishism strategy works to insure that the law is upheld. A central principle of the fetishism strategy is to guarantee that creative energies and vitalities are stifled, perhaps even murdered if necessary.

Since another crucial aspect of the fetishism strategy is masquerade, it is almost impossible to discern in any specific instance, or at any given moment, whether eroticism is regulating and taming violent and destructive urges or whether the death drive is insinuating its presence by painting itself in erotic colors. And this *uncertainty* haunts the pages of *Cultures of Fetishism*. As we go along we shall also learn to tolerate and appreciate the value of uncertainty. Certainty collaborates with the principles of the fetishism strategy. A toleration for uncertainty is the ally of the essential human spirit that opposes and undermines the fetishism strategy.

The fetishism strategy can, and often does, insinuate itself as a deadly, destructive force that opposes human dialogue, the heartbeat of human existence. Each time a child comes into the world, there is a new opportunity to re-establish and preserve the human dialogue. Yet, it would seem that we live in a world dominated by cultures that would interfere with that dialogue. It is ironic that the vital importance of an infant's need for human dialogue should be subverted at the very moment in human history when the complaints of human detachment and alienation are loudest.

As we plunge unthinkingly into the very emptiness we fear, something in us continues to resist. For the time being the human dialogue has not been silenced. Even the increasing robotization of human beings illustrated by Reality TV, or the increasing interference with the parent-child dialogue by mechanical devices that, all too often, substitute for human interchanges and human contact, can be combatted and defeated. This battle begins with the ability to detect the fetishism strategy in all its deceptive guises. So, let us begin.

Two

UNRAVELING FREUD ON FETISHISM

I begin our explorations of the fetishism strategy with Freud's six-page paper "Fetishism." While this book is definitely not about Freud, and does not give much attention to *his* theory of fetishism, I discovered after many readings of his befuddling paper on sexual fetishism, that it has been infiltrated by the fetishism strategy. Therefore, "Fetishism" turns out to be a demonstration of the differences between fetishism, the perversion, and the fetishism strategy that is the central subject of this book.

As I began the process of detecting the fetishism strategy in Freud's paper, I simultaneously began to take in some facts about Freud's state of mind, during the two weeks in the summer of 1927 when he was writing "Fetishism." The state of mind of a person who is suffering can be as much a culture of fetishism as a characteristic of the social order, or a cultural endeavor such as biographical writing, making films, or training psychoanalysts.

Over the years, I have read and re-read "Fetishism," a paper whose formulations about male and female differences have always troubled me. This time around, though, I was guided by my understanding of the fetishism strategy. I therefore could detect how the fetishism strategy had influenced the tone and quality of these formulations. One principle of the fetishism strategy stood out with a striking intensity. As I will be demonstrating, what was meant to be a contribution to a theory of the erotic life, gradually, but surely, degenerates into a destructive aggression toward the female body. "Fetishism" is an example of the death drive tinting itself in erotic color. Recall the fifth principle of the fetishism strategy where this tint of erotic color can make deadly practices invisible to the naked eye. The erogenous color draws a mask right on the skin.

The centerpiece of "Fetishism," situated at its dead center, is Freud's basic theory that fetishism is based on an aversion to the female genitals. The "absence" of a penis signifies that these genitals must be "castrated." The fetish, whatever form it takes, represents a substitute penis. However, the substitute penis cannot erase the "horror" of the sight of the castrated female

genitals. The sight of the female genitals remains as a "*stigma indelible*."[1] The
fetish represents "a token of triumph over the threat of castration and a
protection against it,"[2] yet, "the horror of castration has set up a memorial to
itself in the creation of this substitute."[3] Thus a fetish reassures but also recalls
the horror of castration.

Finally, in the last paragraph of the third page, as if to hammer in the
point, Freud proclaims, "Probably no male human being is spared the fright
of castration at the sight of a female genital."[4]

The fourth and fifth pages are taken up with the exploration of some typical fetishes and one man's unique fetish of an athletic supporter. The entire
last page is given over to men's destructive impulses directed toward the
bodies of women. Apparently these fetishists can only appease their castration
fears, when they are actively engaged in mutilating parts of a woman's body,
or parts of her clothing, which might be snipped off and kept on hand for
future sexual activities, or, at the very least, as with footbinding, obsessed
with worshipping a body part that has already been mutilated. And, the coup
de grace, Freud's final statement about the anatomical difference between
the male and female sexes, will turn out to be as horrifying as the "memorial
to the horror of castration." At the bottom of page six, Freud drives home
what he has been saying with a memorable concluding sentence, a memorial, as it were, to the castrations he has been recounting: "In conclusion
we may say that the normal prototype of fetishes is a man's penis, just as
the normal prototype of inferior organs is a woman's real small penis, the
clitoris."[5]

The characters Freud evokes to illustrate his theory of fetishism are a
prototypical little boy who presumably, somehow or other, catches a sight of
his mother's "castrated" genitals; two young men, analytic patients of Freud
whose fathers died when the young men were children; and four more adult
males—a man whose fetish was the shine on a woman's nose, the gentleman
whose fetish was an athletic support belt, and another prototype, a *coupeur
des nattes*, a braid-cutter, and finally, a variant of braid cutting that afflicted an
entire society—men who endorsed the Chinese custom of mutilating the
female foot and then revered it as a fetish.

In the background, given full attention in the first paragraph, are a whole
host of anonymous males, most of whom were at one time or another in
analysis with Freud. Though each of these analytic patients recognized the
abnormality of his fetish, he did not suffer from using it, or see it as a symptom worth analyzing. In fact the patients were quite satisfied with it, sometimes
even praising "the way in which it eases their erotic life."[6]

The fears of the female body, and the mutilations that men sometimes
inflict on women's bodies to counteract these fears, are not figments of
Freud's imagination. Many men do fear the female body and they do sometimes participate in the mutilation of women's bodies in order to alleviate this
fear. However, the manner in which Freud puts his argument together, and
his unrelenting attack on the so-called castrated female genitals, reveal some
of his own destructive aggression toward the female body.

This time, as I re-read "Fetishim," once again my insights into the fetishism strategy have given me a better sense of what was troubling Freud's heart, body, and soul at the time he wrote it. Indeed, now I must wonder at my earlier shrinking away from some facts that I could have registered more consciously much earlier. What I must have been aware of long ago, what I must have known but did not want to know and therefore disavowed, was all the information about the emotional and physical "castrations" that had befallen Freud prior to his writing "Fetishism."

Four years before his sudden impulse to write "Fetishism," Freud had been struck down by the gods twice, one bolt right after the other; in fact, almost simultaneously. The first blow, in April of 1923, would be bringing him the first of thirty-four operations on his cancerous jaw, the placement of a prosthesis in his mouth that made it almost impossible to speak or hear, and sixteen years of nearly unbearable physical pain. The second blow, the death of his grandson, killed his enjoyment of life and was experienced by Freud as far more unbearable than his cancer.

In June of 1923, as his four-year-old grandson, Heinz, lay in a coma, Freud had already begun to speak of him in the past tense: "He was indeed an enchanting fellow," and "I have hardly ever loved another human being, certainly not a child, so much as him."[7] Heinz was frail and skinny, nothing but bones and hair and eyes.[8] There was no hope of survival, and yet he would occasionally open his eyes and act and talk just like his old, charming, enchanting, clever self, making it hard to believe that he was really dying. Freud said, "I find this loss very hard to bear. I don't think I have ever experienced such grief."[9]

Three years later, in a letter of condolence to Ludwig Binswanger, a colleague who had recently lost his eight-year-old son to tubercular meningitis, Freud does not immediately tell him about the death of his grandson from the same illness. Instead he begins by recounting his reaction to the death of his twenty-seven-year old daughter, Sophie. "That was 1920, when we were crushed and miserable, after years of war, against which we had steeled ourselves against hearing that we had lost a son or even three sons. Thus, we had been resigned to fate in advance."[10] Freud was trying to explain to Binswager (and to himself, I imagine) that Sophie's death had not affected him so profoundly as the death of her child, his little grandson, Heinz, or as Freud called him, Heinerle.

It was not Freud's resignation to fate, however, that had made the death of Sophie bearable. In telling Binswanger about Heinz, Freud said, "To me this child had taken the place of all my children and other grandchildren."[11] The presence of Heinz had consoled Freud and helped him to recover from the death of his favorite daughter, Sophie. As so often happens when a parent dies, a part of her or him lives on in the child who is left behind. The clever, enchanting Heinz embodied those precious aspects of his mother that Freud could not bear to lose. If Heinz were still alive, Sophie was not altogether dead.

The full emotional impact of Sophie's death did not register with Freud until Heinz dragged what remained of his mother into the grave with him.

In August of 1923, three months after Heinz's death, Freud was aware he might never recover from this loss. To his colleague Max Eitingon, he wrote, "I am obsessesed by impotent longing for the dear child."[12] He confessed to his cherished friend Oscar Rie, "He meant the future to me and thus has taken the future away with him."[13]

This loss of the future had been immediately preceded by another calamity. In April of 1923, a leukoplakia in Freud's mouth was thought to be pre-cancerous. The growth was removed, but the surgeon had not taken any of the necessary precautions to prevent or minimize shrinkage of the scar. Four months later, two months after little Heinz had died, Freud wrote to a friend that he had not been out of pain since the surgery. However, Freud said that what troubled him most was the emotional pain of losing his grandson. "It is the secret of the indifference—people call it courage—toward the danger to my own life."[14] He felt he could never love anyone else again, not even his other grandchildren.

When a human being feels "castrated" and humiliated by the suffering he is enduring, the erotic colorations of life diminish in intensity, very often yielding to destructive fantasies and actions. What happened to Freud in the years immediately following the calamities of 1923, and some of his own insights into how it changed the ways in which he looked at life, can show how this particular culture of fetishism—the humiliation of a physical or emotional wound that cannot be assuaged—might affect any human being.

Initially, I will be going into some detail about the physical sufferings that attended the surgeries on Freud's mouth and nasal passages. Later in this chapter I will be connecting these details with some details in Freud's theory of female sexual development. I will be suggesting that the mutilating surgeries performed on his mouth had stimulated an unconscious feminine identification that was intolerable to a proud man like Sigmund Freud. These feminine identifications, which are unconscious aspects of every man's masculine identity, are frightening to most men, often inducing a defensive misogynist coloration to their erotic life, imbuing it with a degree of destructive aggression toward the female body. Moreover, as we shall see, some of these defensive reactions are connected with an envy of the power of the female body.

Between the physical and emotional castrations of 1923 and the writing of "Fetishism," were four years consumed by a variety of physical assaults on Freud's mouth. Some were drastic surgical procedures undertaken to control and conquer the cancerous growth. Others were efforts to ameliorate the ghastly physical effects of the surgeries. His physical state, "which varied only from severe discomfort to real torment," began in 1923 and "persisted more or less constantly for the next 16 years."[15]

In late September of 1923, a new and distinguished oral surgeon, Professor Hans Pichler, was elected by a colleague of Freud to take over the case from the first surgeon. Pichler examined Freud's mouth and discovered a malignant ulcer in the hard palate that had already invaded neighboring tissues "including the upper part of the lower jaw and even the check."[16] Pichler, in consultation with the first surgeon, decided that a radical surgery was needed, and he performed this major operation in two stages on October 4 and October 11. In the first stage:

> the external carotid artery was ligatured and the subanillary glands, some of which were already suspiciously enlarged, removed. In the second operation, after slitting the lip and cheek wide open the surgeon removed the whole upper jaw and palate on the affected side, a very extensive operation which of course threw the nasal cavity and mouth into one. These frightful operations were performed under local anesthesia.(!)[17] [The exclamation was inserted by Ernest Jones, who reported the details of the surgery.]

Much of Freud's suffering was due to the outcomes of the second surgical procedure, which had joined the mouth with the nasal passages. This drastic surgery required the insertion of a prosthesis, a huge denture-like apparatus, designed to block off the gaping wound in his mouth, separating it from the nasal cavity. Those who saw the device described it as a "horror."[18]

Since the prosthesis made it impossible for Freud to open his mouth wide, it was difficult to remove it for a few hours of relief from the pressure it caused, or to replace it afterwards. One day, for example, after more than a half hour of the combined efforts of Freud and his daughter Anna had failed to achieve the re-insertion of the monstrous device, they were forced to send for Pichler to do it for them.[19] The tight fit, though necessary to close off the nasal passage from the mouth, "produced constant irritation and sore places until its presence was unbearable."[20] If the horror were left out for longer than a few hours, the tissues would shrink and the prosthesis would have to be altered.

Ernest Jones described the effects of the first "horror" (there would be three more replacement prostheses within the next four years and finally a fifth that was constructed by an orthodontic specialist in Germany):

> From now on Freud's speech was very defective, though it varied a good deal from time to time according to the fit of the denture. It was nasal and thick, rather like that of someone with a cleft palate. Eating was also a trial, and he seldom cared to do so in company. Furthermore the damage done to the Eustachian tube, together with constant infection in the neighborhood, greatly impaired his hearing on the right side until he became almost entirely deaf on that side. It was the side next to his patients, so the position of his couch and chair had to be reversed.[21]

Freud's inability to give up smoking caused further irritation to his mouth and encouraged new leukoplakia, which then had a tendency to proliferate. Soon after the creation of prosthesis number two, Freud writes to a friend in Germany, "I want to thank you again for sending me those good cigars—150 of them. . . . Since it is not my intention to forgo this source of gratification for the short remainder of my life, please take any future opportunity you have to send me additional supplies."[22]

From 1926 until his death, there was an "endless cycle of leukoplakia, proliferation and pre-cancerous lesions. Each of them had to be treated surgically by excision, electrocoagulation, or a combination of both."[23]

A year after his first surgery, Freud had written to his colleague, Karl Abraham, "You must make a real effort to put yourself in my position if you are not to feel ill-disposed toward me."[24] Those words kept reverberating in my mind as I grappled with the motives underlying Freud's descent to destructive mysogenism in "Fetishism." As I put myself in Freud's place I felt enormous sympathy for him and could appreciate how his physical and emotional torments might have influenced the crudely aggressive tone of the 1927 "Fetishism."

In a letter to Lou Andrea-Salome written on the occasion of his sixty eighth birthday, two years before "Fetishism," Freud commented on the "crust of indifference that was slowly creeping up around me; a fact I state without complaining. It is a natural development, a way of beginning to be inorganic. The 'detachment of old age' I think it is called."[25] And then in his next sentence, where he attempts to explain the underlying cause of his detachment and indifference, Freud arrives at the crux of what I am describing as a *"gradual descent from a discourse of eroticism to a discourse of bodily mutilation and destruction."* Freud tells Salome, "It must be connected with the decisive crises in the relationship between the two instincts stipulated by me."[26] Since he had several years earlier written *Beyond the Pleasure Principle*, a revolutionary monograph on manifestations of the death instinct, we can infer that he was referring to the inability of Eros, the life instinct, to tame and modulate the furies of Thanatos, the death instinct.

I am proposing that the catastrophic loss of Heinerle, and the surgeries and ensuing horrors performed on Freud's mouth, those two simultaneous "castrations" that continued to plague Freud during the four years preceding the writing of "Fetishism," foreshadowed and precipitated the castrations executed in that paper. Even if it were possible to discount the death of little Heinz, the surgical procedures alone would provide context enough for Freud's emphasis on "the horror of castration," and his incongruously nonchalant presentations of the mutilations performed by men on the bodies of women. Perhaps the horrors that had befallen him might even have something to do with his confusing a fantasy about the female genitals with their reality. His reference to the clitoris as an inferior penis, a *real* small penis (*itals* mine), demonstrates this confusion between fantasy and realty that pervades "Fetishism." Another example is Freud's habit of referring to female "castration," another fantasy about the female genitals that he writes about as if it were a real mutilation.

Plausible as my proposal may be, we should pursue further inquiries in order to have confidence in its validity. Had Freud approached the question of fetishism and female sexuality differently before the calamities that befell him in 1923? Had something fundamental changed in the way Freud went about pursuing his studies? And if so, what was the nature of that change?

Since I am about to make interpretations about a person's mental state without their consent or cooperation, it is best to begin by giving Freud an opportunity to answer these questions himself. As we saw in his letter to Salome, his own observations about himself seem to confirm that there was a fundamental change in Freud's attitudes after 1923.

In a postscript written ten years after the 1925 publication of "An Autobiographical Study," Freud says: "Shortly before I wrote this study it seemed as though my life would soon be brought to an end by the recurrence of a malignant disease; but surgical skill saved me in 1923 and I was able to continue my life and my work, though no longer in freedom from pain."[27]

As he looks over his post-1923 accomplishments he emphasizes that though he did not cease his analytic work, "*a significant change has taken place*"[28] (*itals.* mine).

After mentioning that he had carried out some significant bits of analytic work since then, among them his revision of the problem of anxiety (1926) and a simple explanation of fetishism (1927), nevertheless:

> It would be true to say that, since I put forward my hypothesis of the existence of two classes of instincts (Eros and the death instinct) and since I proposed a division of the mental personality into an ego, a super-ego and id (1923b), I have made no further decisive contributions to psychoanalysis. . . . This circumstance is connected with *an alteration in myself* with what might be described as a phase of regressive development. (*itals.* mine)[29]

In connection with this regression, Freud speaks of his return to his earliest interests in religious, moral, and cultural issues: "interests which I had acquired in the later part of my life have receded, while the older and original ones become prominent once more."[30]

While it would be far afield from the central concerns of this chapter to delve into the possible connections between Freud's growing awareness of his now always imminent death and his return to his youthful thoughts on religion or morality, it is surely to the point that Freud acknowledges the "significant change" in his analytic attitude, and along with it "a significant change in myself."

Before I contrast Freud's earlier studies of fetishism and female sexuality with his post-1923 studies, I turn, once again, for a moment more, to another of his self-observations, which, quite to the point of this contrast, appears in his 1925 paper, "Some Psychical Consequences of the Anatomical Distinction between the Sexes."

He introduces that paper with an apology for bringing forth findings that have not yet been proven. Asking himself why he does not postpone publication until he has the necessary proof, he responds, "Because the conditions under which I work have undergone a change, with implications that I cannot hide."[31] In the past, says Freud, "I was not one of those who were unable to hold back a discovery before it was confirmed or corrected."[32]

> But in those days I had unlimited time before me—"oceans of time". . . and material poured in on me in such quantities that fresh experiences were hardly

to be escaped. . . . But now everything has changed. The time before me is limited. The whole of it is no longer spent in working [he meant working analytically
with patients], so that my opportunities for making fresh observations are not
so numerous. If I think I see something new, I am uncertain whether I can wait
for it to be confirmed. And further, everything that is to be seen upon the surface
has already been exhausted: what remains has to be slowly and laboriously
dragged up from the depths.[33]

With these remarks, Freud justifies publishing a work before its value or
lack of value can be established. In other words, in 1925 there was, in contrast
to his earlier days, an urgency, a pressing need to tackle certain psychoanalytic
problems, in this instance, the problem of the differences between the sexes.
A tone of agitated urgency, which was not present in his earlier work on the
subject, begins to enter into Freud's writings on gender distinctions.

Putting his prolonged apology for his hasty conclusions behind him,
Freud posts with all dexterity to positing some relationships between the
anatomical differences between the sexes and what he proposes as the corresponding differences between the castration complex in males and females.
From there he makes a further precipitous leap into suggesting a direct
relationship between the anatomical differences (biological facts) and the
social traits of masculinity and femininity (sociological or cultural influences).
Or, as he put it in a paper written the year before, "Anatomy is destiny."[34]

According to Freud's 1925 version of the castration complex, which
advances and consolidates the theory put forth in his 1924 paper, when the
boy first catches sight of the girl's genital region, he sees nothing there or
disavows the nothing that he does see. It is only later when, for one reason or
another, the threat of castration "has obtained a hold on him,"[35] that the
early observation becomes a threat. After that, when the boy recollects his
first sighting, "he must take seriously what he was previously able to laugh at
or ignore."[36] This combination of circumstances determine the boy's later
relations to women, "horror of the mutilated creature or triumphant contempt for her."[37] Freud's portrayals of the origins of the little boy's castration
anxiety and its potential effects on the adult male are plausible and, in fact,
seem to correspond to the ways that real human beings might think about
these matters. Many men who would otherwise be terrified of the female genitals triumph over this terror through their macho defense of a triumphant
contempt for the female.

Freud then turns his attention to "the mutilated creature." And this is where
the serious trouble begins. Until the writing of this essay, Freud had represented infantile sexuality as if the female's sexual development and even her
Oedipus complex were mirrors of the little boy's developmental trials. As Peter
Gay remarks in his biography of Freud, "these were technical issues, a subject
for research rather than polemics."[38] But, Gay then raises a forceful criticism of
Freud's re-examination of the developmental schedules of boys and girls.
When Freud now claimed "that the little girl is a failed boy, the grown woman
a kind of castrated male," he "put a match to inflammable material."[39]

As Gay depicts the changes in Freud's thinking, "his robust and caustic language" represented "a turn to the right, subverting his own idea,"[40] so congenial to the feminists of that time, that males and females have very similar psychological histories. "There was nothing in the climate of the 1920's that would make him propound his controversial, at times scurrilous, views on women."[41]

However, while Gay attributes this sea change to Freud's attempt to puzzle through some difficulties in his new way of thinking about the Oedipus complex, I am, as I mentioned earlier, attributing these "caustic" and "scurrilous" attitudes toward women to the physical castrations that Freud had endured and continued to endure until the end of his life. No doubt, there is some measure of truth to Gay's assumption about the theoretical issues motivating these changes, but his explanation is not sufficient to account for the destructive misogynism expressed in Freud's later views on female anatomy.

In comparing the little girl's Oedipus complex to the little boy's, Freud says, "The situation is quite different for a little girl, who does not turn to disavowal or wait for later experiences to confirm her perceptions and feelings."[42] The little girl knows at once that she is castrated. When she first catches sight of the boy's genital, the girl "makes her judgment and her decision in a flash. She has seen it and knows that she is without it and wants to have it."[43] Moreover, the hope of someday obtaining a penis in spite of everything and so of becoming like a man may persist. Or, "a girl may refuse to accept the *fact* of being castrated, may harden herself in the conviction that she *does* possess a penis, and may subsequently be compelled to behave as though she were a man (*itals.* mine)."[44] Furthermore, "after a woman has become aware of the *wound* to her narcissism, she develops like a *scar*, a sense of inferiority."[45] The words I have italicized in these quotations play into my interpretations of the motives underlying Freud's misogynism.

Let us make a special note of Freud's phrasing: a *horror of the mutilated creature* on the boy's part, and the *fact* of being castrated on the little girl's part. The ideas that the female is mutilated and castrated are here represented as facts and not fantasies. And also note that ominous *scar* that results from the *wound* to her narcissism. Do these eccentricities in language and thought in his 1925 paper reflect Freud's unconscious responses to the mutilations and scars and wounds that his mouth had been subjected to—especially the surgically created cavity that joined oral and nasal cavities? Or, had such language and thought been present in his pre-1923 writings on fetishism, castration, and the anatomical differences?

The thoughts were present long before 1923. But the eccentricies in language and the assaultive tone and the urgency came after the catastrophes of 1923.

As early as 1905, in "Three Essays on Sexuality," Freud had referred to the clitoris as a less than adequate masculine organ. He theorized that it was the little boy's fear of his own castration that might urge him to create a fetish like a garter belt or high-heeled shoe later in life. This fear of castration was said to be partly an outcome of the boy's Oedipus complex and his secret wish of wanting to displace his father in his mother's affections, and partly an outcome of chance sightings of the female genitals.

From 1905 onward, the eroticization of the foot had been Freud's favorite example of fetishism. In his earlier descriptions of this popular and typical form of fetishism, Freud's attitudes toward the female were more friendly and toned with erotic vitality. The dramatic change that took place after 1923 is the relative balance between the erotic and destructive elements in his thoughts about women and the female body. Before then Freud's thoughts on fetishism and castration were linked to a theory of eroticism and to the "adhesiveness" of early "libidinal" attractions.

Themes that associated fetishism with castration and the fundamental inferiority of the visible female genital—the clitoris—were present in Freud's earliest writings. However, when these ideas are re-iterated and reinforced in his post-1923 writings on female sexuality and femininity, they are presented in the context of a project that stood on its own. It was after 1923 that Freud, suddenly, for no apparent reason, began to devote entire essays to the subject of the female sexuality and her castrated genitals. It was then that the "caustic" and "scurrilous" language about the female genitals began to take over his writings.

I am proposing that the intensity of his focus on the topic of female castration was, in part at least, a response to his own "castrations." Perhaps, by emphasizing the differences between the mutilated creatures and the penis-possessing creatures of the male sex, he was disavowing the feminine identifications that had been aroused by the mutilations that were being inflicted on his own body?

Until now we have seen how Freud acknowledged, on several occasions, the changes that had taken place in the way he pursued his psychoanalytic research in the years after his surgery, changes that corresponded to emotional alterations taking place within himself. Moreover, though Freud doesn't acknowledge this directly, a brief review of his pre-1923 writings on fetishism has demonstrated an emphasis on the erotic and libidinal precursors of fetishism, rather than the emphasis on the "horror" produced by the sightings of the castrated organs of the female.

There was another change, a more subtle change in himself, that Freud also noticed. He tries to explain the nature of this alteration in self-experience in the same letter to Lou Andreas-Salome, where he speaks of "the crust of indifference . . . slowly creeping up around me." In this context, he continues:

> The change taking place is perhaps not very noticeable; everything is as interesting as it was before; neither are the ingredients very different; but some kind of resonance is lacking; unmusical as I am, I imagine the difference to be something like using the pedal or not. The never-ceasing tangible pressure of a vast number of unpleasant sensations must have accelerated this otherwise perhaps premature condition, this tendency to experience everything *sub specie aeternitatis*.[46]

And finally, in a concluding passage of that letter, Freud tells Salome: "I still have important work to do, but I must hurry. I must fight against the inexorable Chronos, I must do this before the resonance becomes even more muted."[47]

Certainly the diminution of resonance or intonation could transform what might have been some discriminating nuances in his perceptions of the female genitals into crude and untamed expressions of the same ideas—what Gay referred to as "caustic" and "scurrilous." Also, in reading through "Fetishism," one cannot discount a possible connection between the hurried urgency Freud was experiencing and the awkward way he strings together the multitude of ideas and themes that he raises, one after the other, in rapid succession. In other words the "descent into destruction" could very well be an outcome of these less tangible side-effects—his loss of resonance, his sense of urgency.

With these considerations in mind, let us take a closer look at "Fetishism," and the characters Freud selected to illustrate his theory. Along the way we will come across some valid and potentially valuable ideas about *fetishism, the sexual perversion*. I will be stressing, however, the loss of resonance, the sense of urgency and, most important, the gradual descent from a discourse of eroticism to a discourse of destructive aggression, which is a manifestation of a major principle of the fetishism strategy. As I said at the outset, by describing fetishism, the sexual perversion that is the focus of Freud's paper and the fetishism strategy that is the focus of this book, side-by-side, I will be clarifying the differences between the two forms of fetishism.

I begin with the young man who devised a shine on the nose as his fetish, more precisely the young lady whose nose was blessed with that luminous shine—a blessing that very often only he could perceive. Freud uses this example, which he selected from the numerous men he had studied analytically, all of whom made the choice of a loved one on the basis of her possession of a special feature in her physical make-up. In this instance, as in so many cases like it, the fetish is not a concrete object, but rather a tangible characteristic of the loved one that became essential to the young man's sexual enjoyment.

With his case of the luminous nose, Freud wanted to demonstrate the accidental circumstances that are decisive in the choice of a fetish or the choice of a loved one. Strangely enough, however, the example Freud has chosen does not clarify just what these accidental circumstances might be. The young man's choice of love object seems to have little or nothing to do with an early libidinal attraction or the sighting of a "castrated" genital. His fetishistic obsession hinges on a twist, one could say an accidental coincidence, in language translation. I must wonder, in that connection, why Freud chooses such an idiosyncratic example and then, having made that choice, doesn't bother to explain the connection between the "shine on the nose" and the missing penis of the woman, the woman's castration, all the subjects that then become the central focus of "Fetishism."

All that Freud tells us about this particular young man is that when he was a very little boy, he and his family lived in England, where one day or perhaps on several occasions, he happened to "glance" at a woman's nose. When he was a few years older, his family moved to Germany, where he learned to speak German, which then became his primary language. The word "Glanz" in German means "shine." And thus, explains Freud, the boy became fixated on the idea of a woman with a shine on her nose. [48]

This is all that is said about the young man and his lady friend with the luminous nose. We are left with a halfway explanation of the origins of his fetish. And then suddenly and abruptly Freud changes the topic. The flow of ideas is rushed and urgent, as though there was no time or energy to explain things further or to draw out the connections between the "shine on the nose," and the topic that follows. Perhaps Freud thought the entire matter was simply too obvious to explain further? Or perhaps his next paragraph, though it appears to be a non sequitor, is an attempt at explanation? It suggests that the nose was one of those all-too-obvious phallic symbols. Nevertheless, this going from one topic to another is not characteristic of Freud's literary style, where usually the logical connections between ideas were as important as the ideas themselves.

In the first sentence of the next paragraph Freud explains that in all cases of fetishism that he has treated, the purpose of the fetish turned out to be the same:

> When now I announce that the fetish is a substitute for the penis, I shall certainly create disappointment; so I hasten to add that it is not a substitute for any chance penis, but for a particular and quite special penis that had been extremely important in early childhood but had later been lost. . . . To put it more plainly: the fetish is a substitute for the woman's [the mother's] penis that the little boy had once believed in and—for reasons familiar to us—does not want to give up. [49]

At this point Freud has forgotten the young man who was attracted to his lady friend's luminous nose. His comments on the mother's penis carry his attentions to some little boy or other, probably alluding to all little boys, who are inevitably, sooner or later, "faced" with the sight of a woman without a penis. Freud explains that the little boy's perception of this fact of life, this sight of a woman without a penis, is too threatening for him to accept. After all, to fully acknowledge that a woman had lost her penis (for why else would she not have one?) would mean that he too might lose his penis, the organ of his body that is so heavily invested with his own narcissism and self-worth.

So, what does the little boy do? Does he deny what he has seen in an effort to preserve his narcissism and own bodily integrity? Or, does he acknowledge what he has seen? Apparently neither of these distinct possibilities are open to the little boy. Or, rather, he must have it both ways. [50] He retains his belief that the woman has a penis by constructing a substitute for that missing organ. He appoints a substitute, which inherits the interest formerly directed to the female genitals. And that substitute, as we already know, is the fetish, which is both a memorial to the horror of castration and a protection against it.

What sorts of objects are adopted to assume such a mighty and contradictory task? Freud tells us that the objects chosen to be substitutes for the absent female penis are not, as we might expect, always or usually symbols of the penis. It would seem that the same process that arrests memory in traumatic amnesia is operative in the choice of fetish. The little boy's interest comes to a halt at the halfway mark. The last impression before the traumatic moment becomes the fetish: "Thus the foot or shoe owes its preference as a fetish to the circumstance that the inquisitive little boy peered at the woman's genitals from her legs up."[51] Fur and velvet, which represent the pubic hair that covers the genitals, are also favored fetishes. Similarly, pieces of underclothing crystallize the last moment that the woman could still be regarded as phallic.

At this point in his explanation, Freud drops the discussion of the childhood origins of fetishism and dashes off to a new topic; something that had been of theoretical interest to him for a long time. He was employing the topic of fetishism to take him toward a more satisfactory explanation of the difference between neurosis and psychosis. When he wrote *The Ego and the Id* in 1920, he had thought that in neurosis, the ego suppresses a piece of the id, whereas in psychoses the id suppresses a piece of reality. But now, seven years later, he realizes there is another possible solution. Freud begins to explore the possibility that a person could simultaneously avow a piece of reality but also disavow it. In connection with this new theoretical possibility Freud brings in two young men who had lost their fathers when they were children.

Freud does not enlist the childhood histories of these two young men because they were involved with castration or horrifying discoveries of genital absence, or sexuality, or, in fact, with any concrete fetish object. However, their responses to their fathers' deaths do express succinctly the defensive structure of the fetishism perversion. Each child had thought about the death of his beloved father in much the same way that a fetishist thinks about a woman's body. Each of them knew that his father had died. Yet, at the same time, they did not know and had not acknowledged this death. They were, so to speak, of two minds.[52]

Disavowal, the psychological defense of having it both ways, is now thought to be one of our primary defense mechanisms, prior to and more fundamental than repression, originating in the earliest years of childhood, when the blurring between what is and what is not is characteristic.

Disavowal is the sine non qua of sexual fetishism. According to Freud, a sexual fetishist devises his fetish so that he can have it both ways. He can disregard reality and all the facts to the contrary and continue to believe that a woman *has* a penis. Yet, all the while, he will continue to take account of reality and recognize that she *does not* have a penis. Thus the fetish is both a substitute penis, *she does have a penis*, and "a memorial to the horror of castration," therefore she does not have a penis. Freud's likening of fetishism to death sounds the note of destruction that will be echoed in his concluding remarks on the mutilations of women's bodies.

Very often the defense of having it both ways shows up in the elaborate mental convolutions that determine the construction of the fetish. To show how this works, Freud brings in the example of the man whose fetish was an athletic supporter.[53]

This garment, an elaborately constructed jock strap, was often worn as part of a man's swimming suit. It covers up the genitals entirely and thus conceals the difference between the sexes. But Freud's apparently simple example of the athletic supporter fetish has in it more than a few befuddlements. Only one thing is certain, the garment is masculine. But who is wearing the supporter? Is it the fetishist himself? Or does the man require that his female sexual partner wear the supporter and cover up her female genitals with a masculine garment that disguises the sexual difference? Usually the woman wears the fetish garment, the white garter belt, the blue velvet bathrobe, the black leather boots, the rubberized raincoat. Or, sometimes, the fetishist simply fondles, smells, or gazes at his fetish. Or, at other times, the fetishist wears the garment himself.

Freud's comments do not help us to decide who is wearing the fetish. However, they do clarify the accidental circumstances leading up to the choice of the fetish. According to Freud, the transformation of this ordinary supporter into a fetish was inspired by a fig leaf seen on a statue when the fetishist was a little boy. But this solution just leads to another conundrum. Although we might presume that a fig leaf on a statue is intended to cover up the male genitals, this is not necessarily the case. On some statues, the fig leaf masks the reality of the female genitals. Thus the fig leaf solution, though clarifying with regard to the accidental circumstances that lead to the choice of a fetish, only deepens the ambiguity with regard to which sex is having his or her genitals covered up. At this point in Freud's tale of the athletic supporter, the sex of the wearer of the garment *and* the sex of the statue with the fig leaf are both in doubt.

Though Freud does not stop to clarify these matters, it may be that his own ambiguity is an objective correlative of the fundamental purpose of the athletic supporter fetish. Unconsciously, the garment was meant to leave the differences between the sexes ambiguous and thereby to have it both ways. Thus man could be a male engaged in the masculine activity of sexual intercourse, but leave open the possibility of identifying with a female person—and without anyone being any the wiser, including himself.

And here, though the point remains ambiguous, Freud is hinting at something that *is* quite relevant to the topic of fetishism. Most fetish objects are adopted to allow a man to express his shameful and dangerous wishes to be female and yet remain male. In many typical fetishistic fantasies, where the male or his sexual partner is wearing a fetishized female garment, the fetishist unconsciously (or consciously) imagines he is a woman, but a woman with a penis. But what about a man who is wearing a male garment? Is he then a male impersonator? As Freud would point out in later years, the repudiation of femininity—a man's struggle against his feminine attitude toward another male—is the bedrock of male psychology.[54]

By masking his genitals with a garment that allows for genital ambiguity but is still reassuringly male, the protagonist of Freud's tale of the athletic supporter identifies with some powerful, idealized "phallic" male. At this juncture in Freud's paper, the overall drift of his commentary is toward the fetishist's identification with his father, his father's position in the world, his father's position in sexual intercourse, his father's attitudes toward the female sex.

It would seem that the man with the athletic supporter fetish has created a different sort of memorial from the one created by a fetishist who employs a female garment to attain erection and penetration. It is derived from contrary ideas: the woman is both castrated and not castrated. It is, in part, a memorial to his mother's absent (castrated) genital, her *inferior* genital, her *real* small penis, and that last moment before he discovered her castration. At the same time, since it covers over the male genitals, it is derived from two ideas: that a male could be like a castrated female, and yet the fetish could also serve as a "memorial" to his father's *superior* genital.

Freud goes on to report that this divided attitude is exemplified by the *coupeur des nattes*, and other men who create their fetish to assert their strong identifications with the father: "For it is to him that as a child he ascribed the woman's castration."[55] The *coupeur des nattes* action of cutting off a lock of hair or scrap of female clothing or, in a pretense of more civilized behavior, merely stealing a woman's handkerchief, expresses two mutually incompatible assertions: "the woman has still got a penis" and "my father has castrated the woman." In this way he is able to treat his fetish both with reverence and at the same time, with the contempt and hostility deserving of someone who has been castrated.

When Freud concludes "Fetishism" with his observation, "the normal prototype of inferior organs is the woman's real small penis, the clitoris,"[56] it is not clear whether he is alluding to a little child's fantasy or an adult fetishist's fantasy. In my opinion, most likely the phrase "real small penis" represents Freud's own irrepressible infantile version of the female genital regions. Freud's intimacy with the workings of the unconscious mind did not exempt him from a prototypical, albeit unconscious attitude toward the female genitals, an attitude that expresses simultaneously an idealizing reverence and a hostility based on all the unwelcome news that is called to mind by the female genitals.

Like the perversion itself, Freud's "Fetishism" unsettles the boundaries between the *real* and the *not real*. Freud's concluding sentence about the female's *real* small penis is tantamount to a disavowal of the enormous and terrifying and humiliating significance of the actual female genitals. The female genitals are the emblem of that unwelcome news that Mother and Father share a desire that excludes the little child. The mother does have some genitals of significance and the father does desire her for having them. The little boy, of course, is competitive with his mother for his father's love. He wishes to be in her submissive position with the dominating father.

He envies her the power she has over his beloved and mighty father and would just as soon imagine her genitals as insignificant and puny—castrated, if necessary, and definitely inferior to his own.

Yes, the crucial point, which keeps peeking through the misogynism of Freud's "Fetishism," is the male's unconscious wish to fulfill what would otherwise be his *shameful* feminine longings, as well as his unconscious envy of the female's extraordinary sexual powers. As most contemporary psycho-analysts would acknowledge, their clinical experience with male patients brings this point home, over and over again—very subtly in most patients, quite emphatically in some others.

There are, for example, those ultra-macho men who are fascinated by "studying" the sexual allure of female prostitutes and call girls. As they speak about their desperate hunt for more and more contacts with professional sexual partners, who "know all the moves," they eventually reveal their iden-tifications with these powerful women, their wish to be like them, their wish to be as sexually alluring as they are. Some men exhibit this by dressing up like women and then masturbating. Others, more secretively, wear shreds of female undergarments under their business suits, workman's overalls, or police and military uniforms. Still others exhibit this feminine identification by giving up their apparently tranquil domestic life in order to devote them-selves to their "studies" of female sexual behaviors. Very often, the biggest turn-on of all for these super-macho males is observing lesbians making love to each other. That way they can have it both ways. They can be both sub-missive-femme and macho-butch;—categories that have more to do with their own fantasy life than what the lesbians are experiencing when they assume top and bottom and in-between sexual positions.

For a short while, the TV series *The L Word*, which features a wide variety of sexually alluring females who seem to be empowered with a variety of erotic ingenuities, took over the place in male imaginations previously held by the departed *Sex and the City*. On posters and in newspaper ads *The L Word* was promoted as VENUS ENVY. Now that this Venus envy is out in the open, we might look back at *Sex in the City* and detect something we might never have noticed about its appeal to some men—an opportunity for them to identify with females and give passive expression to their unconscious feminine identifications.

Two years before his death, in one of his last papers, Freud asserted that the rock bottom of the female personality is her penis envy, her unconscious wish to assume a masculine role in her sexual and domestic arrangements and in society.[57] Most females would protest that they do not have such wishes, or that those wishes are in fact quite conscious and nothing to be ashamed of, except for the sad fact of society labeling such wishes as "masculine." The corresponding rock bottom for the male is his unconscious wish to assume a feminine position in a relationship with a male. Since this feminine position is shameful to a man, he must make every effort to repudiate it. His so-called masculine protest is but the outward sign of his "repudiation of femininity." A possibility Freud never considered, however, was that his own insistent and re-iterated proclamations on female castration, the female absence of an adequate genital, the inferiority of her genitals, and penis envy, were, at least in part, a masquerade, a duplicity, a very elaborate and clever cover story for Venus envy.

Behind every proclamation of female inferiority lurks a forbidden and shameful identification with the powers of female sexuality. When a man feels castrated and humiliated by the conditions inflicted on him by his society, his shameful feminine identifications are aroused. A popular response to these social humiliations is the desire to silence the sexuality of females.

We do know that in cultures where the vast majority of male citizens are treated as if they were beasts of burden or less than human, these men identify with their oppressors. Rather than experience himself as a "castrated" woman, the man acts toward females the way that their oppressors act toward him He denigrates and punishes females for exhibiting their femininity. In such cultures, dominating and humiliating the woman is the screen, the cover story that protects a man from having to acknowledge his own vulnerability. In politically oppressive cultures, women have usually been the most oppressed and humiliated members.

The tumultuous social, political, and religious upheavals that plagued the country of Iran during the last half of the twentieth century and that now continues into the early years of the twenty-first century, testifies to these observations.[58] In 1957, after a succession of premiers finally restored some degree of order to Iran, there was a temporary end to the oppressive laws that had existed for sixteen years. Muhammad Reza Shah Pahlavi, who had assumed the reigns of authority from his father, instituted a series of reforms that would give land to the poor and establish closer relationships with the West. His project of industrialization, modernization, and Westernization created extraordinary and ostentatious wealth in some sectors of the population but alienated and humiliated the urban and rural poor, who grew more and more restless and dissatisfied.

The SAVAT, the Shah's secret police, kept a close watch for signs of discontent and punished those who objected to the Shah's regime with public humiliation, torture, imprisonment, and death by stoning and execution. The humiliation of the female population in the less-advantaged social classes was accomplished by beatings, desertions, and denigrations by their husbands and fathers. On the other hand, under the Shah's regime, the Westernized middle- and upper-class women were encouraged to serve in public offices, and allowed to vote, dress as they wished, listen to Western music, and read Western books.

One of those who objected to the policies of the Shah, particularly his adoption of Western values, was the Iranian Shiite, Ayatollah Ruhollah Khomeini. His outspoken criticism of the Shah's regime led to his exile to Iraq in 1964. In Iraq he developed a strong religious and political following, which led to Saddam Hussein forcing him to leave the country. Speaking from Paris, Ayatollah Khomeini called for his fellow Iranians to depose the

Shah. Counting on the fervent religious Islamism and desperate social unrest of the lower classes, he returned and led a religious revolution that led to the defeat of the Shah, who fled to Western Europe.

In 1981, Khomeini issued a decree transforming the nation of Iran into the Islamic Republic of Iran. Soon afterward, due to a dispute over a shared waterway, the Islamic Republic of Iran was attacked by Saddam Hussein's Iraq. From the Iranian point of view it was a war of the holy Islamics against the heathens, the Satanic forces of Hussein. This war would last eight years, killing over a million Iranians and leaving many Iranian cities and streets and homes in shambles.

Throughout these chaotic times, from 1979 until 1989 when Khomeini died of a mysterious illness, two things remained constant: the oppression of women of all classes by the Ayatollah's ruling government, and an unabating effort to eradicate any remaining vestiges of Westernized femininity and female power. The lower-class women, most of them religious Islamics, continued to suffer their husbands' denigrations, but after 1979 it was the previously liberated middle- and upper-class women who suffered the brunt of Khomeini's fanatical de-Westernization.

Azar Nafisi, an upper-class Westernized college professor whose mother had been one of six women elected to Parliament in 1963, reports the situation in *Reading Lolita in Tehran*.[59] When she returned to Iran with her husband after studying literature in the United States, the laws governing female rights had regressed to what they had been before her grandmother's time. After the revolution, two women who had risen to the post of cabinet minister were sentenced to death and summarily executed for warring with God and spreading prostitution.

The shah's SAVAT had been replaced by Khomeini's "Blood of God" militia, who focused much of their attention on the improprieties of the female population. They drove around the streets in their white Toyotas trying to ensure that women were wearing their veils and chadors properly without a speck of skin showing, were not wearing makeup or fingernail polish, were not walking through the streets with men who were not family members Young women who disobeyed the official Islamic rules were thrown into the patrol cars, "taken to jail, flogged, fined and forced to wash toilets and humiliated."[60]

Nafisi tells the story of what happened to one of her female students. This story captures the essence of what happens to females in a country where the vast majority of men are oppressed and humiliated; men whose only opportunity to survive and advance their careers and obtain food and shelter for their families is to become an Islamic thug, who drive around in a patrol car with a semi-automatic weapon looking for young women who don't dress or behave like proper Islamic women.

Her student, Sanaz, a very intelligent, pretty, charming girl, did not disobey Islamic strictures. But sometimes she could be obstinate and insist on doing what she wanted—no matter what. She didn't always listen to the advice of her parents, who lived in terror of the morality squads. She and five of her girlfriends had gone to a villa by the Caspian Sea for a two-day holiday. The first day they were there they decided to visit a nearby villa, where the fiancé of one of the girls lived.[61]

Suddenly, "they"[62] came; the morality squad had jumped over a low garden wall and surprised them. They had had a report of illegal activities and had a search warrant. Finding nothing wrong with the girls' dress, they searched the house for alchohol, CD's, and tapes. And, even though they found nothing, "the guards took all of them to a special jail for infractions in matters of morality."[63]

The girls were kept in a small, dark room for forty eight hours and not allowed to sleep. Members of the morality squad would come by periodically and wake them up and insult them. The girls were not allowed to call their parents. They were taken to a hospital where a female gynecologist gave them virginity tests in front of a group of male medical students. Not satisfied with the gynecologist's verdict of innocence, the guards took them back to jail and gave the girls' their own tests. Sanaz was too embarrassed to explain what these various tests were. Finally, Sanaz's parents located the girls and had them set free. But not before the girls were given a summary trial where they were forced to confess to their sins against Islamic Law and each given twenty fifth lashes as punishment. Sanaz, who was wearing a T-shirt under her robe, was given some extra lashes, to make sure she really felt the pain.[64]

The nation of Iran, even in the "good old days" under the Shah and his SAVAT secret police, but especially when it was transformed into the Islamic Republic of Iran, created a social order that bred and nurtured the fetishism strategy. Thus a religious belief, a social or political regime can be as much a culture of fetishism as the personal humiliations suffered by an individual, the making of films, the writing of biographies, the training of psychoanalysts, the designing of Reality TV shows that commodify human beings.

With this in mind, I return now to Freud's "Fetishism." I go to the three lines immediately preceding "the normal prototype of inferior organs is a woman's real small penis, the clitoris."[65]

Referring to a variation of the *coupeur des nattes* that he viewed as "a parallel to fetishism in social psychology,"[66] Freud takes his readers to "the Chinese custom of mutilating the female foot and then revering it like a fetish after it has been mutilated. It seems as though the Chinese male wants to thank the woman for having submitted to being castrated."[67] Were husbands and lovers grateful to women for having submitted to being mutilated? How did they demonstrate their gratitude? Did their appreciation help to mitigate the woman's pain and the torment of having been mutilated?

These unanswered questions stimulated my imagination. I wondered which features of the Chinese social psychology might have inspired a cultivation and nurturing of this custom? I wondered about the feelings of the women who had been subjected to footbinding as children. I wondered about the miseries suffered by the female children who were forced to submit to footbinding.

As a result, I became an impostor-poet. I invented a memoir, purportedly written by a woman who had her feet bound when she was a small child. I gave her the name, A-Hsui. I hoped that writing about A-Hsui's plight, in this special way of becoming one with her, being her, and being inside her head, would offer some new insights into the cultures that breed and nourish the fetishism strategy.

THREE

FOOTBINDING AND THE CULTURES OF
FETISHISM THAT BREED IT

So much has been written on fans and paper,
Every word is soaked in blood[1]

—"Song of Female Writing," *Nu shu**

The first few times I came to Freud's lines on the mutilation of the Chinese women's feet, I tried to imagine what it might be like, for me and for her, if a woman who had been subjected to this mutilation had come to me for psychotherapy. But eventually I realized that could not have happened. First of all, the woman would have had to question the fetishistic demands of her social order and then question her own motives for submitting to these demands. She would need to consider how she participates in perpetuating the practice of footbinding.

From early childhood she would have been told that the smaller her feet, the more she would be revered by her husband. As a child, before she achieved any of the promised advantages of her bound and mutilated feet, she might have had moments of rebellion, complaining, and crying. Occasionally she might have removed her bindings to get some relief from her pain. But after marriage, active rebellion would have been extremely difficult, if not impossible. Why would a woman, whose bound feet had brought her the promised husband, want to question the way things were? As with men who rarely question their fetishes until some time after they come to analysis for help with their job problems, insomnia, violent outbursts, or miserable marriages, a fetishized woman might begin to question her condition

---

* *Nu shu* is literally "female writing." According to Ping, (pp.160–61) it is a language created by women, a secret script passed down by Chinese women for centuries. It is a syllabic representation of a local Hunan dialect.

only if she came to a psychoanalyst for some other distress: the inability to find the right kind of man, loss of her husband's veneration and attention, headaches, insomnia, phobias, depression, or a miserable marriage. Of course, the major obstacle would be that during the centuries when all upper-class and middle-class little girls had their feet bound—by their mothers or grandmothers who also had bound feet, or by emissaries of the mother, servants whose feet were usually unbound so that they could serve their masters and mistresses—there was no psychoanalysis or anything like the psychotherapies we have today. In fact, it would have been impossible for such a treatment to have existed in the traditional Chinese culture, where centuries-old dictums discouraged sharing private thoughts and feelings, where putting emotions, feelings, and fantasies into words in the presence of a stranger would not have been acceptable.[2]

There is a tradition in China that, like psychoanalysis, encourages moving away from the external or material world in order to delve into the internal domain of thought and reflection. However, even within that tradition, silence, meditation, and introspection would be valued at the expense of revealing these thoughts directly to another human being. Even writing directly in a personal memoir would have been unacceptable.[3] But some forms of writing, such as writing on fans and writing on one's body, are secret ways, women's ways, of expressing otherwise forbidden fantasies, feelings, and thoughts.[4]

Soon after I began to notice the fetishistic structure of Freud's paper on fetishism, I read some books on footbinding. And what I learned from these readings made me even more determined to write for a woman who could not write for herself.

Footbinding is believed to have originated in China, in the twenty-first century BC. At that time it was confined to concubines and dancing girls and a ruler's mistresses. The practice was infrequent among commoners and fairly localized, until the beginning of the Ming Dynasty (1368–1644 AD), when it began to spread all over China.[5] Footbinding became a widespread enthusiasm in the late Ming period and reached its peak in the Qing Dynasty (1644–1911), during the mid-seventeenth century, when its popularity seemed to be a response to cultural crises arising during that time.[6] Feminist scholars attribute this crisis to the apparent increase in gender ambiguity in the previous century, which then stimulated a generalized anxiety about the erosion of a clearly defined place of women, and with it a male fear of woman's competition for supremacy, a fear that she might subvert the patriarchal order.[7]

As gender and class hierarchies were shaken up, they encouraged the spread of Neo-Confucianism. Footbinding then became an expression of the contradictions inherent in Neo-Confucianism, whose slogan was "maintain *li* (reason of the cosmos)" and "eliminate *yu* (human desire)."[8]

It is sometimes said that Zhu Xi, the founder of Neo-Confucianism, introduced footbinding as an efficient method of keeping women in their place. By hampering women from moving around freely, he hoped to eliminate *yu* and keep women chaste. This story, true or not, reflects these fundamental contradictions. Footbinding was designed to keep women chaste to meet the teachings of the Neo-Confucianist edict against human desire. And yet footbinding was highly eroticized. Critics of the practice of footbinding have frequently observed that the binding of women's feet embodied "China's oscillation between two extremes: neo-Confucian moral restraint to eliminate desires," while everywhere a person was surrounded with "indulgence in extravagance, expenditure and sensual pleasures, particularly in food and sex."[9]

The dual nature of footbinding is a reflection of China's oscillation between reason and indulgence, high moral purification and a corrupting of the flesh.

I was reminded here of Foster's essay on the fetishistic structure of the seventeenth-century "Pronk" still-lifes. You may recall that these images also reflected similar contradictions in Dutch culture. While very different in religious outlook and economic structure from the culture of seventeenth-century China, the contradictions in Dutch culture arose out of similar circumstances, as a consequence of conflicts over the dictates of religious fundamentalism and economic excess, extravagance, affluence, and financial speculation. Foster said this conflict reminded him of the contradictions in the Reaganomics of his day. Certainly that conflict has come back to life in a more virulent form in our own Bushomic era, in which the contradictions between the high moral stance of religious fundamentalism and the program of increasing the affluence of the already affluent and supporting the financial extravagances of the rich are plainly evident.

The Chinese had their footbinding; the Dutch had their "pronken." What are the cultural forms that express the contradictions in our culture? I hope to be able to answer that question, as I continue along in my explorations of the cultures that breed and nurture the fetishism strategy. For the moment, I can offer only a tentative outline of what that answer might turn out to be.

All of these cultural phenomena, Neo-Confucianism and footbinding, Dutch Protestantism and Pronk paintings, American fundamentalism and financial greed, have a similar fetishistic structure. In each instance, the moral stance allays the anxiety that arises in connection with the expression of human desires, whether these desires take the form of eroticism of the bound foot, or gustatory excess, or simply plain old financial greed.

My studies of Chinese footbinding stirred up a few other questions in my mind. Some scholars have proposed that footbinding might be an expression of a female opposition to the cultural contradictions inherent in male culture. In other words, females are said to have been attracted to footbinding because they saw it as a method of transmitting female culture to females. While initially I disagreed strongly with this hypothesis, after thinking some more about the contradictions that are inherent in the fetishism strategy, I was willing to consider that it might have some merit.

For example, in the late sixteenth century, just around the time that footbinding reached its peak of popularity, there was an outpouring and flourishing of poetry written by females and transmitted to other females orally. Much of the writing took the form of embroidery and painting on

fans.[10] Even the traditions and techniques of footbinding were regarded as a
sacred form of writing meant to be transmitted from woman to woman and
from mother to daughter. Most of that writing on the body, especially the
word-of-mouth "words" that described and perpetuated the accouterments
of footbinding, such as the weaving of the binding cloths and the intricate
embroidery on the satin shoes that would encase the tiny mutilated feet, were
fetishizations that turned against those who created it. Nevertheless, footbinding is often depicted as an art form, a form of writing on the body that
women created. All in all, it is generally believed that the practice of foot
mutilation was not entirely a creation of males. As I would see it, footbinding
embodied certain contradictions that are typical of gender role conformities.
It was a female capitulation to a fantasy of male desire, posed, however, as a
form of resistance to male domination. You might say, a sort of *Sex in the City*
of ancient times.

When I assimilated the possibility that the Chinese woman needed to
perpetuate and immortalize her mutilation, I realized how helpless I was in
the face of such a woman's helplessness to alter her fate. It was then that I
decided to become an impostor-poet. I invented a memoir and pretended
that it was written at the beginning of the twentieth century by a woman who
had had her feet bound as a child. I chose those years in Chinese history,
because it was a time of sweeping social change, when the Natural Foot
Societies that had been formed in the late nineteenth century by missionaries
and educated Chinese women were taking hold all over China. The natural
foot began to be more valued and revered than the bound foot. And as my
memoirist will explain, this positive change in social values, which included
greater equality between women and men, did not ameliorate her suffering
but brought with it pain and unhappiness of other kinds. After I recognized
the extent of the bodily torments that would begin and end my heroine's life,
I decided to give her some of the erotic pleasures that purportedly accompanied
having bound feet. And to advance that purpose, I also gave her a husband
who showed her his appreciation for her bound feet by introducing her to a
few of the extravagant eroticisms that exploited the advantages of the bound
foot. I did all this with the full knowledge that many Chinese husbands
treated their wives like chattel, beat them for their minor disobediences, and
had sexual intercourse only with their mistresses and concubines. But since I
was about to offer my fictional heroine a cure, I couldn't bear to make her
entire life a litany of unspeakable sufferings.

Writing is a form of expression that can be transformative, very much like
the expression of one's life narrative through remembrances, dreams, fantasies, and wishes, in psychotherapy. So, while I am not in any position to heal
an actual Chinese woman who submitted to footbinding, I could read the
books that contained some of the early poetry written by women. I could
read the interviews with women who were willing to talk about their footbinding and to reveal their feelings about the resulting mutilation of their
bodies. I could compare these revelations with the life narratives of my female
patients, many of whom suffered from female perversions, like extreme

sexual submissiveness, delicate-cutting, and eating disorders, that were tantamount to a self-fetishization of their bodies and minds and all in the name of their quest for love, admiration, adoration, veneration. Thus my clinical understandings of contemporary women, who also inscribe their fantasies on their bodies and minds, enabled me to give my invented Chinese heroine the gift of expression. Her name itself, and many of the words and phrases in her *faux memoir*, are derived from the interviews[11] I read. However, the psychological insights and narrative cohesiveness I am attributing to this woman would not have been available to an actual Chinese woman at the beginning of the twentieth century. The verbal forms I am inventing for her would feel alien to her. Nevertheless, my methods of writing words on paper are the only healing I can offer. The memoir of my imaginary patient is a composite of the voices of the many women I have read about and listened to. I imagined her writing the story of her life for me so that I could listen to her words and then transcribe them in my book for others to read.

Now, even as I am just beginning to inscribe her story on paper, I am already recognizing that many aspects of this story of self-fetishization will turn out to be a reflection of my own magical thinking. Footbinding, a form of writing transmitted from mother to daughter, and from one woman to another, is a form of magical thinking that turns against its creators.

And so, as an impostor-poet, who holds the magical belief that words can heal, my tale will surely turn against me. For example, why did I choose to emphasize certain details and not others? Why did I decide that erotic pleasure should compensate for my heroine's horrific bodily sufferings? Surely there must be something fetishistic about my strategy of offering pleasure to my heroine as a form of cure. Perhaps it is an illustration of Derrida's idea that the death drive tints itself in erotic color; that the impression of erogenous color draws a mask right on the skin? Perhaps this offering of pleasure has something to do with an erotic surface disguising and covering over the absences that would otherwise force us to think about the pain of trauma? *Maybe* several years from now, or maybe very soon after I finish writing this entire book, or *maybe* even sooner, as I come to the conclusion of this book and am trying to integrate my ideas on footbinding with my other depictions of the fetishism strategy, I *may* look back on this imposturous memoir and comprehend the fetishistic nature of the words I have attributed to my invented author, who I named A-Hsui.

MY BELOVED AND TERRIBLE LOTUS*

by A-Hsui

Until I was seven years old I was a lively child. My mind was alert and as frisky as my body. I looked everywhere at every thing. My imagination was riotous. I asked intelligent questions. Not all of them could be answered. But most of

---

* The basic outline for *My Beloved and Terrible Lotus* is derived from Levy's report of an interview with a woman named A-Hsui, "A Precaution to Lotus-loving Gentlemen," 210–12. However, her memoir is my invention and a composite of several of Levy's reports, 203–285.

them could and usually were. So, even though I studied at home and only in the mornings, I learned faster than my brothers, who went to school for a full day. In the afternoons I liked to jump about and dance. We had a big space of grass in our courtyard where I played jumping and hopping games by myself until my brothers came home. Then I would challenge them. Usually I could jump higher than any of them—except for the twelve-year-old.

Then on the lunar moon of the first month of my seventh year mother told our wet nurse to start binding my feet. I was so excited that I wanted to shout the news to the whole world. I laughed as I told my younger sister and my cousins that from the next day on I would have the prettiest feet in the family. I had heard three inches was the prettiest and that night I dreamt of three-inch lotus feet under a half-moon sky.

At that time, when I was still an innocent child, I didn't know why they had given feet the name of a flower. Nor did I consciously realize that the half-moon in my dream was the big toe hanging over the other four petals. I had seen my mother's feet without the bindings. They did not look like a lovely flower. They looked squished and pointy and her big toe was a hideous lump. But I tried not to think about what I had actually seen and kept dreaming about a luxurious, languorous lotus with petals moist with evening dew and all lit up by the shining moon. Now, at the age of forty-five, after so many tragedies have come to me because of my lotus feet, I understand the misunderstandings of my childhood. I can recognize that I was denying what my eyes had told me. I was softening the harsh and ugly image with a dream of softness. I wonder now whether I really deceived myself the way I am saying now. In any case the deception soon began to crack and wither away.

Before binding, my nurse softened my feet in a basin of warm water. The idea was to soften my toe bones so they could be bent into the proper shape without too much pain. As I gazed into the friendly warm water, I was aware that I was one of the lucky little girls. My nurse, who came from Hunan Province, had let me know that there were other bone-softening techniques. Nurse herself, who had never had her own feet bound because lotus feet were not convenient for a working woman who needed to be on her feet at all times of the day or night and walking from here to there whenever their mistress or master needed them, had been taught that the urine of a young boy[12] was the most reliable softening medicine. However, and fortunately, my mother, who was an elegant and enlightened upper-class woman, did not believe in the superstitious methods of country folk.

Indeed I was a fortunate girl to have such a wise and considerate mother. Since the time when I was three years old I had been hearing about the little girl who lived in Ta-T'ung near my cousin's village, who had had her feet softened by having them stuck for nearly two hours in a slit-open lamb's belly brimming with the hot blood of the lamb who was still crying out piteously for an hour before he finally expired.[13] My cousin was told that the girl's screams of terror were as much about the lamb and its bloody torment as about the suffering she was experiencing now and imagining she would endure after the binding began.

My binding cloth was made of hand-woven white cotton about five feet long and two inches wide.[14] After my toes were softened, Nurse placed one end on the top surface of my foot just below my ankle and wound it once around the four small toes; then she pulled the cloth toward the outside of my foot and turned it back toward the sole in order to bind the four toes more tightly. As she went along, Nurse would be pressing down on the binding around the toes as hard as she could. Pulling from the inside of the foot, she guided the binding toward the point made by the backward tilt of my little toes and then pulled the binding around my big toe. After that she pulled the cloth from the outer side of my foot and wrapped the heel guiding the binding toward the point of my little toes and wrapped it around the point, covering all except for the big toe. She wrapped the cloth over the instep and went once around the ankle and returned to the instep. Once again, she turned the binding toward the heel and wrapped it from the inner side of the foot to the point, which was becoming more pointed with each turn of the binding. After wrapping the cloth over the instep to the outer side of my foot, Nurse finished her task by pulling the binding around the heel and pulling that end of the cloth toward the end of the cloth covering the instep. The procedure, which looked complicated, actually had a certain pristine precision. It had been passed on by word of mouth from one generation of women to the next. The goal was to create a binding that would press my four small toes as far backwards toward the heel as possible until their tips reached nearly to my heel. Nurse wrapped the cloth around the front part of my foot two times and the rear part three times. Eventually, after several re-bindings, the big toe was also supposed to reach to the heel. To finish off, the front and back ends of the cloth were then sewn into place with needle and thread.[15]

The cloth was soft. My feet had been softened to mold more easily to the cloth. But the pain was unbearable, nevertheless.[16] When I tried to stand up to walk, I could not take even one step. Nurse had to carry me to bed. Mommy came to kiss me goodnight and praise me for my bravery. As I said, I had a wise and thoughtful mother. Though she was upper-class, she clung to the ways of her social order even though some mothers of her class no longer believed in footbinding. It was toward the end of the nineteenth century and already, in the big cities, many men and women, especially the intellectuals, were joining Natural Foot Societies. The best friend of my mother even drew up leaflets to pass out in the public demonstrations against footbinding. But mother would have none of these new-fangled notions. She was sure the natural foot fad would come and go just like so many other foolish ideas of the time. She wanted me to grow up to marry well just the way she had. Her certainty about the ways of the world enabled me to undergo the long and often painful process, with my own dreams and fantasies as her allies. She was determined to make it as easy for me as possible. As she told me many years later, she still remembered how painful it had been for her. And in her days, mothers didn't bother to console and comfort their daughters.

Nurse's mother, who was our cook and laundress, had woven six cloths for me on her loom. It was finer and softer than my cousin's binding cloth.

Cousin, whose family was not quite as wealthy as ours, had only two for changing twice a month. Her feet smelled. And her skin peeled. My mother never relented about the binding even when I pleaded and described the terrible pain. However, she made it as comfortable for me as she could. She instructed Nurse to change my bindings a few times a month, even though it meant removing her neat little stitches and re-sewing each time. When, on a few occasions, Mother discovered that I had opened the stitches and loosened the cloth at night to give my poor little toes a special treat of cool breeze, she Never beat me on the shoulders with a sugar cane. She simply gave me another lecture on how the tiniest feet were the most precious and how each night of unbinding defeated the shortening process and how one day I would be grateful for the pain and discomfort, and how one day a rich, handsome man would fall in love with my lovely lotus feet.

And sure enough, shortly after my fifteenth century birthday, this very man came along He fell in love with me the moment he looked at my three-and-one-half-inch lotus, which of course he could not see but only imagine, since they were clad in the gold-rimmed, satin slippers embroidered with a green and yellow dragon,[17] which peaked out from beneath my long black satin trousers. He agreed to the marriage with, what seemed to me at the time, a hurried, surreptitious glance up to my face, which my mirror and my family had told me was exquisite.

I had delicately slanted ebony eyes that were brilliant with the vitality of my questioning intelligence. The vivid impressions of the world I had seen were reflected in them. I was also blessed with the requisite tiny squat nose and rosebud mouth set in a jade oval that was whiter and more sensuously curved than the languorous bulb of a night-folded lotus flower.

The next day, when I was formally introduced to my husband, I noticed his eyes light up with pleasure as he watched me walking toward him. I no longer walked about with a cane or with my nurse supporting me. By the age of thirteen, I had learned the walk that went with lotus feet. It had not been a matter of studying or practicing that walk. It came naturally as a result of the physical effects of footbinding and my attempts to lessen the pains of walking on lotus feet.

After several years of being bound, as my feet grew shorter and more pointed, as the arch of my foot grew more bowed, the section from my knee to ankle became stunted in growth. Consequently when I walked I could only take very tiny steps and had to place my weight on my thighs and hips. This way of walking exuded a promise of exquisite sensuous delights. No one had to tell me this. It came as naturally to my mind as the lotus walking had come to my body. Although I never talked about it with my mother, I was aware that my method of walking caused the outer folds of my vagina to rub against each other.* As husband-to-be watched me walk toward him, it was as if he could see through my satin pants. First eyes lit up; then a moment later

* The walk that resulted from binding and its effects on the body and genital organs. From a Taiwanese doctor (Levy, 34). Ku Hung-ming, a scholar who advocated footbinding, describes the "wondrous" folds of the vagina. Levy (141). Buttocks full and large: Levy (151). General physiological effect: Levy (295–99).

the corners of his lips curled into a smile of pleasure. As for me, his looks and the sensations between my thighs were telling me of the unspoken advantages of lotus feet. I took note of the long, lush pigtail that announced the sensual possibilities of my-husband-to-be.

Later I learned that many men, my husband among them, believed that a woman whose thighs and hips undulated when she walked could also press her vagina forcefully during sexual intercourse, giving intense sensations to the man's penis.

But there was more to it than that. Soon after we were married my husband would begin to teach me the genuine value of diminutive feet. I actually didn't do much walking about after I got married. I did so only when serving tea to my husband and his business friends. If I went into town, which I rarely did, I was carried about in a covered sedan chair. Most of the time, I spent the day at home, lolling about, reading, learning the lute, embroidering, trying out a new face powder or hair lacquer, while waiting for my husband's return from his office. When I knew he was on his way, I would call my personal maid to dress me. My husband would greet me with his usual smile of pleasure. After dinner, he would carry me to bed.

About three years after I married him, I found out that when my husband was a young man still in school he had begun to learn the ways of lotus feet from expensive prostitutes who all had golden lotuses, which they knew how to employ in golden ways. There is a difference between one lotus and another. The golden were said to be three inches or less. These were the kind I used to dream of as a child. Mine turned out to be somewhere between slightly more than three inches and yet not nearly four. They were called Silver Lotus. Those that were any longer than four and yet still in the shape of a lotus were Iron Lotus. Phoenix Head meant that the tip of the foot was small and pointed, like the head of a bird. New Moon was supposed to indicate that the tiny foot was encased in white silk stockings that enhanced its elegance and made it look as slender as a sliver of moon. Jade Bamboo Shoots, which is what my husband liked to call my tiny lotus, was a term of endearment meaning that the foot was warm and glossy-white and soft as jade with a tip as pointed as a bamboo shoot.[18]

The tiny foot, in its flesh, personified the beauty of the entire body. It glistened like the white skin, it was arched like the eyebrows, pointed like the jade fingers, rounded like the breasts, small like the mouth, and when worn with the red embroidered shoes it was like the lips. Since the foot was hidden away it was enigmatic, like the vagina, the clitoris, the vulva, and all the private inner parts of a woman's body. The odor was more delicious than the armpits, legs, or vagina and also more seductive because a man could put the tiny foot all the way into his mouth.[19]

There were many ways to caress a lotus that would arouse the man, but if he was a gentle and sensitive man these gestures could carry the excitements to the woman's body, arousing her to peaks of exquisite joy. My husband's arousal depended very much on his ability to bring these sensuous excitements to me. He was not like some other husbands of the time who cared only for his own pleasures and might have three or four wives who he wanted to humiliate sexually. My husband was a liberal in all ways and even believed that one day Chinese girls might be given an education equal to that of their brothers. It wasn't until later that he realized that equality would mean the end of footbinding. And when he did come to that realization, everything between us changed. However, for the first fifteen years of our marriage, he was a Lotus lover and loved only me and loved to teach me the many ways of the Lotus.

He began with the average, ordinary way of caressing my lotus. After he carried me to bed, he would simply hold my left Lotus in his right hand. With the point of the Lotus face-up, he would tightly grasp the side of the Lotus in his palms and press his thumb and forefinger on the toes, covering the instep with his other fingers. After a few minutes he would reverse to the right Lotus and perform the same gestures with his left hand.[20]

A few months later, my husband introduced me to more complicated pleasures. At the time I didn't always know what he was doing. But he seemed practiced in his methods and sure of himself. His confidence was very exciting to me. As I think back now and recall his methods of grasping and caressing my Lotus, they seem rather studied and artificial, almost ridiculous. But in those days whatever my husband did with my body seemed just right to me. Even when the pressure of his hands and fingers verged on pain, ultimately his carefully calculated touches on my Lotuses could make my entire body sing sweetly like a lute.

He would press with his palm and four fingers on the tip of the lotus and instep and then, placing his thumb and forefinger across and under the middle of the arched sole, he would grip tightly and twist his wrist around. Tightly covering my instep with his palm he would lock it under the sole with his thumb, index, and middle finger. His ring finger and little finger would support my heel. He would place the big toe in the center of his palm and press his lit-tle finger down on it. With his thumb and middle finger forming a circle around my shoe he would press the center of the sole against the thumb and forefinger. At a certain moment in this ritual of Lotus caressing, he would ask me to caress his pigtail between my thumb and forefinger. Usually, that would be the moment before the moment of his ejaculation. Sometimes though he would require these pigtail caresses many times during our scenario of love.[21]

After our first year of marriage, my husband supplemented the Lotus caresses with little scenes that he might have learned with the prostitutes, but that soon became our personal joys.

He would instruct me to sit at the edge of the bed and lean backwards, supporting my upper body by placing my hands behind me. From this half-reclining position it would be easy for me to spread my legs upwards and apart. As he stood facing me, he put my right foot on his left shoulder and grasped my left foot in his right palm. He could gaze at the right foot and feel the left one soft as cotton in his hands. I would gaze up into his eyes and he would lean forward to bite my tongue. He timed the frequency and vigor of his movements with the upward and downward motion of the right lotus on his shoulder and convey his mounting excitement to me by grasping the left lotus tightly between his thumb and forefinger. By then I knew to caress his pigtail at just the right moment of his excitement.[22]

Sometimes he would sprawl across the edge of our bed, facing inwards with one foot stretched out and the other hanging beside the bed. He instructed me to sit and rest my thighs on his stomach. My left thigh crossed his knee so that my red shoe could face upwards. My right thigh crossed over my left thigh in such a way that I could draw up my knee to a position that placed my bare lotus in his left palm. He had the red shoe for his visual pleasure and my slender, pointed, soft, glossy bare lotus for sensuous pleasures and for all kinds of playful caresses. Intercourse in this position, although a bit uncomfortable for me, gave my husband exquisite sexual excitement. His rising excitement would make my own excitements rise to heavenly peaks.[23]

The basic formula of the alternating red shoe–bare white lotus scenarios my husband had learned from prostitutes. But he invented many of the variations, and his inventiveness enabled me to participate willingly in the joys of these scenes. There was one that particularly excited me.

Our courtyard garden, which was enclosed by small trees and hidden from view, was open to the sky. On moonlit nights, my husband would like to sit on the stone stool in our garden. He liked me to start out wearing my red embroidered slippers and stand before him fully dressed. He instructed me to clasp his neck with my right arm and balance myself on my right foot only. My left foot was to be drawn upwards. I would take off my left shoe and place the exposed lotus in his left palm. He would encircle my waist with his right arm and kiss me as I leaned forward. He would bite my tongue and then begin caressing it with his tongue as he caressed my left Lotus between his palm and three middle fingers. With our tongues caressing and one Lotus touching earth like a red pepper and the other in his palm like a slender bamboo shoot, we needed no other pleasures.[24]

In the first five years of our marriage we had two sons. Our last child, who came to us almost as a surprise, ten years after our second son, was a girl. A year or so after our daughter's birth, my husband had begun to become a stranger to me. Though he had been a devoted Lotus lover throughout his youth and the first fifteen years of our marriage, each year after the turn of the century he became more and more aware that footbinding was considered politically incorrect. If it got around that he favored such an antiquated practice, it would diminish his prospects for advancing his career in the government and probably severely curtail the profits from his business dealings. He had always been a man who kept up with the times. When he heard that pigtails would soon be outlawed, he immediately cut off his beautiful long pigtail, which for all these long years he had regarded as a mark of his manhood, much as my Lotuses had been the mark of my womanhood. He had worn his pigtail with pride and dignity. Now, he prided himself on his liberal political and social ideas. Yet, despite his willingness to give up his pigtail and despite his advanced social ideals, he had managed to resist the foot emancipation movement until after the earliest years of the century.

However, the 1910 Revolution, with its emphasis on social equality and the emancipation of women, would set in motion the nationwide events that would eventually bring an end to footbinding in China. After nearly four thousand years (2100BC–1900AD) it took only a decade or so, less than one generation, for the practice to almost disappear. By 1910 most well-to-do families had decided that their daughters would have natural feet. Very few girls born after 1920 had their feet bound. The tragic generations were woman my age and older, any woman who had been born before 1907.[25]

As early as 1897, foreign missionaries were running a natural foot society in Shanghai. They petitioned the Emperor that children born after 1897 should not be recognized as citizens unless they had natural feet. The year after my second son was born the Empress Dowager, under pressure, issued "The Anti-Footbinding Edict of 1902." After the 1910 Revolution, there were foot emancipation edicts announced every day.[26] There were public demonstrations and newspaper editorials denouncing the practice as a sign of barbarism and reactionary political directions. In most towns and villages the local governments recommended coercive measures to assure the abolition of bound feet. Girls under fifteen were told to unbind their feet, or were forbidden to bind them if they were still unbound. The fine for disobedience was five silver dollars. Women over thirty were advised to let their feet out, but were not fined if they did not. Female investigators were appointed to assist village elders in conducting periodic examinations of young girls' feet. In some places, women with bound feet were publicly shamed. In some places, cast-off bindings were collected into mountains of shame. Little red shoes were collected and lined up along the corridors of schools and other public buildings.[27]

The public shaming became the private and personal shame of the woman with tiny feet. Almost every household where a woman with bound feet lived was affected. My husband was ashamed to be seen in public with me. In private he disdained my lotus feet and all the rest of my body and never again did his eyes light up with excitement at the sight of me. He turned his gaze from my face, trying not to look at me, and only did so when absolutely necessary. He was afraid that his new friends and business colleagues would laugh at me because my tiny feet were so ridiculous. He stopped inviting his friends and business acquaintances to the house. He would no longer invite me to attend banquets with him. He now praised natural feet with the same fervor with which he had sung the delights of the Lotus. He soon took a mistress ten years younger than me who had large natural feet and a high position in the revolutionary government.

My husband's harsh treatment deprived me of the love that had brought my erotic senses, my entire being, into existence. It made me feel as though I, myself, whoever I had once been, no longer existed. For a few years, I no longer knew who I was. Who I had been had been so much enmeshed in my silver lotuses. I suffered deeply but there was no one I could talk to about my sufferings. Only one thing made me happy. My husband forbade that our daughter have her feet bound. I was spared having to inflict this painful experience on her. But I feared that when she grew up she would have contempt for me. She would laugh at my preposterous lotuses.

My mother, who had died several years ago, had believed that she would enhance and insure my marital happiness by insisting that I have my feet bound. But my beautiful silver lotuses turned out, in the end, to be the source of my greatest misery and unhappiness. Like many other women of my generation, I tried to get my feet to revert to their natural form.

Compared to the excruciating torture of letting the foot out, the discomforts and pains of foot binding were relatively minor.[28] In spite of my growing hatred for him, I wanted my husband back. I wanted to become an emancipated woman. I was ashamed that I could not participate in the world outside my garden walls. I wanted to set a positive example for my little girl.

I tried soaking my feet in cold water every night but this remedy did nothing except to make my feet swell up. I tried walking about without bindings. But this brought extreme pressure on my four toes, which until then had been curled up under the sole of my foot. I endured these tortures for two months. But there was no sign of any improvement. In fact, my instep became puffy and my legs were becoming more and more swollen. I was hearing what had happened to other women of my generation who tried to let out their feet. In the winter their feet and legs were very sensitive to low temperatures and suffered from cold sores. In the spring, as the days grew warmer and warmer, the flesh would decay and make it impossible to take even one step.

A year or so after I had tried to let my feet out, the government printed specific instructions for letting out the feet.* These instructions were circulated to every household and posted in prominent places on public buildings. The instructions said that it was essential to begin the letting out by making a shorter and looser binding cloth. By no means should a woman suddenly eliminate use of binding cloth. This would only succeed in causing the blood to flow so violently that pain and swelling would be the inevitable result. This disastrous outcome, of course, I had discovered on my own. The next directive said to wash the foot nightly in hot water, adding a little vinegar to the water. And here how mistaken my own judgment had been. I, like so many women I knew, had been using cold water. When retiring to bed, we were supposed to remove binding cloth and stockings to allow the blood to circulate. We were to stuff cotton between our four toes, thus encouraging them to gradually expand outward.

I tried following these steps. Using hot water with vinegar did help to ease the pain. My toes did begin to expand outward from the cotton between them. But these measures achieved just a tiny bit of expansion, barely noticeable. I followed the instructions with half a will. In my heart of hearts, I knew all too well that the extreme bowed bone structure that had been created by the bindings of my childhood could never be restored to anything vaguely resembling a natural shape. The flesh on my feet eventually

---

* The instructions for letting out were printed in 1927, long after A-Hsui would have let her feet out. Nevertheless I am assuming that similar instructions would have been available to her.

did expand somewhat. But my feet expanded into bulky and shapeless lumps. I bought the larger shoes that were recommended in the foot emancipation directives and put cotton in the toe region so that the shoes wouldn't fall off my feet when I walked. Of course, I couldn't really walk. All I could do was stumble along like a beast. A few times I fell down and couldn't even stand up again until my youngest son came home from school and helped me. He had a contemptuous grin on his face. But I was his mother and he helped me to get up.

Compared to the way I became when I started to let out my feet, I had been relatively spry and vigorous with my Lotuses. I missed my Lotuses, which still seemed very beautiful to me. I loved the red embroidered slippers that had adorned them. I hated the new natural shoes I was forced to wear. My husband's mistress had natural feet that she could fit into delicate shoes with high heels and thin straps across her instep. When she and my husband went to banquets together, she wore these fashionable high-heeled shoes. In her office at the Bureau of Intelligence she wore plain but stylish flat shoes. With my shapeless lumps I could never wear a beautiful shoe again. I could not feel comfortable in the natural flat shoe, either. Now that I had lost my Lotuses, I didn't know what to do with the exquisite embroidered slippers that lined the shelves of the cupboard that had been built to house and cherish them.

Throughout the land the tiny-footed woman was looked down upon and made to feel ashamed. In my cousin's city the tiny-footed woman was forbidden to appear in public places. In some towns they were prohibited from walking in the streets. Police were sent to search out the hidden tiny-footed and strip off their bindings. In Changehow, the local citizens were encouraged to whip the feet of any tiny-footed woman seen in public. I heard that some women committed suicide rather than face the shame of exposure.[29]

It wasn't until my cousin, who had also suffered the shame and dishonor of her Lotuses, encouraged me to write about the injustices that had befallen me as a child, as a young bride, and as a grown woman, that I began to grasp the fuller implications of what had been done to me. After I started to write my memoir, I gained back some sense of who I had been and realized how different that was from the person I was now. My writing of words brought me back into existence. I will leave these pages as a legacy to my daughter, who has strong and capable natural feet. *Maybe* other women will read my tale. *Maybe* throughout the ages to come women will resist those forces that encourage them to mold their daughters into objects of desire. *Maybe* women will become subjects in their own right. *Maybe* even the natural-footed woman, who wears sensible work shoes by day but then, like my husband's mistress, cripples her own feet by squeezing them into high-heeled alluring shoes in the evening, might question if she is any freer than her shameful sisters who had their feet bound as children, and now sit at home in mourning. *Maybe.* Or *maybe* the image of the bound foot is irresistible, endlessly compelling newer and more extravagent versions of the Lotus.

Though the writing of A-Hsui's memoir did not cure her sufferings, it offered me a "cure" for my fixation on Freud's "Fetishism." It was, as all such cures inevitably turn out to be, a passing flight into health and therefore only temporary. Every now and then, thoughts of A-Hsui's silver Lotus crept into my mind as if to warn me that my focus on her dramatic plight had been a diversion that enabled me to avoid some of the more complicated aspects of the fetishism strategy. I sensed that the vivid images of bound feet were preoccupying the foreground of my mind. I suspected that those images remained so insistently in the foreground in order to obscure something more threatening that hovered in the margins and background. In other words, these images were a device modeled on the foreground-background principle of the fetishism strategy, and not far removed, in their unconscious motivations, from the standard lists of fetish objects that sexologists and other medical experts parade before our eyes in order to banish the traumatizing social forces that breed these fetishes. The object of such fetishistic devices is to keep hidden and silent the traumas that keep trying to press their way out of the background and into the foreground of our minds. For the moment, at least, my symptomatic clinging to the spectacular images of A-Hsui's tortured feet was allaying my anxieties about what I might discover if I tried to look more deeply into the "cultures" that sponsored A-Hsui's affliction.

I started thinking about something else—another way in which women's bodies are exploited. I turned my attention to the film medium and the various ways that film writers and directors exploit the body of a woman as a distraction from the traumatic elements that hover in the backgrounds of their films. This tactic, I reasoned, would bring me halfway to where I needed to go. Or, at the least, a bit closer to confronting the traumatic elements that hide in the shadows of our cultures of fetishism.

In order to get started on this uncertain journey, I decided to use a psychoanalytic method on myself. I let my mind roam freely from one seemingly irrelevant thought to another. Every now and then I thought about the images of skin-cutting that appeared in the 1997 film *Female Perversions*. However, for the moment at least, these images of women cutting into their own bodies did not seem to express what I was trying to explain about the cultures that breed and nurture the fetishism strategy. At last I came to an image that replaced my preoccupation with A-Hsui's plight with a "healthier" occupation.

I decided to write about the way women's bodies are exploited in films. However, the initial image that caught my mind seemed to have very little to do with films. Since I was then, as always and still, disturbed by the fetishistic structure of the medical profession and the insidious infiltration of the medical approach into psychoanalysis, I decided to introduce my ideas about women's bodies in films with some sort of medical representation of the body of a woman.

It was not exactly a bolt from the blue that encouraged my mind to revisit and review a famous painting that depicted the body of a woman bent over backwards, collapsing onto the arm of a doctor whose medical specialty was hysteria. Although, presumably, I had forgotten all about that dramatic image, it was only lying dormant, ready to come to life when I needed it. It was not an image from childhood or adolescence. Nor did it come to me directly from my psychology internship, where very likely I might first have seen it, but not yet been ready to take in its fetishistic significance. I was ready to receive and register that broken-backed figuration of a woman's body when a photograph of it was used as an illustration for a paper I had edited for *American Imago*, "What's love got to do with it? Woman as the Glitch in the Postmodern Record."

As the thoughts I wanted to express began to take shape in my mind, the photograph I had seen several years earlier, sprang back into life and I realized at once that if I simply wrote down my thoughts about this photograph, it would turn out to be exactly the right image to introduce my ideas on how the fetishism strategy is employed in the making of films.

FOUR

THE BODY OF A WOMAN
MAKING FILMS

In Andre Broulliet's 1887 painting of Jean Martin Charcot giving a clinical lecture at The Saltpetriere, the brightly lit foreground is dominated by the figure of Charcot and his hysterical patient, Blanche Wittman.[1] Charcot's left hand supports his patient. His right hand supports his lesson in hysteria. Wittman's body is compliantly collapsed across Charcot's left forearm in the characteristic back-arched posture of the hysterical fit. The hysteric's eyes are shut, her head and neck are twisted to the side, her bosom and shoulder are partially bared. The doctor's right hand is posed in the fist of authority, the index finger extended in emphasis.

The room is filled to capacity with bearded, black-suited medical students, and all of them, whether standing against the windows and walls or seated, are leaning forward as though captivated by the authority of Charcot's words. Or, at second glance, perhaps they are transfixed by the spectacle of Miss Wittman's artful fit? In the shadows, on the back wall of the lecture hall, behind the students, hangs a series of large medical illustrations. These illustrations within the painting are of prostrate women, stretched out on wooden floors and slabs with their backs arched in the helpless ecstasy of a hysterical fit.

In the late nineteenth century, there was a fondness for images of collapsing, broken-backed women. The technical name for this posture was *opisthotonus*, "a spasm of muscles of the neck, back and legs in which the body is bent backward."[2] Sometimes, it was stressed that the posture represented the spasm of a hysterical fit. At other times, the posture was said to be the outcome of some spasmodic sexual excitement. But either way the emphasis went, the meaning was actually the same. The confusion between female sexual desires and hysterical fits is generic to the study of hysteria. The images in the Charcot painting convey the centuries-old gendered script where mentality and rationality were assigned to the doctor (typically a male), while bodily spasms and irrationality were assigned to the patient (typically female).

Charcot's students were told that mild hysterias were not a real illness, "but one of the varieties of female character. . . . One might even say that hysterics are more womanly than other women."[3] And, like the most womanly of women, hysterics were said to be "impressionable, malleable, coquettish, seductive, lazy."[4] At the same time, men were warned not to be taken in by the hysteric's womanly arts, because the hysteric can be "unjust, violent, she recriminates with bitterness, gives herself over to scenes, tears and extravagance, makes a show of her passions"[5] And, obviously such a woman is in no way suited to "bring happiness and calm to the conjugal hearth."[6]

Charcot's students were also taught how to make the diagnostic differentiation between epileptics and hysterics. "The hysterics were the ones who adorn their medical charts with artificial flowers, ribbons, pieces of mirrors, pictures with bright colors."[7] Hysterics, unlike the epileptics, are untruthful, recalcitrant, and tricky. The helpless ecstasies of the hysterical fit very often turned around into displays of power, acts of rebellion and rampant sexuality.[8] Thus these most womanly of women with their stereotypical femininity could be almost virile in their masculinity. The students of Charcot, compassionate as they might have been as they found themselves entranced, perhaps seduced, by the dramatic spectacle of Blanche Wittman's *opisthotonus*, were being taught that hysterics were tricky deceptive females, as enigmatic and elusive as the female herself.

Whether in medicine, art, psychology, politics, or religion, it has been a long-standing tradition to employ the enigmatic body of a woman with its mysterious desires and perplexing, unpredictable movements as a fetishistic emblem. As I shall be demonstrating, the fetishism strategy displays with suspicious urgency a narrow or partial representation of the body's experience, in order to mask or repress a fuller experience that might otherwise constitute a trauma. We must ask, "Are the images of broken-backed, hysterical women so flagrantly dramatic that they foreclose the possibility of the trauma of loss, perhaps specifically, the loss of childhood innocence?" If we look past the glittering spectacle of the foreground image, we gain access to the images of loss that loom in the background. At the same time we do not banish the foreground but retain it, so that we may decipher the dynamic relationship between both images. It is crucial to the fetishism strategy that while it focuses the viewer on the foreground, it also allows that some expression be given to the potentially traumatic experience that lies in the background or margins. Like the fetish, which is both an item of concealment and an item of revelation, the images of women in films both mask the traumas and expose them.[9]

In a film, what the female (and, of course, sometimes the male) performer does and says is, in part at least, a product of how the directors, writers, cameramen, editors, costumers, hair-dressers, and make-up and lighting artists decide to use her body. At a certain point, though, the performer is *the* artist, who must transmit an emotional experience to the audience. The body of the performer is the essential creative medium. In the films I will be discussing, the bodily presence of the film star—her posture, gestures, facial expressions and voice—achieve the two opposing but reciprocal psychological functions that are characteristic of the fetishism strategy:—concealment and revelation.[10]

In proposing these reciprocal functions for the body of a woman in films, I am also proposing a method of film interpretation derived from clinical experience with the fetishism strategy. Fetishistic transactions are desperate, fixated, ritualized, repetitive. They preoccupy a patient's life and seek to occupy the total space of the psychoanalytic therapy. Similarly fetishistic transactions in film are those that occupy the center or foreground of the visual field and thereby preoccupy the conscious attention of the audience to the detriment of some other less conscious or unconscious theme. Whether in life, in an analysis, or in a film, these efforts to dominate and preoccupy the conscious field of experience are designed to push the trauma or traumatic elements to the background or margins of experience. Thus whenever images of a woman's body are a hyperconscious, dominant focus of a film, we must suspect the fetishism strategy at work, rendering other aspects of the film unconscious. Nevertheless, the body of the actress also serves an opposing or reciprocal function, which is to undermine foreclosure and disavowal by exposing an unconscious theme that has eluded the many persons engaged in the manufacture of the film.[11]

Not every film calls for interpretations informed by the foreground-background strategy of fetishism. Moreover, even when a film is clearly structured along fetishistic lines, that is, even when there is a conspicuously vivid, preoccupying foreground, the dynamic reciprocities between foreground and marginal texts are not easily discerned. They must be interpreted. Therefore, I am not suggesting that psychoanalytic interpretations of films should eliminate the central or foreground text in order to arrive at some *true* unconscious marginal or background text. The crucial factor that must be discerned and interpreted is the discordance or discrepancy between a foreground statement and those elements that have been cast into the margins or background.

I begin with an image that once was, and still is, dramatically present in the popular imagination: the bodily presence of Marilyn Monroe—a bodily presence that both exposed and screened out the catastrophic traumas of her life both in and out of films. Norma Jean Mortensen alias Norma Jeane Baker alias Norma Jeane Dougherty alias Marilyn Monroe was then (and is still now) an American icon. Marilyn Monroe was the fabricated cultural commodity.[12] But where is Norma Jeane? The virtual annihilation of the abandoned child who was Norma Jeane is the pre-condition and prerequisite for the manufacturing of Marilyn Monroe, the sex goddess.[13]

Even after we know and acknowledge what happened to Norma Jeane, we go on worshipping the goddess; we go on worshipping this glittering image of womanly womanliness to repress any knowledge of the range and complexity of actual female sexuality. We shall be seeing how Monroe's films exploit the glittering white light of her body and how that fetishistic device serves to obscure the deceptions and lies of the American social order.

However, the sad, hurt eyes and trembling baby voice of the lost Norma
Jeane defeat the exploiters. The eyes and the voice transmit the ways in which
the body was exploited. The lies are exposed. All we have to do is bring them
out of the shadows and there they will be—right before our eyes.[14]

To illustrate, I will outline the plots of the two films that generally serve as
the markers for the official beginning and official ending of Monroe's stardom:
Niagara (January 1953), in which she was given her first major role, and *The
Misfits* (February 1961), her last completed film. As in *The Misfits*, the central
or foreground plot of *Niagara* unfolds against a background theme of
redemption through a reunion with Nature. *Niagara* opens with a visual
display of Niagara Falls and the voice of a narrator contrasting the torments
of the mind with the peaceful certainties of Nature. As the narrator describes
the universal longing to find peace in the embrace of Nature, Niagara Falls
fade into the background and the human story begins.

In *Niagara*, Monroe was cast as Rose Loomis, the dark woman, the
wicked seductress, whose corrupt and unruly sexuality provides a stark visual
contrast to the innocent boundlessness of Niagara Falls. Rose Loomis represents the untrustworthy, tricky, manipulative, seductive aspect of the hysterical
female. Her bodily presence is employed as the corrupt counterimage that
will reinforce and enhance the background theme of redemption through a
return to Nature.

Rose leads her latest lover, Ted, to murder her husband, George, played by
Joseph Cotton, whom she manipulates into alternate fits of sexual ecstasy and
insane jealousy in order to lure him to the scene of his murder—the Niagara
Falls. When Rose explains to Ted, "There's always a way to get around
George," the viewer knows she is referring to unmentionable sexual acts.
Rose gets around George but, within minutes afterwards, George reverts to
his paranoid suspiciousness as he watches Rose getting all dolled up "to go
shopping." He discovers the plot to murder him, murders Ted instead,
disguises himself in Ted's clothing, and then stalks and lures Rose to the
Niagara Tower, where he strangles her.

Rose's corpse stretched out, back-arched in the generic *opisthotonic* posture
against the striped shadows of a corridor within the Niagara Tower mimics the
hysterical bodies illustrated in the Charcot painting. The sensational image of
her *opisthotonic* corpse marks the midpoint of the film.

The second half illustrates George's redemption and cure, which he
achieves first through a good woman and then through the natural goodness
of Niagara Falls. The good woman, Polly Cutler, played by Jean Peters, is the
loyal wife, the nurse-mother, who is properly indignant when her newlywed
husband, Ray, invites her to contort her trim body into a seductive pose á la
Rose Loomis. By rescuing Polly from drowning and allowing his own body
to sink into the swirling waters of Niagara Falls, George's tormented soul
finds peace in the embrace of Nature.

Aside from a few minor scenes in a souvenir shop and a hospital room, the
entire film takes place in three settings, the Niagara Tower, the motel over-
looking Niagara Falls, and the motor launch that carries Cotton and Peters

into the currents leading to the falls. George's emotional switch from the corrupt, amoral, seductive Rose to the honest, supermoral, proper, asexual Polly is crucial to the plot. Rose is the hysterical, childlike woman whose unruly sexuality threatens to undermine the sanctity of marriage. Polly is the motherly redeemer whose kind nursing, empathic listening, and compassionate attunement to George's emotional plight initiate the process of psychological redemption that will ultimately lead George back to the body of the primal mother.

Monroe would never again undertake a role that entailed the blatantly corrupt, blatantly seductive actions of Rose Loomis. Nevertheless, while *Niagara* was in the public eye, she went along with the publicity that required her to engage in and cooperate with crude exploitations of her body. She went everywhere clad in the skin-tight, body-revealing dresses appropriate to a seductive manipulative woman. Joe DiMaggio was outraged and refused to accompany her to these highly publicized spectacles. The Hollywood gossip columnists described her as a vulgar exhibitionist. Joan Crawford shook her finger at the shameless Monroe for conduct unbecoming an actress and a lady.[15]

In her last film, *The Misfits*, written by Arthur Miller and directed by John Huston, Monroe is cast in the mythic form that had became her trademark—sexual availability filtered through a glow of innocence. Still an exploitation, but a more subtle and deceptive one. Huston invented and developed the mythic Monroe image when he directed her in her first serious role as Angela in *The Asphalt Jungle*. His direction and Hal Rosson's camera work filtered Angela's voluptuous bosom, thighs, and buttocks through the soft focus of Monroe's glow of innocence, as if to state that Angela was a victim of the Jungle and not one of its predators. Despite his honorable artistic intentions, Huston did not hesitate to exploit her body in that early film or in *The Misfits*.

Miller had worked for three years, transposing his short story *The Misfits* into a screenplay as a "valentine for Marilyn."[16] By the time the film went into production, Monroe had had two miscarriages, her marriage to Miller was over, her affair with Yves Montand was petering out Miller's valentine love had so frequently alternated with anger that his ambivalence had tilted over into a palpable, barely disguised hatred, which Monroe must have sensed and responded to with a certain mistrust of valentines. Despite her wariness of Miller, she still trusted Huston. Besides, she was desperate to do another movie and therefore desperate to go ahead with the filming—no matter what.

The film was a disaster. Monroe was blamed for everything that went wrong. All her emotional problems were exaggerated to cover up Huston's gambling debts and the huge squandering of money on the production.[17] Monroe was always late and always demanded infinite retakes. Clark Gable, one of her costars, complained, "I damned near went nuts waiting for her to show." When he died shortly after the film was finished, gossip had it that the strain of working with Marilyn had contributed to his untimely death.[18]

In *The Misfits*, Monroe is cast as Rosalyn Tabor, a childlike vagabond. The opening scenes portray a Rosalyn who is always memorizing her grown-up lines and looking to find herself in a mirror. Rosalyn is the shyly seductive, uneducated but intuitively knowing, sensitively sweet, malleable little girl with a woman's body, whose glowing innocence captivates Guido (Eli Wallach), Gay (Clark Gable), and Perce (Montgomery Clift), the three misfit cowboys, who are meant to symbolize all the physically powerful but socially castrated Men of America. Miller's cliches inhabit and pervade the movie and assign to Monroe the most vivid expressions of his customary bland, less-than-thoughtful liberalism.

Rosalyn is the nurse-redeemer who will attempt a cure and rescue of the cowboys by restoring them to the bosom of Nature. As Rosalyn conceives of her mission of redemption, she must relieve the cowboys of their hard-edged, upright (phallic?) defenses by inspiring their softer, feminine, caring natures. However, Rosalyn is an unbelievable redeemer. Miller has given her the mentality and lines of a four-year-old. Unlike an actual four-year-old, Rosalyn is depicted as an adult imitating a child who is imitating an adult.[19] Rosalyn the redeemer is indistinguishable from the cowboys' broken bodies and souls, the trampled lettuce, hunted rabbits and the lassoed wild mustangs she is striving to save and protect. As a child might do, Rosalyn hugs a tree and watches her garden grow and plays house first with Guido and then with Gay. To win the rodeo money for Perce, Rosalyn plays paddle ping-pong in a skin-tight, low cut, polka dot dress. Her buttocks and bosom shake convulsively as Perce and the crowd of men at the bar frantically place their bets, as they count out how many times she can hit the ball.

For another pivotal scene, Huston and Miller collaborated on acting directions. The scene is meant to represent Rosalyn's quest for wholeness. "She flies into a warm, longing solo dance among the weeds, and coming to a great tree she halts and then embraces it, pressing her face against its trunk."[20]

A few days later, Rosalyn and the three cowboys set out for the desert, where the men will be trying to recover their good old days by capturing wild mustangs and selling them to manufacturers of dog food. As they are riding toward the desert, Rosalyn is thinking of the journey as a return to Nature, while the men are thinking only of proving their manhood. When Rosalyn realizes that she has been duped and that, furthermore, she is helpless to stop the cowboys from their ghastly mission, she turns away from the men and strides off into the desert in a fit of rebellion. When she is some forty feet away from the cowboy trio, Rosalyn swerves about and enacts what Miller's screenplay demands of her: "she screams, her body writhing bending over as though to catapult her hatred. . . .'You liars. All of you.' Clenching her fists she screams toward their faces, 'Liars!' "[21] "Man, Big Man. You're only living when you can watch something die. Kill everything, that's all you want."[22]

The conclusion of the film, which comes soon after Rosalyn's hysterical fit, is arbitrary. In order for things to fit together in proper Hollywood style, misfit Rosalyn had to be matched up with one of the misfit cowboys. As Rosalyn and Gay (Huston and Miller had first considered Perce, and then Guido) ride off in the pick-up truck, she speaks of creating a baby who will be brave from the beginning, and Gay points to a distant star of hope. As Miller's script reads, Rosalyn and Gay have found their true selves in their newfound capacity for intimacy. However, by the time that last scene was finally filmed, Monroe and Gable were emotionally depleted and the emotional space Rosalyn and Gay inhabit is dead and emptied of all desire.

Monroe was not oblivious to her exploitation. She particularly resented "having to throw a fit," instead of being given words of reason. "I guess they thought I was too dumb to explain anything, so I have a fit—a screaming, crazy fit. I mean *nuts*. And to think Arthur Miller did this to me. He was supposed to be writing this for me . . . and Huston treats me like an idiot."[23]

The fits, contortions, quivers, and gyrations assigned to Monroe's body, the four-year-old level of the supposedly intuitively intelligent dialogue written just for her by Arthur Miller—in other words, the *way* her body and mind were exploited by the director and writer and cameraman—functioned as unconscious counterforces to the conscious messages of the film The fetishistic uses of Monroe's body undermine and sabotage the film's conscious messages of humanism, naturalism, and the transcendence of Nature. The celebration of a salvation through a return to Nature is exposed as a flimsy lie—a cover-up for the traumas of every misfit, male or female, who has been deprived of the Word.

As Monroe played out the repetitions of the type to which she had been assigned, the stereotype that became the mirror where she sought to find herself, her life was robbed of the diversity and vitality that allows an actress to grow into a believable womanly presence. And she was smart enough to know how she was being exploited. After the filming of *The Misfits*, she said, "All my life I've played Marilyn Monroe, Marilyn Monroe, Marilyn Monroe. I've tried to do a little better, and find myself doing an imitation of myself."[24] Monroe's creative growth was stunted and betrayed by the stereotypes of womanhood she eventually succumbed to in her desperation to find herself. Monroe composed a lyric, "Help, Help, Help, I feel life coming closer . . . When all I want is to die."[25] Julie Suks, another would-be poet, described Monroe as a child playing statues, pleading, "Find me. Find me. Complete this form."[26] But no one ever did find her. Not the several therapists and analysts who treated her, nor the psychiatrists who ministered her a jumbled assortment of medications that were bound to exacerbate the severe depressions that assailed her.

Norma Jeane, the abandoned child, had discovered a self-cure for the depressions, and it was the only cure that seemed to work—at least for brief periods of time. Indeed, it was Norma Jeane's self-cure that had collaborated in the manufacture of the sex goddess, Marilyn Monroe.

Norma Jeane's body knew how to make love to the camera and the camera loved making love to her. While she was never entirely certain of "who or what she was," the camera assured her that her body was beautiful and sexually alluring. Later on, the perplexities of "who or what she was" still spoke in Monroe's mournful eyes, imparting to her sexuality the childlike innocence that became her trademark. When all else failed to confirm her

58   C u l t u r e s   o f   F e t i s h i s m

identity, Monroe could rely on her body and the powerful effects she could
achieve through an exhibition of her body. Finally, though she had longed to
find herself in a different kind of mirror, Monroe only felt alive and real when
she was the sexual object of a powerful and prominent man.[27] She was
desperately "feminine," treating her body as if it were a container on which
she or her retinue of hair-dressers, costume designers, voice and body
coaches, directors must inscribe the designs of femininity. And as any female
impersonator, male or female, will tell you, these bodily inscriptions are
designed to produce a caricature of femininity.

And, if these female, female impersonators, like Marilyn Monroe, are our
designated sex goddesses, we must also wonder if they are not the glaring
white lies that distract us from the potentially traumatic knowledge of the
actualities of female sexuality. While not exactly the "dark continent" that
haunted Freud's studies of femininity, to most men and women, the vitalities
of actual female sexuality are still thought of as enigmatic, ambiguous, unpredictable, difficult to pin down, and therefore dangerous. The justification for
these attributions is that the female's sexuality is internally located and poly-
morphous, not centered on any single erotic zone. While these justifications
do have some basis in actual anatomy, it is not the whole story by any means.
It is as if any knowledge of female sexuality must be continually re-repressed
and disavowed, as if we have some stake in thinking of it as an unmapped
continent.

Marilyn Monroe, the manufactured sex goddess, is an obvious and vivid
example of the fetishism strategy that is symptomatic of the corruptions in our
social institutions of medicine, art, psychology, politics, and religion. What is
being concealed but also revealed in the exploitations of Marilyn Momroe is a
latent text on the cultures of fetishism that collaborate in a perpetuation of the
traumas of a Norma Jeane. Moreover, our worship of the sex goddess is tantamount to a disavowal and repression of the knowledge of female sexuality.
As I pondered the puzzles embodied in the exploitations of the body of
Marilyn Monroe, my mind was automatically carried to *Thelma and Louise*.

What do we make of *Thelma and Louise*, a film that consciously focuses on
the sexual exploitations suffered by women, a film in which the social
corruptions are being exposed and revealed? What is being disavowed in such
a film? In *Thelma and Louise* the disavowal is to be found in the discordance
between the traumas of sexual abuse and violence suffered by the heroines
and the subtext of their flight from the corrupt city toward a rebirth and
magical reunion with Nature.[28] Caution filmgoer: Always watch out for the
return to the embrace of Mother Nature—a device of the fetishism strategy
designed to deny the traumas implicitly and explicitly displayed in the film.
What had been repressed and disavowed in *Niagara* and *The Misfits* returns
in *Thelma and Louise*, where once again the promise of a mystical reunion
with Nature attempts to bleach out the blood of trauma.

It would constitute a symptomatic narrowing vision to focus exclusively on
the manifest violence in the film and thereby overlook the themes of intimacy

and emotional transformation. There is a discordance, however, between the overall violence of the first half of the film and the journey toward a mystical reunion with Nature in the second half. This discordance should alert us to the fetishistic strategy. In order to animate the full text of the film and bring it into full focus, it is essential to discern and interpret the discordance. To attempt to mask a trauma of loss and despair by counterposing an experience of grandiosity and elation is a device of the fetishism strategy, a device that enhances and perpetuates the repression of trauma—which then will always return, perhaps the next time in a more devastating form.

With the trauma still repressed and unconscious, the enigma of female desire was as confounding in the 1990s as it was in Charcot's 1887 clinic. Now, in the twenty-first century, as we look back at *Thelma and Louise*, let us think about the two heroines by first returning for a brief moment to Charcot's clinic. Hysterics were said to be impressionable, malleable, coquettish, seductive, lazy—the epitome of femininity. However, the hysteric is also irascible and violent, she recriminates with bitterness, gives herself over to scenes, tears, and extravagance, makes a show of her passions. She is untruthful, unladylike, willful, troublemaking, rebellious—almost virile in her masculinity.[29] And perhaps, although the doctors seldom thought to mention it, those little trinkets and ribbons that the hysterics often stole were used as fetishes when they masturbated. The hysterics were female fetishists. Unheard of and unthinkable in those days, even though four out of the ten cases of fetishism analyzed by Charcot were females. The dominant idea then, which upheld the gender mythology of the day, was that males were fetishists and females were hysterics.

Thelma and Louise opens with two women imprisoned by a social order that exploits, demeans, and abuses women. Louise (Susan Sarandon) who was once raped by a man she hardly knew, is no longer an impressionable innocent. She has found a self-protective solution in a conformist rebellion of passive-aggression and social isolation. In the early scenes, Thelma (Geena Davis) is a guillible, malleable innocent who submits to the bullying of her husband. However, all this changes after Louise gives up her passive-aggressive defense and responds directly and aggressively to Thelma's rape with a gunshot that kills the rapist. At that point, the gullibility and malleability, the docility and suggestibility of Thelma commences the predictable tilt into willfulness, troublemaking, rebellion, recalcitrance—the other face of the representations of the hysteric. And much like the recalcitrant hysterics who faced a life sentence in Charcot's clinic, the now rebellious Thelma and the no longer *passively* aggressive Louise are undone by the forces of law and order. But, before they can be caught, Thelma and Louise take a magical journey that returns them to the bosom of Mother Nature.

Why am I so condemning of themes that pose Mother Nature as a redeemer? There have been two fundamental flaws in the psychoanalytic theory of sexual difference—the writing out of the mother in classical psychoanalysis *and* the disavowal of female sexuality. In recent years, psychoanalysts have consciously tried to rectify the first of these oversights by stressing the role of the mother and the crucial significance of the earliest mother-child dialogues. Unintentionally, I contributed to that psychoanalytic trend with *Oneness and Separateness*, my 1977 meditation on the vital importance of the infant's relationship with the mother.

However, as I have since come to appreciate, in the process of resurrecting and elevating the mother, we seem to have entombed the sexual woman. The glorification of the maternal principle has had the indirect effect of further obscuring the intricacies of female sexuality.

Surprisingly, but also expectably, this same obfuscation usually occurs in most actual lives. The idealized, unconditional love attributed to the primordial relationship with the active, caregiving mother is lost in the discovery of the reality of the mother's sexual and procreative powers. Indeed, the later knowledge of the mother's sexuality threatens the image of the mother as redeemer. One outcome of this threatening near-knowledge is an attempt to reduce the sexual mother to a breast, a haven of milk and honey. With this disavowal of the mother's sexuality, the idealization of some, largely mythical, earlier unconditional love is preserved. Thus the image of the all-good, all-embracing mother is a retroactive fantasy created in the wake of disillusionments and anxieties that arise in connection with the traumatic vision of the erotic powers of the sexual mother.

With this retroactive fantasy in mind, I think again of *Thelma and Louise* and reflect on the heroines' journey away from the corrupt city and back to Mother Nature. A full analytic reflection requires that we explore the dynamic relations between pre-oedipal and oedipal, between redeemer mother and sexual mother, between foreground and background. The purpose of scrutinizing and animating the margins or background of a film is not to discover the real and true meaning at the margins but to open up a new dimension of meaning. This new dimension can only be discerned by exposing the problematic discordance between the central text (the foreground), which in the instance of *Thelma and Louise* is about sexual abuse, sexual exploitation, violence, and counterviolence, and a marginal or background text—in this instance the emotional transcendence of the mother-child couple, the reunion with Mother Nature.

In *Thelma and Louise*, clearly, but also in *Niagara* and *The Misfits*, a world destruction fantasy is countered by a fantasy of rebirth. Most people have no trouble equating world destruction fantasies with an apocalypse. However, it is usually more difficult to think of the fantasy of a return to Mother Nature as apocalyptic. Apocalyptic fantasies have two aspects; one of destruction and another of redemption.[30] As the psychoanalyst Mortimer Ostow depicts the traditional form of the apocalyptic fantasy: after the scenes of destruction some sort of messianic rescue or magical journey brings the individual into a paradise, which is often recognizable as "a representation of the interior of the mother's body."[31]

Viewed from the perspective of an apocalyptic narrative, the dominant film plot of *Thelma and Louise* concerns the return to mother, and everything else that occurs in the film is a treacherous hazard that obstructs the magical reunion. Thus primal scene renditions of a violent and corrupt sexuality and disturbing issues of sexuality and genital difference are brought into focus (foregrounded), merely as obstacles to the journey back to paradise. Like the winged creatures in biblical renditions of apocalypse,[32] the motor launches (*Niagara*), pick-up trucks (*The Misfits*), the enchanted convertible in *Thelma and Louise*, or any other moving vehicles that regularly appear in contemporary apocalyptic narratives, such as the amazing, technologically proficient, digitally created space-ships designed for *The Matrix* and other sci-fi films, represent a "method of escape from a scene of destruction" and on to the path to the Elysian fields or safe havens that represent the tender mother.[33]

In the second half of the film, Thelma and Louise climb into their magical convertible, and the film switches gears and moves into a dream realm that brings them into a reunion with Mother Nature. The discordance between the first half of the film (the world destruction fantasy) and the second half (the redemption), needs to be discerned and interpreted. To simply celebrate the illusion of rebirth as a solution to the plight of Thelma and Louise is a symptom of the fetishism strategy. The body of the hysterical woman is one conventional disguise for the potentially traumatic sexualties of the female. Yet another disguise is the fantasy of a reunion with Mother Nature. In many films whose structure is regulated by the fetishism strategy, images of the body of a woman collaborate with themes of redemption to bleach out the traumas depicted in the background. It is always an abortion of a full reading of a film, to interpret the illusion of redemption and rebirth as a solution to the traumas of loss and world destruction.

In *Eyes Wide Shut*, writer/director Stanley Kubrick caught the essence of the apocalyptic fantasy. In the first half of the film, Dr. William Harford, played by Tom Cruise, wanders about in an unfamiliar, surreal world of necrophilic sexuality, violent sexual couplings, sexual exploitation, and social corruption. In the second half of the film Bill finds his way back home to a reunion with the redeeming mother, his wife Alice Harford, played by Nicole Kidman, Cruise's then real-life wife. But, in contrast to the Monroe films and *Thelma and Louise*, the reunion and redemption scenes that conclude *Eyes Wide Shut* acknowledge the traumas and affirm the sexuality of the "good mother." As she speaks the last lines and last word of the film, Alice demonstrates the qualities of an ordinary devoted mother, a forgiving wife, and a candidly sexual woman.

The fetishism strategy pervades every corner of the Harfords' world. It is expressed not only through the foreground-background pattern of an apoc-alyptic narrative, but also through Kubrick's depictions of the ways in which the material realities of money and consumerism are substituted for the less tangible, spiritual values of Christmas—charity, forgiveness, and compassion. Almost every setting in the film has a brightly lit Christmas tree. But there is no traditional Christmas music and none of the usual cheery Christmas spirit to be found anywhere in the movie. Everything remotely Christmasy is countered by the desperate consumerism surrounding it.

Moreover, Kubrick makes vividly compelling another principle of the fetishism strategy—the destructive aggression that disguises itself in a dazzle of erotic colors and surfaces. Through the procession of images that Kubrick marches before our eyes, we become witness to a descent into an inventory of perversion; from the relatively innocent-sounding fetishism at the top, to voyeurism and exhibitionism, to sadism and bondage, and finally at the bottom—the necrophilia that characterizes much of the frenzied, orgiastic sexuality exhibited in *Eyes Wide Shut*.

In addition to his unconscious sensitivity to the fetishism strategy, Kubrick seems to have grasped the core of Freud's theory of the defensive structure of sexual fetishism. The very title of his film, *Eyes Wide Shut*, is the ideal phrase to signify the defensive disavowals that Freud described in "Fetishism." Eyes that are wide shut allow the person to have it both ways, both seeing what has happened, what is there, but then again, not perceiving or acknowledging the import of what one has seen, or might have seen, plain as day, right before her eyes—*if* the person's eyes were wide open. Much of the dream life of humans takes place in REM sleep, with eyes wide shut. The dreams and fantasies of Alice Harford are counterposed to the cynical consumer fetishism blatantly displayed in the rest of the film.

As in Monroe's films, women's bodies are exploited throughout this controversial film. In fact, sixty five seconds of the original film had to be digitally covered over in order to obtain an R rating. However, unlike Miller and Huston, who didn't realize or care to acknowledge the many ways in which they were taking advantage of Monroe, Kubrick depicts these exploitations of women's bodies in uncompromising detail, as a way of exposing the widespread abuses of power in the social order in which the film takes place. In *Eyes Wide Shut*, the bodies that are emblematic of this social structure belong to women who, like Monroe, have been deprived of the Word, underclass hookers and some classier call-girls, who rent themselves out as embodiments of the exotic sexual fantasies of the ultra-wealthy and the extremely powerful.

The plot unfolds over three days and nights during the pre-Christmas season, in various homes and various streets of New York City and in a suburban mansion. The film opens with Alice shedding her daytime clothes in preparation for dressing up in her evening gown. After this tantalizing long shot of Kidman's exquisitely sculpted naked torso, Kubrick shuts off the lights, producing a two-second blackout before clicking the lights back on to show us Dr. William Harford all dressed up in his tuxedo, and almost ready to leave for the annual holiday ball given by his billionaire patient, Victor Ziegler. Bill utters the first words of the movie, "Honey, have you seen my wallet?" Bill's wallet will play a considerable role in his misadventures over the next three days, as he pays off all those who supply his various needs. There are frequent displays of the large denomination bills that are tucked away in that wallet. The film is as much about dirty money as it is about dirty sex—the sex that money can buy. Even the mommy-child homework scene with Alice and their seven-year-old daughter, Helena, is about money—one of those typical problems of "If Tom has $2.45 and Jimmy has $1.75, how much more money does Tom have?" When Helena seems baffled, Alice hints that it's "a take-away problem."

Soon after they arrive at Ziegler's ridiculously luxurious four-story mansion on the upper East Side, Alice separates from Bill and wanders through the extravagantly chandaliered ballroom, tossing down glasses of champagne as she moves along.

Eyes Wide Shut also illustrates the difference between women like Alice, who are blessed with the Word, and the inarticulate women who get taken advantage of for their beauty. Alice, either out of boredom or shyness or both, becomes intoxicated. Moments later, an unctuous, elegantly tuxedoed gentleman, who introduces himself as Sandor Szavost of Hungary, starts up a flirtation by kissing Alice's hand and asking her if she has ever heard of the Latin poet, Ovid, who wrote about the art of love. Alice, showing her dis-aproval of Szavost's blunt repartee, but also keen on exhibiting her knowledge of Ovid, his poetry, and his eventual exile answers back, "I heard he ended up crying his eyes out in a place not too pleasant." While Alice is dancing with her sleazy seducer and chatting coquettishly about this and that, she looks over her shoulder into the crowd and notices Bill arm in arm with two models, one on each side. As she turns away she loses sight of Bill. He and the two models have disappeared.

Unbeknownst to Alice, Bill had been summoned to do a favor for their host, who is in one of the rooms on one of the floors above the ballroom. Stretched out on a chaise lounge in an alcove of Ziegler's master bedroom is a stunningly beautiful, bare-breasted woman, entirely naked except for a pair of stiletto sandals. She seems to be either dead or comatose. Bill suspects an overdose of drugs. After learning from Ziegler that the woman's name is Mandy, Bill calls her name several times until she dimly awakens, gazing into his eyes with glazed over, half-opened (wide-shut?) eyes. Ziegler swears Bill to secrecy. All the while Alice is still downstairs wondering where her hus-band has disappeared to.

The next evening, as the Harfords are getting ready for bed, Alice, dressed in a scanty, see-through tank top with matching bikini panties, rolls herself a marijuana joint, takes a few puffs, and is suddenly transformed from the good wife who brings "happiness and calm to the conjugal hearth" into a hysteric who "recriminates with bitterness, gives herself over to scenes, tears and extravagance and makes a show of her passions." Working herself up to a hys-terical fit worthy of Charcot's clinic, Alice starts out calmly by cross-examin-ing Bill about the two models. At this point she could be a seer from Ovid, and not quite yet a full-blown hysteric. However, his claim of innocence is unconvincing. Alice, who has been getting increasingly stoned, decides to get revenge on Bill for his seeming fascination with the two models—an attitude in stark contrast to his seeming indifference to her.

In her jealous fury, she voices her first revelation. Slowly and methodically, she reveals the tale of her amorous fantasies about a naval officer she had noticed when they were on vacation in Cape Cod the previous summer. Though Alice had only looked at this very handsome, sexually alluring naval officer, and never met him, she describes in vivid detail how merely the sight of his face and body had aroused her erotic passions. As Bill stares at her in shocked amazement, Alice goes on to reveal that she would have given up her entire life for one night of love with him. Her *entire* life, her *entire* love, she stresses; not just her marital life with Bill but even her maternal love for Helena. She would have given them both up for the immensity of the sexual arousal and erotic pleasures that could be provided by the naval officer.

It is this revelation of Alice's fantasy of complete sexual surrender that provokes Bill's flight away from her into the streets of New York and finally into the eerie, unknown world of sexual orgies in secret places. Before he sets off for the sexual orgy, three women try to seduce him: a patient's daughter; a kind-hearted prostitute; and the prepubescent daughter of the man who owns the costume shop where Bill rents the tuxedo, cloak-hooded cape, and mask that is required for attending the orgy. Bill hires a yellow-checker taxi—the magical chariot that later that night will carry him back to the Elysian fields—to drive out to the mansion where the orgy is being held. Using the password he had wheedled out of a friend who plays the piano at the orgy, he enters the mansion.

After Bill witnesses the first act of the orgy, where masked "nuns" cloaked in hooded capes disrobe to reveal their naked bodies, he moves on to an outlying room where he views the antics of copulating couples. Before he can take in very much of this apocalyptic scene, a masked servant leads him back to the room where the first act took place. Here Bill learns that his disguise has been discovered. He is interrogated for his "crime." But, before the "judge" can pronounce his sentence, Bill is rescued by one of the naked women, who begs that she be allowed to "redeem" the intruding stranger. Her entreaty is granted. Bill gains his freedom, gets into his magical chariot, and returns home to Alice, in a mood of reconciliation.

Thus Kubrick's apocalyptic fantasy begins with a flight away from the disappointing mother, the mother who disrupts the conjugal hearth with revelations of her sexual desires. The fantasy ends with a flight away from the scenes of corruption and back into the arms of the redeeming mother.

In *Eyes Wide Shut*, background and foreground *seem* to be reversed. The traumas seem to be in the background. The redemption theme seems to be in the foreground. But the scenes of corruption are so vivid and compelling that they sometimes assume the foreground. The film begins with a discordance between the apocalyptic background and the foreground of domestic tranquillity that characterizes the Harford residence: their minimalist furniture, their nineteenth-century European paintings, their delicately lit Christmas tree, Mother and Child wrapping presents (while Daddy is examining patients in his well-run office) their refrigerator door covered with a child's drawings, their prototypically well-protected, well-fed, well-scrubbed, chubby-cheeked, darling little girl, whose only naughtiness is to stumble over her math homework, or to stay up late to watch "Nutcracker," or to renew her request for a puppy for Christmas. Kubrick's film is a commentary on the discordance between the Harford's tranquil, domestic hearth and the corrupt social order that supports and maintains that illusion.

Eyes Wide Shut is based on Arthur Schnitzler's short story "Traumnovelle" (Dream Story), about the married couple Albertine and Fridolin, whose sexual dreams, sexual temptations, sexual imaginings, and actual sexual adventures are played out against the background of the Viennese social order of the late 1800s.

A historian once called the Vienna of "Dream Story" a "snake filled Eden,"[34] where "the close proximity of nonchalant wealth and throttling poverty led to the sexual exploitation of impecunious young women."[35] Dear old Vienna, dear Golden Vienna, the so-called city of tolerance actually spawned hatred, "as a marsh does feverish diseases," and that festering hatred went on to spawn the holocausts of World War II.[36]

Schnitzler himself did not comment on the social injustices of his time. Nor did he predict, or even realize (who could?) the horrors that would emerge from that feverish swamp. He simply depicts some of the sexual temptations and sordidly frightening events that Fridoline encounters when, in a pique of jealous fury, he leaves his protected domestic environment in order to get even with Albertine, after she reveals some fantasies and dreams about her imaginary sexual adventures.

Kubrick's script is fairly faithful to the plot of Schnitzler's short story. However, Kubrick brings the traumas of the corrupt and mercenary social order of New York City out of the background and intrudes it into the calm, domestic foreground of his film, portraying the deadened sexual life of Alice and Bill as a mirror of the necrophilic times that surround them. Thus when Kubrick transposes "Dream Story" from nineteenth-century Vienna to the twentieth-century golden mecca of New York City, he highlights the social corruptions that Schnitzler merely hinted at. A viewer of *Eyes Wide Shut* would have to have her eyes wide shut not to perceive the nonchalance of the advantaged class and their utter obliviousness to the humiliations they inflict on those who serve their needs and desires.

A Kubrick aficionado or, for that matter, any other sensitive viewer can't help wondering what sort of feverish diseases will be spawned by the cultural fetishisms that Kubrick exposes: What fevers of hatred? What genocides? What Strangelove holocausts? What apocalyptic nightmares?

The second half of *Eyes Wide Shut*, is like a repetition of the trauma of the night before, only this time with a resolution. It opens with Bill arriving home safely from his apocalyptic nightmare. Alice is asleep. After she wakes up, she gives her second revelation. She is giggling with her eyes half open (wide shut?). Bill demands to know what she was dreaming. "We were in a deserted city and our clothes were gone. . . . I was angry at you. I thought it was your fault. . . . As soon as you were gone, I felt wonderful. I was lying out naked in the sunlight. . . . The naval officer stared at me and just laughed."

Bill insists that the revelation continue. "He was kissing me and there were people all around us. Everyone was fucking and then I was fucking other men, so many, hundreds and hundreds. And I knew you could see me, kissing, fucking all these men, making fun of you and I laughed in your face. That must be when you woke me up." Alice's weird dream sounds all too much like the orgy Bill has just witnessed. Were they both dreaming together? Or was Alice *really* there participating in his *real* nightmarish adventure? Though Kubrick suggestively raises this question, in the end he wants to stress the difference between what is real and what is fantasy.

The next morning, his sexual jealousy re-ignited by Alice's second revelation, Bill plays hooky from his afternoon office duties in order to return to the apocalyptic settings he had visited the night before. This time, Bill doesn't rely on taxis. He drives about, from one location to another, in his classy black sedan.

His second apocalyptic journey concludes with a visit to the morgue. Bill wants to check out the identity of an "ex-beauty queen" who the newspapers report as having succumbed to a drug overdose the night before. Her name was Amanda Currin—Mandy, just like the name of the drugged-out, naked woman in Ziegler's bedroom. As he gazes at her corpse, Bill leans over as if to kiss her on the mouth—a gesture that suggests he is still under the spell of the necrophilic sex that he had witnessed at the orgy, where men in masks (and some women too) were engaging in joyless copulations with drugged-out, doped-up, hypnotized, mannikin-like, robotic Stepford wives with impeccably molded breasts and smoothed out porcelain skin, while the masked guests who were not actively participating stood around peering lasciviously through the eye-slits in their masks. The secret passwords, the rigidly controlled script, the heavily ritualized sex, the orchestrated body movements of the naked women, were all part of a scenario designed to drain sexual experience of all its potential vitality; a scenario governed by the fetishism strategy. At the orgy, nothing errant or unpredictable was allowed to happen. If, by chance, the body of a woman were to come to life, even for a brief moment or two, the world the masked figures had built up with such precision and diligence might collapse in on itself, like Poe's "House of Usher."

After his close encounter with making love to a corpse, who may or may not have been Mandy, Bill is summoned to Ziegler's mansion. Ziegler tells him he has had him followed that night and knows of all his visits. Furthermore, he had seen everything Bill did the night before at the orgy. "I was there." "I saw it all." He tells Bill that the entire scene of the naked woman redeeming him by surrendering herself to the judge had been staged. Nobody punished her. Nobody hurt her. She was just "a hooker," who did what she always did and got what she always got, "she got her brains fucked out."

Bill makes his way back home to Alice for the second time. This time he is in a thoughtful mood, frightened, sobered. He feels that he has sinned. He needs Alice's forgiveness. He needs to confess. He awakens her and with a loud sob, throws himself into her arms, crying hysterically, "I will tell you everything." "I will tell you everything."

Alice listens to the tale of Bill's misadventures with compassion, looking at him through half-lidded eyes, all red and swollen, presumably from lack of sleep and crying. By the time Bill finishes his revelation, a grey dawn was already creeping through the curtains. Alice reminds Bill that they had promised Helena a Christmas shopping trip.

Off the family goes to a huge toy store. As Helena bounces about delightedly from one exorbitantly priced toy to another, Alice, wearing the glasses she always wears when she has to look at things closely, such as price tags and math homework and christmas present wrappings, humors Helena's Christmas fantasies, and at the same time tries to get back into an emotional resonance with Bill. Finally, as Helena dashes off to look at some more toys, Bill asks Alice, "What do you think we should do?"

Like that line, which was taken word for word from "Dream Story," nearly all the concluding words of *Eyes Wide Shut* are either paraphrases or verbatim quotes from "Dream Story." However, instead of dividing these words between the couple as Schnitzler did, Kubrick assigns all those phrases of wisdom to Alice. Bill is the questioner, the one who seeks understanding and redemption. Alice is the redeemer. She pronounces her third and final revelation.

Alice, peering at Bill through her eyeglasses, evaluates his question for a moment. "What do I think? Ummm. I don't know. Maybe I think we should be grateful . . . grateful we managed to survive all our adventures, whether they were real or only a dream." Bill asks "Are you sure?" Once again Alice ponders his question and once again paraphrases "Dream Story."

"Am I sure? The reality of one night, even the reality of a whole lifetime isn't the whole truth. No dream is ever just a dream. The important thing is we're awake now and for a long time to come." Bill says, "Forever" Alice rejects his "forever." "Let's not say that word. It frightens me. But I do love you and there is something very important we need to do as soon as possible." She hesitates for a moment, and then utters a word that would have been unprintable and unsayable in Schnitzler's world.

In "Dream Story," after Albertine says, "But, now I suppose we are both awake for a long time to come," she and Fridoline simply lay silently, dozing dreamlessly, very close to one another, as if in a tender affirmation of the bond between them, until a knocking at the door begins a new sunlit day and they hear the sounds of a child's laughter. "Dream Story" ends with a disavowal of the profound experiences of Albertine and Fridoline, as if everything happy and cheerful will go on forever.

In *Eyes Wide Shut* the word that Alice speaks, in response to Bill's question, "What do you think we should do?" derives entirely from Kubrick's imagination: "Fuck."

And that is the last word of Kubrick's film, followed by a two-second blackout before the large white letters of the film credits roll down on the blacked-out screen.

Schnitzler did not need to say "Fuck." Nor did he need to invent a character like Victor Ziegler to exemplify corruption and to insist on the reality of the real. He felt that his "Dream Story" spoke for itself. The ambiguities regarding the differences between dream life and real life were integral to Schnitzler's psychological insights. Though his cheery optimistic ending seemed to foreclose ambiguities and inconsistencies, nevertheless, the unanswered psychological enigmas of the fantasy lives of Albertine and Fridoline, were left by the nineteenth-century writer for his readers to take into themselves, absorb and puzzle through—if they cared to.

Kubrick approaches these enigmas differently. He is intent on asserting the reality of the real—an artistic inclination that, at first glance, seems like an expression of the fetishism strategy. His attempt to reify images and emotions and fantasies that might otherwise have stood on their own as intriguing ambiguities and uncertainties seems, at first, to intrude a note of false resolution to this otherwise expansively cryptic tale. The deus ex machina of the nonchalantly heartless billionaire, Victor Ziegler, who so obviously exemplifies corruption and so insistently claims that he was a witness of everything that Bill experienced at the orgy ("I was there. I saw it all.") removes any possibility that Bill's apocalyptic adventure might have been a dream or fantasy, no more real than his wife's fantasy of sexual surrender to a stranger. But, this was probably what Kubrick had in mind. He wanted to drive home the point that the apocalyptic nightmare that Bill experienced was real and really happened and really does happen in our corrupt social order. It was not imagined. Kubrick poses the fantasy life, the inner life of Alice as a reparation and rejoinder to Bill's *real*, reality. It is her affirmation of the life of the imagination, the life force, that Kubrick poses as an antidote to the consumerism and commodity fetishism that characterizes the social world of the Harfords.

Kubrick exhibited a kind of bravery, in which Schnitzler was thought to be deficient. Unlike Kubrick, who had gained world renown for his bold confrontations with the social injustices of his times and who used the marital deadness of the Harfords to mirror the necrophilic times, Schnitzler was sometimes referred to as a writer who belongs in the boudoir, "holding a bedroom screen up to his times," not to reflect the times but to hide them.[37]

As I thought about the deathlike, porcelain skin of the naked women in Kubrick's film, I was carried back to some images of women's bodies from the film adaptation of my book *Female Perversions: The Temptations of Emma Bovary*.

The 1997 film *Female Perversions* was one of the first of a rash of films with scenes devoted to skin-cutting. The skin-cutters were a thirteen-year-old girl, Edwina, who is trying to come to terms with her menstruation, and the heroine, Eve, a thirtyish female lawyer, who is about to become a judge and who struggles over her hitherto unacknowledged identification with her mother. Then came *The Piano Tecaher*, a film based on a novel of the same name. It describes the life of Ericka, a highly sought-after piano teacher, who sleeps in the same bed with her mother, who cuts into her own skin and puts broken glass into the coat pockets of a younger pianist whose talent she envies so that her fingers will be destroyed, and then, in the bargain, has oral sex with one of her favorite male students in the school's ladies room. In 2002, *Secretary* was on the big screen and focused on Lee, a lonely young woman who finds true love after learning how to combine her skin-cutting with her fetish for being spanked by her boss.

2003 was a big year for movies about people with a fanatical devotion to self-mutilation. In that same year, for the first time the term *fetishism* was used to describe the emotional force behind these self-mutiliations. *Thirteen*, a vivid, nearly pornographic portrayal of the body mutilations and sexual activities of a thirteen-year-old girl and her somewhat older, more experienced best friend, who indoctrinates her into these practices, arrived in the summer of 2003. David Denby reviewed the film for *The New Yorker* and explained that the events depicted in this movie were not just an odd phenomena that applied to single-mother families living in trailer parks, but to our culture at large. "The film could be set in a lot of other places in a country that knocks young girls off their feet with waves of consumer fetishism."[38] In November, movie critic Stephen Holden described Esther, the heroine of *In My Skin*, a thirty-year-old woman who compulsively slices off, cuts, and bites off pieces of her skin, as "trying to hide her fetish from her boy friend."[39] As Holden locates the source of her fetishistic behavior, he captures the essence of what I am calling a "culture of fetishism." Holden says: "In a sterile corporate culture where human appetites are quantified, tamed, and manipulated by market research and where people are rewarded for functioning like automatons, uncontrollable tics [Holden is referring here to skin-cutting] are really the anxious, protesting twitches of an oppressed animal spirit."[40]

Skin cutting is symptomatic of a larger culture of fetishism that is infiltrating every corner of our lives, not just the lives of those rare individuals who are drawn to acts of self-mutilation, not just some odd-ball weirdos—but all of us.

Like footbinding, wearing stilettos, and tattooing, skin-cutting is a form of writing on the skin. In some hunter-gatherer societies, for example, the elders carve into the skin of a pubescent child as if it were a piece of wood, leaving marks that are meant to assure that the youth will conform to the traditional ways and not be led astray by Nature. As we shall see in the next chapter, "Writing on the Skin," skin-cutting can express many different and contradictory emotions and thoughts. While it can sometimes be a mark of rebellion, just as often it can be a mirroring of the corruptions of the social order. Similarly, it can either be a gesture that undermines and opposes the fetishism strategy or an expression of it.

Five

Writing on the Skin

In the middle of the twentieth century, after decades of colonialist expansion, when hunter-gatherer societies were still relatively free to forage the scrap of Earth left to them, anthropologists followed them, lived among them, observed them and diligently recorded their daily life. In hunter-gatherer societies, where it was a matter of survival to stay in close touch with the mysterious and uncontrollable forces of Nature, there was the pretense that social and religious rites could control an otherwise capricious Nature. The growing-up of a child into adulthood was not left to Nature. Writings on the body had to be forceful and declarative—acts of inscription that were tantamount to body mutilations.

Many of the anthropologists were particularly fascinated by the rites of passage, particularly the ceremonial rituals that initiated a girl or boy into adulthood. They took careful notes on the mutilations of the body that these rites usually required; among them (depending on the society): pulling out a tooth; cutting off the little finger above the last joint; cutting off the earlobe or perforating the earlobe or nasal septum; tattooing; scarifying the face, chest, back, legs, and arms; excising the clitoris; perforating the hymen; subincising the penis; cutting off the foreskin.

The anthropologists did not merely record the shapes and sizes of these cuts into the skin, they also interpreted them. Arnold van Gennep, who studied the Barundi of Tanganyika, conceived the theory that the human body was treated like a piece of wood whose surfaces could be trimmed, broken through, written on, whose irregular projections could be carved away or shaped into the forms that a society designates as womanly or manly.[1] From what we know of the fetishism strategy, we could interpret that the body mutilations were the Barundi's method of taming and subduing what might otherwise be a disruptive vitality. Though the Barundi elders, who used fetish objects in their religious rituals, knew nothing of the fetishism strategy, they nevertheless employed that strategy to control the pubescent urgencies of the

Barundi youth. Their carvings into the body were meant to assure that boys and girls would take on the shapes of acceptable manhood and womanhood.

Among the Tiv of Nigeria, the scarifications were interpreted by their anthropologist, Bruce Lincoln, as a method of etching the body with a permanent record of the dilemmas of human existence.[2] To Lincoln's eyes, the scars seemed to posit such contrasts as male/female, line/circle, lineage/age group, ancestors/descendants, and most important past/future. Lincoln thought that the oppositions were resolved in the scars. In the last opposition, that of past and future, the scar was said to represent the emergence of a present moment that is capable of drawing on the past as it creates the future. He then deepened that interpretation by adding, "The present is not thought of as a hairline between 'was' and 'yet-to-be' but as a space filled with history and potentiality."[3]

The scarifications, amputations, excisions, and perforations were permanent body transformations. They were marks of membership in a community of peers, signs of incorporation into adulthood. The ritual initiations into manhood and womanhood also typically included a few temporary body transformations, such as paring the nails; pulling out the scalp hair or cutting off a few locks; painting the body with clay, menstrual blood, semen, or saliva; or wearing special garments, masks, or jewelry. Victor Turner, an anthropologist whose data was primarily from the Nbembu of northwestern Zambia, interpreted these temporary bodily transformations as a method of divesting youthful sexual vitalities of their social threat and transforming them into a source of social rejuvenation.[4] Turner did not know "the fetishism strategy" by name, but his interpretations indicated his intuitive appreciation of how such a strategy of divesting a body of its threatening aliveness might influence the initiation rites of the Tiv.

Erik Erikson, a psychoanalyst with an anthropological bent, studied the Dakota Indian (previously Sioux) initiation rite. The culminating episode in the rite required the young men to "engage in the highest form of self-torture by putting through the muscles of their chest and back skewers which were attached to the sun pole by long thongs. Gazing directly into the sun and slowly dancing backwards the men could tear themselves loose by ripping the flesh of their chests open."[5] Erikson traced the origins of the sun dance to the breast-feeding habits of that culture. Every woman's breasts were freely available to all the tiny warriors of the village. But, after the months of earliest infancy, if a little boy should bite down on the nipple of a breast, then the woman would remove him, thump him on the head, and let him rage with frustration until the next feeding. The devouring rage the infant experienced was later in life directed against enemies, animals, and "loose women"; and, in the sun dance ritual, against his own breast—presumably a stand-in for the mother's breast.[6]

The Dakota girl, in training to give her breasts to tiny warriors, was allowed to participate in the sun dance ritual by bathing the wounds of her brother.[7] The sister-brother bond was composed of entitlements and intimacies that were not accorded to other female-male relationships. The girl was encouraged to be emotionally close to her brother. The brother was encouraged to be respectful of his sister. She would embroider clothing for his wife and children. The hunter-brother would save the fattest animals and most luxurious pelts for his sister.[8]

As for her relationships with other men in the tribe, the girl was taught to be bashful and fearful. As a wife, she was expected to be a hunter's helper and a future hunter's mother. She was expected to cook, sew, and to put up tents. She must not look like a loose woman. "She was trained to walk with measured steps, never to cross certain boundaries set around the camp, and—with approaching maturity—to sleep at night with her thighs tied together to prevent rape."[9]

For the Dakota boy, who was in training to be a hunter, those tantalizing tied-together thighs invited physical contact. It was a challenge commensurate with touching a dangerous enemy in battle. The girl's rite of passage was the Virgin Feast, where she was expected to defend herself against any accusations that she was not a virgin.[10] Various scenarios were enacted that were supposed to compel the girl to admit wrongdoing—on her part. If, for example, a man would claim that he had touched a girl's genitals, she had to prove her innocence. Thus the Dakota girl did not experience an actual, physical body mutilation. Nor was she expected to endure a self-inflicted bodily torment. However, she lived in dread of a man penetrating her body before marriage. The potential body mutilation must have been always on her mind. And when she slept, she was reminded of that possibility by the pressure of the ropes that kept her thighs bound together.

The permanent and temporary mutilations and penetrations of the body (even those merely feared and imagined) among the hunter-gatherer peoples were gestures fraught with social and celestial implications. Whether the mutilations had the same implications for the hunter-gatherers as they did for the anthropologists who observed them was never exactly clear or certain. It was, after all, a matter of interpretation. As part of their professional indoctrination, the anthropologists came to believe that they were able to read the meanings of these cuts onto and into the human skin. The human skin could be written on. The cuts into the body were a text, and like any text, they had a latent meaning and that meaning could be deciphered and interpreted.

Sometimes the writing on the skin is done by professionals, tribal elders, surgeons, parents, tattoo artists. Though the psychological meanings may turn out to be the same or similar, it is nevertheless important to distinguish between personally inspired body writings that are often regarded with distaste and social opprobrium and those that are socially prescribed, as with the hunter-gatherer peoples. In between, there is a whole range of personally ambiguous and socially uncertain varieties of writing on the skin—a compendium of writings that are tantamount to body mutilations: amputations, body slicings; skin-cuttings; tattoos; ear, nose, tongue, and cheek piercing; nipple piercing; navel piercing; and genital piercing. And all of them, no doubt you have noticed, entail a perforation or incision into the envelope of skin that covers the entire human body.

So, let us begin with SKIN.

In the earliest development of the human embryo, the ectoderm consists of the epidermis or outer layer of skin and the dermis inner layer, with its sebaceous and sweat glands and hair follicles. Also present are the organs of special senses such as the eye and the ear, and the nervous system and the brain. Thus skin, nervous system, and brain develop out of the same primordial tissue. The epidermis-dermis skin then becomes a two-sided surface that faces inward toward the brain and other organs, nerves, and muscles of the body and outward toward the external world. Directly or indirectly, the nerve, endings of the skin touch every organ, nerve, and muscle inside the human body. And, the human skin is capable of touching and being touched by everything outside the human body.[11]

In addition to these biological givens, every human being has fantasies about his or her body from the tip of the scalp to the tip of the toes, and also about individual parts of the body, especially the erotogenic organs of mouth, ears, eyes, vagina, penis, prostate, urethra, uterus, stomach, heart, and lungs.[12] Furthermore, most people have fantasies, concsious and unconsious, about the envelope of skin that covers the entire surface of the body, and the mucous membrane of the skin that even reaches into the entrance of the alimentary canal tube that runs from the roof of the mouth to the esophagus and all the way down through the stomach to the anus—another major erotogenic organ.[13]

A human being might be blind and deaf and mute and be deprived of the sense of smell but she would still be alive and have fantasies and wishes simply because she (like Helen Keller) would still be capable of communicating through the sense of touch. Because of her skin, she can touch the world and the world can touch her. Skin brings Eros to the brain and to every other part of the human body. Skin is precious. Skin is everything that makes us human. As the psychoanalyst Didier Anzieu said in *A Skin for Thought*, "There is no human being without a virtually complete envelope of skin. If one seventh of the skin is destroyed by accident, lesion, or burns, the human being dies."[14]

The epidermis-dermis layers of skin are the envelope of the body. The skin keeps us in touch with what is happening in the rest of our body. The skin also makes palpable those myriad events that take place outside the body. Skin is one of the most important contributors to our body image—an image that we can sometimes visualize, sometimes even hear or smell, but always somehow "feel" no matter how much or how often that image is revised over the course of an ordinary human life. Our body image, a mental or psychological outgrowth of having a skin that transports erotic vitality to the rest of the body, is an internal map of the body and all the body's individual parts. Our body image delineates the distinctions between the outside of the body—the skin outside,—and the nerves, muscles and organs inside the body. Though it tends to unify tactile, postural, kinesthetic, visual, and aural sensations, the body image is also capable of dispersal, disruption, dissolution, and disunity. The body image is immensely pliable, intensely suggestive, and amenable to all varieties of biological, psychological, and social transformations of the actual physical body.[15]

Our body image also takes its shape from the infinitely various detachable parts of the body—the voice, the breath, the odor, feces, saliva, vomit, hair, nails, menstrual blood, urine, semen, sperm—which though they may become permanently separated from the body, nevertheless remain forever magically linked to the body image. The body image marks out a differentiation of bodily zones, orifices, curves, and convex and concave spaces of the physical body.[16]

Many theoreticians of the body represent the skin as if it were a Mobius strip of ribbon that twists around to touch on every organ, muscle, and nerve inside the body, and then spirals about to bring the inside surface outward, so that the inside touches every segment of skin on the outside of the body. One of the great advantages of the Mobius strip model is that we need not make sharp distinctions between mind and body, inside and outside, brain and skin, psychic depth and skin surface. While these entities are actually disparate, they do also have the capacity to twist one onto the other. Elizabeth Grosz, a feminist theoretician of the body, put it this way: "It [the Mobius strip model] enables subjectivity to be understood *not* as the combination of a psychical depth and a corporeal superficiality but as a surface whose inscriptions and rotations in three-dimensional space produce all the effects of depth" (my emphasis).[17]

Some theoreticians make a distinction between "civilized" body writings, which typically are read and interpreted for their internal psychic meanings, and "savage" scarifications. Referring specifically to the people of Kau in Kenya, Alphonso Lingis explains that the primitive inscriptions on the body surface function to amplify the skin's erotogenic sensitivity. Instead of reading them as messages or as signifiers of hidden meanings buried deep within the person's psyche, Lingis portrays the welts, scars, cuts, tattoos, and perforations as efforts to increase the surface space of the body, creating hollows and ridges and contours that then give the body an erotic intensity that was not there before:

> The savage inscription is a working over the skin, all surface effects. This cutting in orifices and raising tumescences does not contrive new receptor organs for a depth body [as, for example, the prosthetic additions to the civilized body, do] . . . it extends an erotogenic surface . . . it's a multiplication of mouths, of lips, labia, anuses, those sweating and bleeding perforations and puncturing . . . these warts raised all over the abdomen, around the eyes. . . .[18]

It may very well be that "savage" writings on the skin do serve the function of extending the erotogenic surface of the body. We must keep in mind, however, that Lingis is referring to socially ritualized inscriptions on the body, not to *self*-mutilation, a form of writing on the skin that is personal and àsocial. When, many years ago, I first wrote about self-mutilation, I emphasized that the borders between the more extreme acts of self-mutilation and acts that could pass as "normal" are not clearly or permanently staked out. When we observe an act of extreme self-mutilation, "the mask of Eros that usually masks the grinning mask of Death is *barely* discernible."[19] However, even in these instances, Lingis' observations on "savage" body writings are applicable. Even the most horrific and terrifying acts of self-mutilation express an erotic element. The erotic is not immediately apparent, but if we look hard enough we can detect it—just below the skin.

In the initial chapters, we encountered several examples of body mutilation, beginning with doctors who complied with a woman's request to carve her foot into a shape that would fit more easily into her open-toe stiletto, so as to make visible the toe cleavage which was so much the in-fashion of the day.[20] The doctors performed the mutilation. But, only on request. Foot-carving surgery, therefore, is at the boundary between the social and the personal. Since it is performed by a professional, it is socially condoned. Yet, at the same time, to "request" this mutilation of one's own body is a "sort of" self-mutilation.

Similarly, in the case of A-Hsui's silver Lotus, her mother and her nurse-maid performed the footbinding that would contort A-Hsui's toes into the size and shape of a Lotus blossom. As a young child, A-Hsui wept and com-plained bitterly about the pain she suffered. At night, when no one was looking, she would try to undo the hand-woven linen bandages for a few moments of relief. But in a few years, like most upper-class Chinese girls of her day, she began to grasp the advantages of bound feet and after-ward became an active participant and collaborator in the mutilation of her body.[21]

There are certain kinds of body mutilation that are less socially ambiguous. They are self-inflicted, usually performed in secret, and are not socially approved. The person who performs such secretive acts of self-mutilation is fanatically devoted to the performances. When the urge comes upon her, *the delicate cutter*, so named to distinguish her from the *coarse cutter* who is usually a male, cannot wait to be alone to begin the cuttings or slicings or perforations of her skin. These desperate acts of self-mutilation slide comfortably into the standard definition of fetishism, "an excessive devotion to an irrational practice."

But, how would these acts qualify as illustrations of the fetishism strategy? It would have to be shown that these irrational practices of self-mutilation were inspired by a culture that breeds and nourishes the fetishism strategy. If, for example, a person lives in a social environment that encourages her to behave like a humanoid, an automaton rather than a flesh and blood human being with ordinary human desires, she might cut into her skin as a gesture of stirring up a spark of life beneath her skin. Or she might despise her skin for having a mind of its own and coming between her desire and its satisfac-tion. What better way to achieve satisfaction than to cut through the skin to the nerve endings, so that they might knock at the door of the dulled and stupefied brain and bring it to life? The performance of *delicate self-cutting* might be an instance of hatred masquerading as love, and/or an example of, destruction painting itself with an erotic tint Either way it is an expression of the fifth principle of the fetishism strategy.

The act of self-cutting can also be interpreted as a way of controlling the dangerously unpredictable vitalities of the body. *The more dangerous and unpredictable the threat of desire, the more deadened or distanced from human experience the fetish must be.* Self-cutting, therefore, can be either a way of enlivening the body or a way of deadening it.

So far as we know, only a minority of adolescent girls are *delicate self-cutters.* Nevertheless, almost every adolescent girl is struggling, consciously or unconsciously, with the same emotional and physical conflicts as the *delicate self-cutter,* among them separation from her parents. At the same time, she is trying to come to terms with the uncontrollable physiological effects of puberty that are changing her irrevocably into an adult woman with sexual and procreative urges and capacities. These urges and capacities frighten the girl, for reasons that elude her. To compound these conflicts arising in connection with her changing body she now also is suffering the loss of her childhood illusions and with them the waning of her childhood fantasies of perfection and self-perfectibility.[22]

She may at times, and for a while, force these awesome anxieties and mortifications to the background of her mind by becoming preoccupied with bodily sensations that verge on pain but still seem tinged with pleasure. She tears at the skin of her cuticles, rubs the skin off the bottoms of her feet, plucks her eyebrows and the hairs on her arms and legs, splices the split ends of her hair, pulls out chunks of her hair, even occasionally pricks the skin on her arm until a small spot of blood appears. Or, she might, if the anxieties threaten to emerge from the background of her mind, make a tiny, barely visible, *very* delicate cut into her skin.

Though these actions give her a twinge that she is doing something not quite right, perhaps even sinful, the girl is able to lose herself in these bodily preoccupations and forget about the worries that would otherwise come into the foreground of her mind. The little mutilations take up her mind and enable her to temporarily escape from the frightening implications of being transformed physically and emotionally into a woman with the sexual and moral responsibilities of adulthood. Her self-mutilations are a way of taming and controlling the mysterious promptings of an awakening genital arousal.

The adrenal and ovarian estrogens that brought out the initial stages of puberty, like the elevated nipples and downy pubic hair, have been silently at work effecting changes over the entire skin surface and also the inner surfaces and organs of the body. There will be a rapid fat accumulation on the hips and thighs, a dramatic increase in the size of the wrist, the pelvis, the heart, the abdominal viscera, the thyroid, the spleen, and especially the long bones of the legs, arms, and torso. The expansiveness of the growth spurt is alarming to the adolescent girl, who is already afraid that she will be unable to contain excitement or relieve tension or find comfort.

Delicate self-cutting is a symptom that expresses a resistance to socialization, a resistance to Nature, a resistance to saying farewell to childhood, a resistance to growing up into adulthood. The child-becoming-an-adult does not leave her growing up to Nature. Nor can the elders of her social order tell her what kind of woman she must become. The girl who cuts into her skin is enacting a personal rite of passage And, though no one is there to witness her enactment, the cuts into her skin leave scars as witness to her troubled soul. Later on, she may exhibit these scars as signs of her triumphant defeat of Nature, Society, Civilization, Mother, Father—and the Therapist who is trying to help her to understand the inner meanings of her gestures of self-multination. However, as most therapists of delicate cutters soon discover, cutting is also a resistance to Interpretation.

The girl does not interpret her acts of cutting or her scars as anything more than what they are. In this respect, she is like a "savage," who feels that her identity is fixed on her skin. The mere suggestion that there is an "inside" with depth and psychic meanings is enough to set the girl off on a binge of self-cutting. Those mysterious insides are her major enemies.[23]

Cutting is primarily a resistance to the body. The girl does not have a Mobius strip image of the body, where outside twists around to become inside. Inside is inside. Outside is outside. Only cutting can release what is trapped inside and bring it out into the open. The sight of the blood pouring out of the cut skin brings instant relief from the tensions and excitements that emanate from inside the body.

As she approaches womanhood, the delicate-cutter is unable to anticipate any relief from the menstrual tensions or the sexual excitements induced by the bodily changes of puberty. She is possessed by a desperate need to define and protect the boundaries of her body. Menstrual blood is experienced as an ugly, demonic substance that could leak out of the body and cover the entire world if it were not tamed and controlled. Similarly, emotions like depression, anxiety, sadness, anger, joy, and love are imagined as demonic substances that must be brought under control and then expelled from the body as though they were tears, vomit, nasal mucus, urine, feces, or menstrual blood.

"I felt mad and I couldn't take it anymore." "I was frustrated like I couldn't do anything about anything." "Everything was getting all fucked up; my mother, my father, my teacher, my friends, everybody was really fucking me up."[24] "I felt shitty."[25] "I felt so tense, I thought my body would burst wide open. I had to do something."[26]

Without the cut into the skin to put an edge on the boundaries of the body, everything might leak out—the tears, the feces, the menstrual blood, the rage. As an infant and young child, the girl did not learn how to express her emotions except in the infantile experiences devouring or of a leaking out of bodily substances. As an adolescent, the delicate self-cutter continues to associate any kind of inner arousal with devouring or leaking-out experiences. Moreover, she confuses one kind of inner arousal with another. She confuses rage with sexual arousal. She confuses sexual arousal with rage.

Since the *typical* self-cutter does not anticipate care or help from anyone, she does not seek therapy until either she or her parents have been made frantic by her escalating and increasingly coarse skin-cutting. Her cry for help has to become a shriek before anyone pays attention.

From the self-cutting girls who gradually learned to trust that they might safely have feelings and then safely communicate them to their therapists, we learn something about why self-cutting has the power to provide relief from menstrual tensions and the inner genital arousals that accompany the changes of puberty: "I felt the badness inside me go out."[27] Or, "It's like vomiting—you feel sick and you spit out the badness."[28] Another delicate cutter told her therapist that the trickling of the warm blood, the sight of it oozing through the gap in the skin, [29] was like a calming voice saying, "It's all over now honey. Don't worry, dear. Everything is going to be all right."[30] Still another patient likened the blood that oozed from the "self-made zipper"[31] to a voluptuous bath, a sensation of delicious warmth, "which as it spread over the hills and valleys of my body, molded its contour and shaped its form."[32]

The delicate self-cutter is also expressing the haunting complexity of her confused identifications with her mother. She is relieved when the "mother-blood" warmly flows over her. The deadened mother and the deadened daughter are resurrected and reunited in the act of self-cutting. As the bad, dirty blood flows out, the daughter rids herself of her internal "bad" mother. At the same time she becomes a bleeder in an identification with the denigrated, castrated, bleeding mother. The anticipated passively experienced "castration" of menstruation is transformed into a controlled, delicate cut into the skin.[33]

The delicate cutter thinks of her skin as a container for the dangerous body substances and organs and all the insupportable arousals emanating from inside her body. Whereas the orifices of the body—nose, mouth, eyes, ears, anus, vaginal hole—are vulnerable to attackers from outside and inside, the skin can hold in or fend off the dreaded attacking arousals in a controlled and manageable way. In the place of a cannibalization of the entire inside and outside of the body, there is a localized, focused, *delicate* mutilation.[34]

Shortly after her first menstruation, one delicate cutter used a knife to scratch the letters L O V E on her thigh. The cuttings were neat, precise, and shallow, but nevertheless quite deep enough to allow the blood to color L O V E a violent red. She told her therapist that she had actually had the impulse to carve right down to the bone.[35] As she dramatized the gestures that described her original impulse, her usually sweet, innocent face was clouded over by "an almost palpable hatred."[36] The girl confessed that she had really wanted to carve H A T E into the bone of her thigh. She had restrained herself because H A T E was not a nice thing to feel or think, much less put into words.

It would seem that the male self-mutilator, most often a *coarse cutter*, suffers more extensively from the bodily anxieties that afflict the female delicate cutter and usually, therefore, he inflicts on his body more extensive and devastating damage.[37] Though he might never engage in extreme forms of skin-cutting, many an adolescent boy will engage in self-mutilating activities such as tying strings around his fingers and toes until they turn blue, tearing away at his cuticles until they bleed, plucking at his acne pimples until he creates open wounds and sores, self-tattooing or otherwise scarifying his arms and legs. And these mind-absorbing body preoccupations, as much as they are visible expressions of the boy's fears of mutilation, are also the means of taking his mind off some of the other expectable adolescent anxieties such as mourning the loss of his childhood illusions, separating from his parents, expiating guilt, and becoming a man with adult sexual and procreative capacities.

Coarse cutting, in which a knife or other large sharp instrument is used to penetrate through the skin surface down to tendons, veins, arteries, and bones, sometimes advances to severings or amputations of body parts, in which cases the diagnostic label is adjusted to *self-amputation*.[38] Any body part may be chosen for amputation. The least anxious of the self-amputators will limit the mutilation to the hands, fingers, and toes. Some finger and toe severers make a hobby of their self-mutilating activities and eventually trade personal secrecy for joining a secret society devoted to the practices and ideals of amputation. Here, in the safety of these "therapeutic communities," fellow "hobbyists" can trade memories of their first experiments with self-amputation or recall the childhood origins of their current lust for female amputees.[39] They are able to share, without shame, the imaginary amputations that figured in their adolescent masturbation rituals: the fake peg leg that enabled them to hobble toward orgasm, the masturbatory excitement of cutting off arms and legs from photographs of women. In the letters columns of various girlie magazines, fellow hobbyists can solicit sexual partners, exchange ideas, and share specific preferences with others who have a "mono-pede mania." *Amputee Love*, an erotic comic book with a limited circulation and a highly select readership, is devoted to love among self-amputees and amputees.[40]

Hobbyists particularly enjoy reminiscing about the unwitting doctors who gave them their first lessons in the techniques of proper surgery. How exciting it had been to observe as the doctor applied his scalpel to the botched "small" half-hearted, incomplete, experimental self-amputations and carried them through to the "ultimate" professional amputation.[41]

These days, young men and women share many forms of writing on the skin. Piercing different parts of the face and body—ears, nose, cheeks, lips, brows, tongues, navels, nipples. The favorite shared enthusiasm is tattooing, a writing on the skin that in the past had been the exclusive territory of young men.

The author of *Ink: The Not-Just-Skin-Deep Guide to Getting a Tattoo*, introduces the section on the one-point tattoo technique used by most American and European tattoo artists with a lecture on skin:

> Measuring in at an average six pounds and about twenty square feet is the largest organ of the human body—the skin. And what a fantastic organ it is! With a remarkable ability to repair itself it is the first and best defense that we have against all manner of microorganisms, chemicals and even ultraviolet radiation. . . . The total thickness of human skin averages between one and two millimeters but the epidermis is only a small fraction of that, only one tenth of a millimeter thick. . . . The dermis underneath, however, is a pretty complicated place. Heat, cold, pressure and pain are felt through tiny bulges of the dermis as

it intrudes a bit into the epidermis. Also, the dermis has collagen fibers, sweat glands, hair roots, nerve cells, lymph vessels and blood vessels. . . . Wow, all that in such a shallow space![42]

As we know, a tattoo is pigment that is inserted into the dermis. When you look at a tattoo you are looking at it through the epidermis. An electric tattoo machine punctures the skin with sterilized metal needles, pushing ink through the epidermis into the dermis. The needles that deliver the pigment are in a sterilized hollow tube that acts as a container for the ink, which then coats the needles. Different needle configurations are used for different parts of the design. The needles travel just a tiny distance into the dermis, not too deep, but not so shallow that the ink only gets as far as the epidermis. Finally, after the healing process (which requires considerable time and patience), the ink concentrates between epidermis and dermis. The outline process, usually done in black ink, is more painful than the shading process that comes afterwards.[43]

The choice of tattoo design is personal but also influenced by the traditions of tattoo art. Tradition-oriented young men are likely to chose the homey old-fashioned images of blood-tipped swords, fiery-tongued serpents, skull and cross bones, anchors, fists, flying fish, mermaids, suns, slivers of moon, stars, a portrait of Christ, Christ on the cross, St. John's cross, Sacred Heart, Our Lady of Guadeloupe, national flags, red leaf maple, Statue of Liberty, eagle killing a snake, flower petals, ocean waves, palm trees, clouds, pin-up girls like Betty Boop or Marilyn Monroe, the word "Mother," and Cupid with arrows that aim at the word "Mother."[44] A young man who hires a tattoo artist to tattoo these images into his skin is rarely aware of the fantasies underlying them. If he thinks about them at all, he thinks of the dragons and Cupid arrows as aesthetic statements meant to beautify his body and give his skin an erotic boost. He might be somewhat aware and gratified that his exhibitionistic bravado has excited the eyes of an innocent viewer.

Now that tattooing is considered a fashion statement and even a religious calling, the girls have joined the guys. Butterflies are said to be the most popular tattoo among females, especially the single butterfly on the small of the back, just above the buttock cleavage, peaking out from the low-slung pants or skirt. Females are sometimes even more avant-garde than males when it comes to choosing the latest fashions in tattoo design. Unlike the traditional anchors and Cupids of yore, the most popular contemporary tattoos have "new age" references: There are Western Zodiac signs from Aquarius to Capricorn; Eastern Zodiac signs from the Year of the Rat to the Year of the Dragon; Chinese and Japanese and Arabic letters; Polynesian shapes and geometric designs; the elephant god Ganesha, the beautiful blue-faced Krishna, and the multi-armed dancing Shiva; protective Sanskrit writings of Buddhist prayers; new age animal heroes such as whales, dolphins, and beavers of the Pacific Northwest; cartoons of Calvin and Hobbes and Japanese *anime* sweethearts like Battle Angel Alita or Sailor moon; ghouls and tombstones; Japanese Kanji pictorial letter characters that can be used to spell out names, places, and secret messages; Egyptian hieroglyphs.[45]

There are more extreme tattoo images, such as biomechanical images of the skin ripped open revealing the inside of the body. But that imagined inside is not composed of muscles, bones, and organs. The image of ripped-open skin reveals images of metal rods, pulleys, gears, and tubes;—sort of like "Alien meets Terminator in ink."[46] These seem to be a masculine prerogative, although some women are beginning to favor them. Among the unisex favorites at the turn of the twenty-first century were abbreviated versions of the Japanese *Bushido* "body-suit" tattoo.

Japanese *Bushido*—Bu (military), shi (man), do (way)—is associated with Samurai warriors and their ethics. As with Samurai ethics, *Bushido* emphasizes self-control, inner personal strength, and Zen-like self-discipline.[47] Full-body *Bushido*, which encompasses the entire body from the shoulders to the ankles, requires endurance of severe pain and an extended series of appointments often extending over several years.[48] It requires great patience and diligence, both on the part of the *sensei*,—the tattoo artist—and his client. The Japanese word for tattoo is *gaman*, or perseverance.[49]

The Japanese think of *Bushido* as emphasizing the role of the body in human life. The transient nature of the tattoo, which can only live as long as the body lives, suggests the ephemeral nature of life.[50] The Japanese expression *mono no aware* refers to a deep appreciation of beauty along with a sense of longing or sadness at the transience of beauty.[51] The cherry blossom, which blooms for a week or two and then dies, is a symbol of *mono no aware*.

The tattooed back, which stretches from the neck and encompasses the buttocks and ends at midthigh, is the largest unbroken space on a body to view a single image and therefore is considered the ideal canvas for a Japanese tattoo artist.[52] There is also the split chest body suit for the front of the body and the *Hikae*, or chest panel that covers the chest and goes over the shoulders, across the back and halfway down the arms.[53]

The traditional full-body suit tattoo bears the images of the bodies and elaborate garments of Samurai, of tigers, dragons, fire-breathing foxes, cherry blossoms, Japanese gods and goddesses, butterflies, birds, and fish, especially the carp.[54] These intricate designs are outlined by a tattoo machine and then filled in and shaded in by a "hand poke," in which "needles are attached to the end of a long, thick handle (typically made of pliable materials such as wood or stainless steel), dipped into ink and pushed into the skin by the tattoo, almost as though with a small pool cue."[55]

In these days of globalization and global travel, Japanese are visiting the United States and becoming captivated by American ways of doing things and Americans are visiting Japan and becoming entranced with the Japanese ways. While the Japanese are becoming more casual about their tattoos, Americans are opting for the more painful, time-consuming variations of the full-body, hand-poke tattoo.[56]

Now that tattooing has become a popular form of writing on the skin among late adolescents and young men and women in their twenties, thirties, and forties, the practice no longer seems to belong in the category of the fetishism perversion—a fanatical devotion to an irrational personal practice. Nevertheless, as with the piercings of ear, nose, eyebrow, cheek, tongue, and navel and nipple, tattooing can still be interpreted as an expression of the fetishism strategy. These forms of body writing can still be seen and interpreted as ways of taming and subduing the urgencies of the body—as anchors that hold the unruly skin in place. Or, they could have the opposite meaning—as acts that attempt to undermine the fetishism strategy, which favors organization, control, and social conformity and thus be interpreted as resistances to social inscriptions of the body.

However, perhaps we interpret too much. Perhaps a delicate cut is just a delicate cut and a tattoo is just a tattoo—savage inscriptions on the skin with no inner meanings whatsoever? In which case they can be seen for what they appear to be—attempts to extend the erotic surfaces of the body, as Alphonso Lingis suggested. Theoreticians of the body disagree on these matters. For example, Elizabeth Grosz feels that Lingis' insistence on distinguishing "savage" from "civilized" forms of body writing suggests a "touristlike position of spectatorship."[57] Despite her gesture of protest, Grosz proceeds to give Lingis' basic distinctions between savage and civilized some theoretical twists of her own. For example, she suggests that a civilized person's conviction that she is not merely a surface but a creature with profound depths that can be interpreted, may be an ethnocentric ploy designed to put herself above those who act on instinct or impulse without any understanding of their psychic life. Grosz, therefore, is suspicious of the civilized tendency to give deep interpretations to skin markings such as delicate cuts and tattoos. She asks whether these writings on the skin are really best interpreted as symptoms, signs, and clues to an interior psychic life? Or are they, like the "savage" skin mutilations, actually indications of an equally violent social inscription?[58]

Our civilized bodies are involuntarily marked, but by acts that we believe are voluntary. According to Grosz, "Makeup, stilettos, bras, hair sprays, clothing, underclothing mark women's bodies, black or white, in ways in which hair style, professional training, personal grooming, gait, posture, body building and sports may mark men's."[59] The person who has been inspired to adopt these modes of body inscription thinks of them as perfectly natural, and a true index of who they are beneath the skin.

Grosz argues that the social inscriptions that have left their mark on the surface appearances of the human body are also identifiable if the person is stripped of clothing and makeup and other adornments and stands naked in the world. The body au naturelle would still be marked by its diet, its patterns of body movement, "its disciplinary history."[60] The naked body is not a natural body, for it is marked by "the history and specificity of its existence."[61] A person's biography is written on her body. It need only be read and deciphered. She insists that::

> This history would include not only all the contingencies that befall a body, impinging on it from the outside—a history of the accidents, illnesses, misadventures that mark the body and its functioning; such a history would also have to include the "raw ingredients" out of which the body is produced—its internal conditions of possibility, the history of its particular tastes, predilections, movements, habits, postures, gait, and comportment.[62]

However, the skin does not just yield to whatever is written on it. The skin modifies what is written on it and sometimes even rebels against it. The human skin always has a texture.

"The texture of the skin" is my metaphor for these exchanges between the human body and society. The texture of the skin shapes and contours the messages that the social order tries to impose on the body. Diet can alter the texture of the skin. Body-building and exercise can make it bulkier, tougher, or firmer. Sun can dry it out. Moisture can soften it. Age can wrinkle it. Fires can scar it. But, to the extent that a person's skin has an essential inborn texture, which sets a limit to what, when, and how much the environment or the agencies of the social order may try to impose on it, she is a biological entity—a DNA machine, if you will. However, she is an intricate, inventive machine that is designed to be able to protect its integrity. A human being is not destined to accept everything the social order attempts to write on her skin. Because of the texture of the skin, the socializing pen or stylus cannot inscribe any message it wants to, no matter how much force it applies, no matter how subtly gentle or seductively caressing it may be as it glides its message across the skin.

Some writers, and the vast majority of painters and sculptors, consider the texture of the paper, canvas, clay, marble, and steel they "write" on as crucial to the meaning of the words or images they create. Of course, these days, most writers who write on paper are only vaguely aware of the texture of the paper on which they are inscribing their words, and very likely, do most of their writing on a computer that later prints up the words to a twelve-point font on twenty-pound bond. But texture matters. Calligraphers know this well. The texture of the paper is as decisive for the shape of the words they will inscribe as the textures of the hairs of their brush. These words that I am now writing might have had a different shape if I had written more drafts of them on paper before copying them into my computer. I try to write my first drafts on a soft textured paper that yields to my #2 carbon pencil. The texture of the paper seems to respond to my words. The ridges either absorb and cradle the words that my pencil writes, or resists them, causing me to re-think my words. (Of course, it is me who is inspiring the paper to resist.) In the same way, the texture of the human skin can absorb the pressures put on it or can set a limit to what may be written on it.

Peter Greenaway's film *The Pillow Book* is about the texture of the skin and the words that can be written on the skin. Greenaway explores the several ways in which body surfaces can give expression to the depths of a human psyche. On the surface, the film is about writing on the skin, specifically Japanese calligraphy—although after the Japanese-born heroine meets her lover-to-be, a blond British translator, a lot of words are destined to be written in bold, upper- and lower-case English, French, Yiddish, and finally also in Italian and German.

What I recalled of *The Pillow Book* before I decided to look at it again and study it more closely was an adorable little Japanese girl having her face written on with a calligraphy brush by her adoring father—a famous Japanese writer. I then recalled that in Muslim countries, where sensuous images of any kind are forbidden, religious words written in calligraphy are allowed to be inscribed on temples. By transforming words into images, calligraphy can sneak the sensuous into the holiest of places. Calligraphy is a sublimation of the erotic. From these thoughts, I then recalled that when the heroine grew up, she only wanted to have sexual relations with men who had the talent to write on her body the way her father had done. Engraved into my mind (and probably my skin) were a few scenes between the heroine and her translator-lover where body writing and sexual intercourse were interwoven to produce extravagantly erotic visual images. The images in *The Pillow Book* can either be interpreted as outright sexual fetishism or as examples of the fetishism strategy. As we shall see, it is an amalgam of both forms of fetishism and thus provides a way of distinguishing between them.

The Pillow Book begins with a child's fourth birthday and her beginning appreciations of the written word. On each of her birthdays her father "writes" a face on her face with his calligraphy brush as he speaks, "God created a clay model of a human and painted the eyes, the nose, the mouth and a sex." The word "sex" was written with a finger smudge on the mouth. As God did with his clay model, the father writes his child's name, Nagiko, on her forehead, "lest the owner should ever forget it." And, "If God approved of his creation he brought the model into life by signing his name." And so her father turns Nagiko around, lifts her hair away from her neck and signs his name on the back of her neck as a sign of his approval of what he has created. These markings are an expression of the fetishism strategy. *When the sexual object is alive, with all manner of threateningly, dangerous unpredictable vitalities, her desires must be brought under control.*

For Nagiko, her father's act of writing on her face is intimately associated with a pillow book. A pillow book is a diary of personal thoughts, a treasured book that for safekeeping is tucked away into the carved box that forms the base of a Japanese pillow.

For Nagiko's bedtime stories, her aunt reads to her from an ancient pillow book, written nearly a thousand years ago by a woman whose name was also Nagiko. With her calligraphy brush, the long-ago Nagiko recorded her adventures, her lovers, but also all the marvelous images of the world around her, "a snow mountain," "a bird in flight," "duck eggs," "shaved ice in a silver bowl," "wisteria blossoms," "indigo colored snow," "indigo writing paper," "plum blossoms," "a child eating strawberries," "to pass a place where a child is playing." As these words are spoken by Nagiko's aunt, an insert color image of them is presented over the black and white image of Nagiko lying in bed, listening to her aunt.

And all the while, the background for both sets of images is a thin sheaf of white paper written on with delicate, sinuous, black calligraphy marks. Possibly the background is the text of the original pillow book. The original

Japanese pillow book, the first one of its kind, was written in the year 997 by Sei Shonagon, exactly one thousand years before Greenaway's *The Pillow Book* was produced and presumably one thousand years before Nagiko's twenty-eighth birthday.[63]

By the time Nagiko is six, she is determined to learn how to write and to produce a pillow book of her own. The viewer gathers from the colored images inserted above her head, that Nagiko assumes that the book will be composed of the gentle touch of her father's handwriting on her body and the wondrous words that her aunt has read to her. But in the black and white background, seen through an accidental opening in the shoji screen, is another image, that of her father's publisher, a leery, evil-looking man, taking money from her father and then suggestively closing his kimono and tying up the strings of his pants. Later on, when she is much older, Nagiko realizes that this is blackmail money and that the publisher has violated her father's body and brought sorrow and disgrace into her otherwise magically happy childhood home. But, even if the child Nagiko did not realize it consciously, this shameful image of her perfect father was marked on her skin along with the calligraphied face on her face, and the pillow book images from the long-ago Nagiko.

She is married briefly and disastrously to a young man who had been hand-picked for her by her father's humiliator. He refuses to write on her face. He has contempt for her habit of reading the hundreds of books she purchases with his money. He despises the written word and especially the words in Nagiko's pillow book, which are written in English, a language he does not understand. Finally, in desperation he burns all her books including her precious pillow book. As she imagines the flames devouring her books, Nagiko announces that this is the first world destruction. They are the flames that will take her away from Japan and the world of her childhood. She predicts that there will be a second fire, "marked by major changes in my life." The first fire took her out of Japan. The second fire will take her back.

After spending a few dismal years in Hong Kong as a kitchen helper and secretary, Nagiko (Vivian Wu) decides to perfect her English by acquiring "an American accent." She flies to Los Angeles, where she soon becomes a famous runway model whose mark of distinction is that she sometimes poses in backless garments with calligraphy written on the bare skin of her upper back.

Now wealthy and successful, but also a little spoiled and petulant, especially since she is now the proud possessor of the most powerful accent in the world, she returns to Hong Kong, where she tries to recapture her childhood via the habit of picking up men in a bar "cum" brothel, and inducing them to write on her flawlessly textured skin. She does not care if they are good, indifferent, or awful sexual partners. It is the quality of a man's handwriting that interests her. She says that she would rather have an indifferent lover who is a good calligrapher. She dismisses all those who do not pass the test of writing on her skin with style and finesse.

Enter the beautiful blond Jerome (Ewan Mc Gregor). His writings on her skin are heavy-handed and ugly and English. He writes his name, JEROME, on her arm with big black upper-case letters. Nagiko rejects his writing style. But she permits him to try some other words in other languages, even the Yiddish word for breasts, which she instructs him to write on her chest. She grows more and more irritated with his writing style. "This is not going to work." "You are not a writer. You are a scribbler." "Get out." Jerome is not easily dismissed. He says, "Show me. Write on me. Use my body like the pages of a book. Your book." This invitation intrigues Nagiko. Through Jerome, Nagiko discovers that the best writing of all is when she is able to write on the skin of men.

Hoki, her photographer friend, discovers her talent for writing on men's skin. He begs her to write on his skin. "No. Your skin does not make a good paper." The photographer, who follows Nagiko everywhere and appears to be totally smitten with her, does not give up. "I could help you." He suggests that he take photographs of the calligraphy characters she writes on other mens' skin. He will make the photos into a book, which he will then bring to a publisher. Nagiko agrees.

But then Nagiko gets her first rejection letter: "This book is not worth the paper it is written on." She blames the paper for her rejection. "The skin was not good." At that point Nagiko's female servant suggests that Nagiko seduce the publisher. Nagiko visits the publisher's book store. While she is waiting to speak to him, the publisher opens the door to his office and she sees him kissing Jerome tenderly and lovingly on the cheek as he says "good-bye." She realizes at once that Jerome is his lover. She also realizes that he is the same publisher who violated her father. She decides to seduce the publisher's lover instead of the publisher.

She invites Jerome to her home. The moment the two naked bodies touch, we know that Nagiko and Jerome are exquisitely matched. As Nagiko is seducing Jerome, Nagiko is being seduced by Jerome. Nagiko and Jerome spend many hours writing on each other's skin and then bathing and washing away the writings into the drain of the bathtub. The delights of the flesh and the delights of literature are intertwined. Sexual ecstasy and religious ecstasy are intermingled, as Jerome writes the words of the Lord's prayer—"We forgive those who trespass . . ."—in several languages on all the surfaces of Nagiko's skin. After several days and nights of writing on the skin and having sexual intercourse in and out of the bathtub, Nagiko suddenly recalls the point of her mission. "I would like to honor my father by becoming a writer." Upon hearing this, Jerome writes on Nagiko's face just the way her father used to. And it is just right. She tells him she wants *his* publisher to publish her writings. "But," says Jerome, "he rejects you, and he loves me. I could be your messenger. You could write on me."

So, Nagiko writes FIRST BOOK OF THIRTEEN on Jerome's skin, from his neckline to his wrists and ankles, back and front. And Jerome delivers the book to the publisher.

When Jerome slowly removes his clothes to reveal Nagiko's "Book," the publisher reads the "words" and then licks the ink on Jerome's chest. The publisher calls in his copiers who, blandly and without comment, copy the words written on all the visible surfaces of Jerome's body. Nagiko's book is on its way to being published. Jerome's plan has succeeded. But in the process he loses Nagiko, who is wildly jealous of the sexual relationship between Jerome and the publisher. No doubt her frantic emotional outburst is also a result of remembering the publisher's sexual relationship with her father.

She decides to get revenge on Jerome by continuing her writings without him. She takes two men home from the bar, writes two more books and sends the men off to the publisher to show him the writings on their skin. Once again the copiers are summoned. She then brings home an indifferent lover who had once written some fairly sensitive words on her back and writes BOOK OF THE IMPOTENT, the fourth book. Later the same week she writes BOOK OF THE EXHIBITIONIST on the skin of an obese American with a minuscule penis. When Jerome sees this ridiculous body covered with Nagiko's words, lying prostrate in the publisher's store, he realizes that Nagiko is managing to write even though she no longer has access to his skin. He dashes off to her apartment to apologize for his absence. When he knocks and knocks at her door, however, she refuses to let him in.

Jerome goes to the bar where he first met her. He asks the photographer why Nagiko won't talk to him. Hoki, probably in a mood of spiteful jealousy, tells Jerome that he should try to scare Nagiko. Handing him some jars of pills, he suggests that Jerome follow the script of *Romeo and Juliet*.

Jerome rushes off to Nagiko's apartment. The door is open and the apartment is empty. He enters and as he gradually removes all his clothing, he swallows down dozens of pills, one after the other. He collapses onto his back on Nagiko's bed. Nagiko enters a few minutes later, crying out, "I'm sorry, I'm sorry." Thinking that Jerome is alive but sleeping, she takes out her calligraphy pen and ink and proceeds to write a book on his skin. After most of Jerome's body is covered with the words of Nagiko's book, her brush touches on his mouth. A rivulet of blood oozes out of one corner. The blood is so darkly red that it looks like ink. Only then does Nagiko realize that Jerome is dead. After allowing a few minutes, or perhaps a few hours, for sadness and quiet thought, Nagiko continues writing her latest book on the body of her dead lover.

After the funeral, the photographer tells the publisher about the death of Jerome and the book written on his skin. The publisher hires some hoodlums to dig up the grave and bring him the body of Jerome. He then hires some "professionals" to help him slice off the chemically treated skin from Jerome's body, which is covered with the words of Nagiko's BOOK OF THE LOVER.

In *Bushido*, a book on the art of Japanese tattoo, the authors describe a method for preserving the artwork that has been tattooed into human's skin. It is called "flogging," which I presume is another word for skinning. Some tattooed skins that were flogged after the death of their bearer have been donated to the Skin Museum in Tokyo. Of course, after the skin is flogged, "many qualities of the living work of art are lost."[64]

After Jerome's skin has been flogged, the remainder of his body parts are dumped into a garbage truck. The publisher folds the skin into his own personal pillow book, taking it out both day and night, unfolding the pages and pressing them against his skin—as though the unfolded pages were Jerome's still-living, physical skin.

When Nagiko hears of this latest calumny of the publisher, she tries to make a bargain with him by trading in the remainder of the thirteen books for BOOK OF THE LOVER printed on Jerome's skin. Though he gazes longingly at the male bodies whose skins are covered with Nagiko's words, the publisher refuses to surrender his pillow book. Nagiko does not give up. The publisher's vile act inspires Nagiko to become a calligraphy virtuoso. For example, the words of the ninth book, BOOK OF SECRETS, are written on various hidden parts of a young man's skin, behind his ears, on the crown of his head under his hat, on the inside of his fingers ("a hand cannot write on itself"), and between his thighs and his crotch. The thirteenth and final book is sent to the publisher written all over and everywhere on the body of a huge, muscular Samurai-type wrestler. It is the BOOK OF THE DEAD. Some of the words indicate that the time has come for the publisher to pay for his crimes. "I am Nagiko Yutokino, and I know that you are the man who blackmailed, violated and humiliated my father." Then, finally, Nagiko has written the worst crime of all on the wrestler's skin, "You desecrated the body of my lover." The publisher picks up his pillow book composed of Jerome's skin, unfolds the pages and holds them against his body for one last time. He bares his neck, giving permission to the wrestler to slit his throat. The wrestler does so and then returns the BOOK OF THE LOVER to Nagiko.

She leaves Hong Kong and returns to her childhood home in Japan, where she plants three pillow books under a blossoming bonsai in a beautiful ceramic pot; most probably her own pillowbook, the pillowbook of the long ago Nagiko, and BOOK OF THE LOVER, written on Jerome's skin.

Soon afterward, on her twenty-eighth birthday, exactly one thousand years after the writing of the first pillow book, Nagiko gives birth to the child she and Jerome created. The last scene is of Nagiko holding her baby in her arms and writing on its face, "eye," "nose," "mouth," and "sex." The expression on the baby's face indicates that he/she is absorbing the words of love written on its skin a wondrously tender image that has the bizarre effect of erasing the violent and traumatic events preceding the birth of Nagiko's baby.

In my earlier discussions of writing on the skin—the social inscriptions made by the tribal elders, delicate and coarse self-cutting, tattooing—I detected the fourth and fifth principles of the fetishism strategy. Now, as *The Pillow Book* concludes, we must question, Which principles of the fetishism strategy have been revealed? We have already interpreted that Nagiko's father (unconsciously) used his calligraphy pen on his daughter's skin to control her wayward impulses and impress on her the importance of tradition and obedience. Certainly, though, by smudging her mouth with the word Sex, he is simultaneously conveying an opposite message. Writing on the skin is often composed of an amalgam of erotic expression and an attempt to tame and subdue it.

We must question further. When a film ends with a resolution that focuses on a mother-infant couple, what is the trauma that is being disguised and disavowed? When a woman's body dominates the foreground of a film, what is being pushed into the background? As we came to understand in the chapter "The Body of a Woman," if we look past the glittering spectacle of a woman's body placed prominently in the foreground of a film, we can gain access to the images of loss and trauma that lurk in the background.

A full understanding requires that we explore the dynamic relationship between both sets of images—foreground and background. The crucial factor that must be detected is the discordance between a foreground image and those images that have been cast into the margins, shadows, and background. A film that concludes with an image or reference to the redeemer mother, the holy mother-infant couple, or the face of Mother Nature herself in a tree, a waterfall, a desert landscape, is an expression of the fetishism strategy. As I warned in the last chapter, "Always watch out for the return to the embrace of Mother Nature—a device of the fetishism strategy designed to deny the traumas implicitly and explicitly expressed in the film." In most films that employ this device, a world destruction fantasy is countered by a fantasy of rebirth. The destruction-rebirth theme signals an apocalyptic narrative. I stressed that, "Most people have no trouble thinking of a world destruction fantasy as apocalyptic. It is usually more difficult to think of the fantasy of a return to Mother Nature as apocalyptic." However, in an apocalyptic narrative both fantasies are working in tandem.

Applying these thoughts to *The Pillow Book*, we ask: What are the traumas that are being disguised and pushed into the background? Where is the apocalyptic narrative? My discussions of apocalyptic narratives such as *Niagara*, *The Misfits*, *Thelma and Louise*, *Eyes Wide Shut* illustrated one way that these two fantasies might be expressed. When a violent and corrupt sexuality and disturbing issues of sexuality and genital difference are foregrounded in the first half, they are depicted as obstacles to the journey back to the paradise that once was, in the second half.

Greenaway's narrative structure is more convoluted and difficult to decipher. Like a delirious Mobius strip that staggers capriciously from inside to outside, from past to present, from one skin layer to another, Greenaway's redemption theme interweaves with world destruction fantasies of various sorts. *The Pillow Book* is an extravaganza of naked bodies. All of them, save for Nagiko's, are the bodies of men. Jerome's beautiful body is followed by a parade of nude men of assorted shapes and sizes. A devastating trauma is unfolding but the continual stream of naked male bodies keeps distracting the viewer from realizing what is going on in the margins and shadows. The primary aim of the fetishism strategy is to tame and subdue those human vitalities, which otherwise might overturn and destroy the universe. In most of the examples I have used, the feared and dangerous vitalities have to do with human sexuality and human creativity. But, the fetishism strategy can also be evoked to give expression to a male's feminine erotic longings. Or it may be evoked to give destructive impulses just enough of an erotic tint to contain the wish for total annihilation. Only when the fetishism strategy can no longer sufficiently disguise or regulate the underlying shameful, frightening, forbidden, and dangerously unpredictable impulses, fantasies, and wishes does outright madness, rampage, violence, rape, body mutilation, incest, and murder result. *The Pillow Book* expresses several principles of the fetishism strategy. But there is one I haven't mentioned in this context. The eternal writing on the skin in *The Pillow Book* is also an effort to contain and regulate aggression, violence, and destruction. We are usually so preoccupied with the destructive and dehumanizing aspects of the fetishism strategy that we might overlook how it can also be a mediator between erotic and destructive impulses.

However, in *The Pillow Book*, the fetishism strategy has failed. Destruction runs amok. To compound matters, this total annihilation of the universe is disavowed by the closing image of the mother-infant couple.

The film begins in a time of innocence, a time when the world, a world of writing on the skin and pillow books, was seen by Nagiko as protective and loving. It is also a time of illusions about her parents and an innocence about her father's sexuality. Hints of the destruction of that world are briefly revealed through the open shoji screen. When Nagiko's ceremonial wedding limousine takes her to the home she will share with her callous and unfeeling husband, we can see written on her pouting, disappointed face the beginnings of the destruction of her childhood illusions.

We can interpret the rest of the film as Nagiko's attempts to restore the presence of her father, a presence that represented the childhood innocence she once believed in and then lost. When Jerome dies by committing suicide, or accidentally from an overdose of sleeping pills, Nagiko enacts the second world destruction by setting fire to all her books and clothing and shoes and jewelry and furniture. After recovering the skin of Jerome, imprinted for all eternity on the pillow book designed by her father's humiliator, Nagiko once again returns to her childhood home, where she embodies her father by writing on the face of her child.

Greenaway's swiveling, apocalyptic journey that goes from one world destruction to yet a second one, ends abruptly in an eccentric twist of plot simplicity. First there is the "planting" of the three pillow books under the blossoming bonsai, as if Jerome's dead body might somehow be resurrected and blossom again. Then finally there is the closing scene of the mother-infant couple. When so many human lives have been laid to waste, so many bodies corrupted and violated, to conclude a film with a reunion with Mother Nature is a disavowal of the vast human dilemmas the film has been presenting.

At one point, just after the first world destruction and just before she embarks on her quest for a calligrapher lover, Nagiko says, "Writing is an ordinary thing but how precious. If writing did not exist what terrible depressions we would have." She is suggesting that writing can be a form of therapy that protects the writer from succumbing to the fevers of depression.

Writing a biography, the topic of the next chapter, is different from writing on the skin. It may, and often does, simultaneously express contrasting aspects of the fetishism strategy. It can be a precious thing that resonates with the creative vitalities of the human spirit and thereby oppose and undermine the fetishism strategy. Or, the biographer might surrender to the fever that is inherent in the task of writing about human lives. In the process of writing a biography, some biographers succumb to archive fever and thereby unknowingly give voice and expression to the fetishism strategy.

Archive Fever
Writing Lives

Long before fetishism was named as a perversion of the sexual life, religious pundits, anthropologists, philosophers, poets, and economists employed the concept of fetishism to illuminate a vast assortment of cultural activities. A recurring theme in all these disparate ventures into the frailties and vagaries of humanity has been the duplicity inherent in fetishism. This duplicity is expressed most clearly in the fetish object, whose concrete substantiality is mistaken as a sign that the object embodies some living substance or spiritual essence, when, in fact, that very materiality and tangibility represents decay, de-vitalization, and morbidity. In speaking of the deceptions of commodity fetishism, for example, Karl Marx would warn, "All our inventions and progress seem to result in endowing material forces with intellectual life and stultifying human life with a material force."[1]

Writing a biography is an enterprise fraught with the dangerous duplicities of the fetishism strategy. There is a susceptibility in the biographical impulse that makes it one of the more telling illustrations of the insidious manner in which material force may be employed to stultify human life. Desiring only to bring to life the flesh-and-blood essence of another human being, the biographer unknowingly stands at the abyss between Life and Death, always haunted by the prospect of drowning in the fathoms of facts she amasses, always verging on crushing her subject under the weight of the archival detritus she has marshaled in her earnest efforts to be true to life.

In his monograph *En Mal d'Archive*, translated in English as *Archive Fever*, Jacques Derrida, the French philosopher, plays around with the differences between the original French and the English translation, thereby capturing the double edge that accrues to archives. "*En Mal d'*" refers to lacking something which you need and must have, but the translation, "Fever," gives voice to the burning desire or yearning for something that verges on a sickness.

As Derrida describes that fever:

> It is to burn with a passion. It is to never rest, interminably, from searching for the archive right where it slips away. It is to run after the archive, even if there's

too much of it, right where something in it anarchives itself. It is to have a compulsive, repetitive and nostalgic desire for the archive, an irrepressible desire to return to the origin, a homesickness, a nostalgia for the return to the most archaic place of absolute commencement. No desire, no passion, no drive, no compulsion, indeed no repetition compulsion, no "*mal-de*" can arise for a person who is not already, in one way or another, *en mal d'archive*.[2]

Before beginning to write, the biographer must locate, recover, and collect data relating to an already dead or still living subject. These acts of retrieval are supposed to bring to life what might have remained silent, unseen, unknown, unfelt, and, for all intents, therefore, dead. On the one hand archives are in the service of life. On the other, archive fever is an expression of the death drive. The problem or dilemma of archives is that the yearning for more and more data leads to a burning up, a veritable consumption and destruction of the psychic vitalities of the subject. The act of storage and accumulation is thus inherently a kind of essential destructiveness.

Lytton Strachey had a sure-fire remedy for archive fever. He said that the biographer, if he wishes to avoid drowning in data and facts, must "row out over that great ocean of material and lower down into it, here and there, a little bucket, which will bring up into the light of day some characteristic specimen from those far depths, to be examined with a careful curiosity."[3]

Referring to the traditional overstuffed biography, Strachey said: Those two fat volumes, with which it is our custom to commemorate the dead— who does not know them, with their ill-digested masses of material, their slipshod style, their tone of tedious panegyric, their lamentable lack of selection, of detachment, of design? They are as familiar as the *cortege* of the undertaker, and wear the same air of slow, funereal barbarism.[4]

Virginia Woolf echoed Strachey's funereal theme. She mockingly proclaimed that the first duty of a biographer "is to plod without looking to right or left, in the indelible footprints of truth; unenticed by flowers; regardless of shade, on and on methodically till we fall plump into the grave and finis on the tombstone above our head."[5]

These two eminent writers, although they wrote long before the time of Derrida's *Archive Fever*, captured the *anarchic, archiviolithic drive* underlying his *mal d'archive*. Since Strachey and Woolf appreciated the force and power of the deadly impulses that could murder a biography, they mustered every possible means to bring vitality to the biographical enterprise.

Strachey's exhuberant aphoristic style ridiculed the pompous sanctities of his subjects—from Cardinal Manning to Florence Nightingale, and even those of the ostensibly plain and simple Queen Victoria, who got a biography all for herself. Woolf, with deliberate intentions of keeping the realities of time and place and person at bay, challenged every biographical propriety. She wrote a biography of the fictional character Orlando, who lived for several centuries and changed sexual identities whenever impulse or circumstance called for it.[6] *Orlando* mocked calendar time, gender conformities, and conventional biography. Woolf followed that up with *Flush*, a biography of Elizabeth Barrett's cocker spaniel, portraying the love and elopement of Miss Barrett and Mr. Robert Browning through the eyes of Flush.[7] Woolf's impudent biographical virtuosity taunted those pathetic souls who plod along, "without looking to right or left."

In 1961, as Leon Edel was plodding through the third volume of his five-volume biography of Henry James, he presented a lecture entitled "The Biographer and Psycho-analysis" to a group of psychoanalysts. After calling attention to certain similarities between biographer and psychoanalyst, Edel focused on the unconscious motives underlying a biographer's compelling attraction to his or her subject.

As Edel gave his psychoanalytic interpretation of the origins and effects of the biographer's compelling attraction, he unknowingly expressed the essence of Derrida's archive fever. This attraction, Edel stressed, was always "mixed up, in different degrees with all sorts of drives"—curiosity, voyeurism, the drive to power and the need for omniscience.[8] He concluded his compilation of the compulsions and impulses that accompany the biographer's compelling attraction to his subject, with that other, even more powerful drive, that ever-present susceptibility so characteristic of biographical study— the digestive factor, "the impulse toward accumulation and ingestion of data."[9] He cautioned that the gratification of the digestive impulse can, and usually does, result in a very cluttered biography or a biography that never gets written. And thus the stored-up accumulation of data, rather then bringing a subject to life, crushes his or her vitalities and inevitably buries the remains of the dead.

How might a biographer protect himself from the dangers of the unconscious forces that inhabit the biographical enterprise? Edel explained to his audience of analysts that a biographer had an interpersonal relationship with his subject much like the analyst has to his patient. And, like an analyst with a patient, the biographer must know *himself* before he can know his subject.[10] Prior to commencing, even before beginning to collect data, the biographer must ask questions like the following: What are the qualities in my subject that arrested my attention? Why did I chose this poet? this painter? this composer? Why not that one? What are the forces underlying my attraction?[11]

Moreover, in order to pursue the difficult time-consuming task ahead of him, the biographer must identify with his subject.[12] How else to re-experience and appreciate his subject's feelings, dilemmas, struggles, passions? Yet, Edel cautions that, in these very identifications, there is another danger. In becoming this other person for the purposes of biography, the biographer risks everything. He might lose himself in his subject or lose his subject by making him a mirror of himself. The antidote to these potential maladies is for the biographer to ponder his identifications and to make them conscious, or as conscious as possible.

Early on in his lecture, Edel reprimands the traditional biographer who is disinterested and unaware of his personal reasons for choosing a subject, "innocently boasting that he is *objective*, and even 'scientific' in his biographical methods."[13] However, because he has assembled his facts by the light of his *unconscious* preconceptions, he actually "arrives at a work that is an image *of an image* of himself, and of his identifications and distortions."[14]

The biographer must question the forces underlying his attraction to his subject and ponder the nature of his identifications with that person. Here Edel reminds the analysts of another way in which biographer and analyst are alike. "The dangers of a kind of countertransference* exist for him as they do for you."[15] Without fully realizing it, Edel's countertransference fears bring him to the central dilemma and tension of his lecture, an ambivalence toward transference that would haunt his future writings on biography. Edel's transference ambivalence would turn out to make him susceptible to the archive fever he deplored.

Should the biographer disengage from his subject? If he does, he might then lose his desire to write biography. If he doesn't, he loses his objectivity and the subject's life will become entangled in the biographer's counter-transferences.

When I first read Edel's lecture on biography and psychoanalysis, I was puzzled by his fear of countertransference. But, after all, the analysts he was addressing were also suspicious of countertransference. At that time, analysts had recognized that an understanding of a patient's transference to the analyst yielded valuable insights into the patient's psychic life. However, countertransference was a thorn in the side of psychoanalysis—to most analysts, something dangerous and menacing that could only act as an impediment or interference with the analytic process. However, even as early as 1950, some analysts in England and France were already viewing counter-transference as perhaps the most crucial dimension of an analyst's ability to understand his patients. Some analysts went so far as to claim that counter-transference is a prerequisite for analysis, rather than an impediment. And that, furthermore, without countertransference the necessary talent and interest for conducting an analysis are absent. Nowadays, countertransfer-ence is widely considered the analyst's friend and ally, if she understands and uses it to advance her patient's availability to the psychoanalytic process.

Over the years, as I became friendly toward countertransference, my analytic experiences began to teach me that *my* countertransferences, when I was able to be aware of them and make them conscious, were as much

---

* The psychoanalytic terms, *transference,* and *countertransference,* have various meanings depending on the particular school of psychoanalysis. In this chapter on biography, I am using the term transference in its most direct and usual sense. Transference is about the feelings, thoughts, fantasies, wishes, and infantile conflicts aroused in the biographer in response to her subject's character, actions, feelings, thoughts, fantasies, and infantile conflicts. When these transferences can be made conscious, they are a source of information and vitality in the writing of the biogra-phy. However, since a biographical subject, unless he is still living, cannot have a transference to his biographer, the biographer cannot have a countertransference in the most technical sense of that term. While some analysts still believe in the idea that countertransferences represent inter-ferences and impediments, most present-day analysts believe that the analyst's countertransfer-ences to her subject are not only useful, but indispensible to the psychoanalytic process.

a source of my analytic insights as were my patient's transferences. At some point during my reconsiderations of countertransference, I was reminded of Edel's fear of it. I re-read his paper and indulged myself in some private interpretations, which I now make public.

According to Edel, identifications were acceptable, even necessary to the biographer's sympathies with his subject's plight—*if* the biographer could make these identifications conscious. It was the transference-countertransference that had Edel worried. The way I reasoned the tensions in Edel's remarks, they had something to do with the differences between rationality and irrationality. Identifications, whether conscious or unconscious, are understood to be ego/superego/ego-ideal formations, and therefore, however nonrational and conflict-ridden these internal structures actually are, the word "ego" dignifies them with the stamp of reason, order, and rationality.

Transferences,—the patients' responses to his analyst that derive from certain elements in his own psychic life;—and countertransferences,—the analysts' various responses to his patient's transferences,—are responses that derive partly from the analyst's psychic life and partly from his sympathy with the patient's psychic life, and are not part of the supposedly rational everyday world we live in. Edel, I interpreted, was made anxious by the irrationality of those mysterious, vagrant, and mischievous life forces that are inherent in writing lives.

In *Writing Lives*, Edel's *Principia Biographica*, transference issues had become central to his biographical wisdom. Nevertheless, despite his increased understanding of the process and his greater awareness of the differences between identifications and transferences, he still had a profound mistrust of transference.

Before tackling the problems of transference, Edel invites us to imagine the surface of the biographer's table—buried under piles of books, certificates of birth, certificates of death, diaries, testimonials, newspaper clippings, and so on. Edel gives considerable attention to the vast assortment of items that clutter the biographer's worktable, which obviously has to be much larger and stronger than the tables of other writers, as if the image of that impressive collection of data could overpower the menace of transference.

It is worth pursuing the possible relationship between Edel's persisting mistrust of transference and his unrelenting apprehensions about archives. Throughout Edel's *Principia*, the two ostensibly distinct topics incessantly rub against one another, embracing in an unacknowledged liebestod.

In the first chapter of *Writing Lives*, Edel addresses the common dilemmas and challenges that biographers must face up to. He cites the wisdom of Lytton Strachey, who had described biography as "the most delicate and humane of all the branches of the art of writing."[16] In an emotionally resonant passage, Edel elaborates the full meaning of Strachey's words:

> Delicate because the biographer seeks to restore a sense of life to the inert materials that survive an individual's passage on earth . . . and to shape a likeness of the vanished figure. Humane, because inevitably the biographical

process is a refining, a civilizing,—a humanizing process. And because it is a delicate and humane process, it partakes of all the ambiguities and contradictions of life itself. A biography is a record in words, of *something that is mercurial and as flowing, as compact of temperament and emotion as the human spirit itself.* (*itals.* mine)[17]

Edel then points to the biographer's main dilemma: The biographer "must be neat and orderly and logical in describing this *flamelike human spirit which delights in defying order and neatness and logic*" (*itals.* mine).[18]

Edel's ambivalence about the human spirit arrested my attention. On the one hand, his words are a radiant testimony to that spirit. On the other, they confirm my interpretation of his fundamental fear of the irrational. Edel worried about what might happen if that vagrant, flamelike spirit were given expression without the restraints imposed upon it by archival data. Although there is a certain ambiguity in Edel's position *vis à vis* order and neatness and logic, in the end he favors reason over the unknowable and uncontrollable human spirit—which so delights in defying the forces of law and order.

Obviously, I see these matters differently from Edel. Archive fever, the impulse to accumulate data, is not merely an expression of lawfulness, but also a device that deprives biographies of the transference vitalities that bring a subject to life. The bulking material reality of archives and facts is employed to still the flow of psychic reality, to squelch the flamelike human spirit that defies order and neatness. After all, the uncertainty and ambiguity of those mercurial and flowing vitalities of the human spirit pose a threat to the emotional and intellectual certainties of the biographer. To put it bluntly, biographers sometimes use archives to silence their transferences. However, when a transference is allowed to speak up and make itself heard, the biographer can use it to help her understand her subject. *Unacknowledged* transferences are the troublemakers and it is these that breed and nourish archive fevers.

Writers like Edel, who not only write biographies but write about biography, are reluctant to welcome transference as a potential ally in the struggle with archive fever. A biographer, however, can no more rid herself of transference than she can do away with her need for archives. The archival instinct can act as a restraint on transferences. Transferences, if they are made conscious, can serve as an antidote to archive fever.

A biographer always has a transference to the person she is writing about. It can be a most valuable tool for illuminating the psychic vitalities of a biographical subject. However, biographers, in their efforts toward achieving objectivity, tend to view their personal feelings and thoughts and fantasies about the subject of the biography as an impediment, something to be deliberately ignored, denied, repressed, and, whenever possible, silenced altogether. Sometimes, when transferences might press forward to become recognized, they are regarded as intrusions and banished.

David Hoddeson, the editor of two special issues of *American Imago* "Transference and Biography," introduced the issues by describing the outcomes of biographers trying to ignore and banish their transferences:

> That in many biographers' workrooms transference phenonomena are deliberately and programmatically set aside wherever and whenever that is possible—or denied or otherwise repressed where it is not—in every sense goes without saying; until very recently, whatever transferences were recognized in the biographer's workspace were considered intrusions. That many of these repressions return in some (dis)guise during the long labor of researching and writing biography is also predictable; although helping to mask any such conflicts are the conventional attachments to more acceptable and widely understood biographical materials (which often come to carry their own transferential investments): the archives, letters, official documents, and circles of contemporaries; the biographer's deepening relationship to a lengthening text.[19]

Edel struggles with archives and he struggles with transferences, seldom perceiving the fearful symmetry that binds them. He expresses his fear of transferences with a series of reprimands to some biographers who had succumbed to them.

He begins his litany of transference laments with his best-case scenario, Andre Maurois, the transference-ridden biographer of Shelley, Disraeli, and Byron. In the late 1920s, Maurois was invited to give a series of talks at Trinity College, Cambridge, where he had the innocent audacity to praise his infatuations with his biographical subjects. "Biography is a means of expression when the author has chosen his subject in order to respond to a secret need in his own nature."[20] It was as if Maurois were inviting Edel's censure, "From the moment a biographer responds to 'a secret need in his own nature' he is tangled in his emotional relationship with his subject—he is in trouble."[21]

Maurois, who had never anticipated an Edel, had no awareness of the dangers of his transference, and probably had never heard of the term, persisted in his argument, boldly claiming that his kind of biography was written with "more natural emotion than other kinds of biography, because the feelings and adventures of the hero can be the medium of the biographers' own feelings. To a certain extent it will be autobiography disguised as biography."[22] Maurois' confessionals in defense of his biographical method were proof enough to Edel that Maurois had been afflicted with transference fever.

After disposing of Maurois' incurable transference misadventures, Edel devotes a few paragraphs to the pathetic case of Mark Schorer's enmeshment with his subject, Sinclair Lewis. In "The Burdens of Biography," Shorer confessed to the affinities that he discovered between himself and Lewis. They were both "inept and unsuccessful boys" in a Midwestern world of muscular masculinity.[23] They were both guilty of "careless writing," "ill-conceived ambition," "bad manners," "fits of temper," and "regrettable follies."[24] Edel, in reporting how Schorer's transference shifted from positive (blind love?) to negative (blind hate?), seemed to grasp, for a moment at least, the ubiquitous relationship between (unconscious) transference and archive fever. "The confusion in his psyche undermined his project and he was ultimately swamped by his too abundant materials."[25]

There were times when Edel seemed almost possessed, even terrorized by the evils of transference. He always posed it as a problem. In his analysis of Lytton Strachey's transferences, he inadvertently exposes some possible motives for his fears of transference.

Strachey's subject was Victorian hypocrisy, and the four characters he chose to illustrate the hypocrisies of the English spirit were Cardinal Manning and his ruthless use of religious power; Thomas Arnold with his Christian Bible and respectability; General Gordon, a warrior who posed as a saint; and Florence Nightingale, the "lady of the lamp" who turned out to be a tough and unrelenting adversary when it came to defying those who would dare to interfere with her humanitarian gestures.

Summing up Strachey's biographical sketches, Edel says that they "pit strong queenly women against puny men. He endows the women with masculine strength, feminine endurance and feminine-masculine action."[26] What family drama might have motivated these cross-gendered fables? According to Edel, it all boils down to Strachey's complex relationship to his own queen mother, Lady Strachey. Directly from his references to the "queen" mother, without so much as a pause to present some data in support of his ensuing wild analysis, Edel strikes out at Strachey's homosexuality, those vagrant ambiguities of the human spirit that seem to terrify Edel. "He learned to cope with his own manipulative and assertive homosexuality by becoming the very queens of his stories. In his fertile imagination he could be the mother of his numerous boys—and at the same time their lover."[27]

Edel further claims that Strachey found a perverse delight in identifying with Florence Nightingale, who became the mother "of an entire army of men,"[28] and that he found equal delight in portraying powerful men like General Gordon and Arnold, an educator of boys, as "ridiculous male figures."[29]

In this context of Strachey's homoerotic predilections, Edel reminds his readers of Strachey's strategies for eluding archive fevers. In his preface to *Eminent Victorians*, Strachey recommended that a biographer should, "attack his subject in unexpected places; he will fall upon the flank, or the rear; he will shoot a sudden, revealing searchlight into obscure recesses, hitherto undivined."[30]

It is understandable that the "plodding" Edel might resent Strachey's cavalier dismissal of archives. Edel wrestled for decades with the stubbornly unyielding archives of Henry James, who had thrown most of his letters and documents into his fireplace. James had hoped this would prevent some biographer from biographizing him after he was dead. That didn't stop Edel from developing archive fever in his pursuit of James's life. Despite his phobic-driven animus toward Strachey's homoeroticism, he acknowledges that there is some value in Strachey's remedy of dipping a little bucket into the vast archival waters. The "little bucket" could balance out "the sober monotony" of compiling facts and sorting through all the debris of birth certificates, genealogies, photographs, letters, old manuscripts, diaries, newspaper clippings, and death certificates.[31]

Edel tosses to and fro as he tries to confront the dilemma of archives; at one moment giving tribute to their importance and then, in the next, giving yet another example of their excesses. He admits to being overwhelmed by them. But the instant he hints of his defeat, he finds it necessary to defend archives. "I am not for one moment deprecating their importance or value."[32]

Finally, he weaves a sobering tale of the newest menace that has invaded the archive scene. Universities and libraries are paying writers for every scrap of their legacies, even before they are dead. Many of these artists make more money from their pre-paid archives than from publishing their poems, stories, and biographies.

"In the old days," Edel tells us (probably thinking of his own archive nemesis, Henry James), "houses were blessed with fireplaces and much paper was automatically consigned to flames."[33] In the age of the archive, however, "Every chance scribble belongs to posterity."[34]

As we approached the turn of twenty-first century, the malady of archives became a severe affliction, a veritable epidemic that seemed to thrive and reproduce itself as one of the symptoms of a general culture of fetishism, where material goods of one kind or another are traded in for the vitalities of the flamelike human spirit.

In 1999 alone one could hardly read a review of a biography that did not make some disparaging comments about what Richard Eder called "the contemporary fashion for megalography: cutting the biographical suit too large for the subject and with cloth yards to spare."[35]

No pun intended, but, I have come to regard these yards of spare cloth, as a surfeit of material or factual reality, a characteristic symptom of archive fever. From my point of view, it is not the number of words and details nor the size and heft of a biography that would identify it as a victim of the fetishism strategy, but rather the way in which a heavy burden of facts and data serves to stifle the vitalities of the subject. To call up the words of Marx once again, such use of details is tantamount to "endowing material forces with intellectual life and stultifying human life with a material force."[36]

The fetishism of biographical writing concerns the various ways that facts and details end up murdering the subject. There are those times when the subject strikes back. If the subject is still living, a biographer can sometimes be seriously wounded, especially if the biographer has idealized and idolized his subject, which would be evidence enough that the biographer's transference remained unexamined and unconscious. And then there are occasions, probably more often than we realize, when megalography and unexamined transference operate in tandem. Because it is such a dramatic instance of my point, I begin with one of the later travesties of transference and then work my way back to the turn of the century.

In 2004, after publishing the last of his three-volume, 2,251-page biography of Graham Greene, Norman Sherry was interviewed by Dinitia Smith in *The New York Times.* He openly confessed his wholesale, irrepressible, blatant transference to Greene. With indignation, Greene's son and literary excecutor, Francis, confirmed Sherry's self-analysis: "This book [referring to the third volume], is not about Graham Greene but about Sherry. . . . His obsession with brothels far surpasses that of his subject."[37]

In my opinion, this was not the more usual case of the biographer making over his subject into his own image. Sherry's variety of transference was distinctive. It was an instance of a biographer's enthrallment with his subject allowing the subject to consume and demolish the biographer.

Sherry told Smith that he dismissed the bad reviews from the English press as "poppycock, piffle and balderdash."[38] However, he did not deny bringing himself into the biography. In fact, he seemed to brag about it, as if it were a badge of honor. "Especially when Greene died, I was very moved by his death, so inevitably I had to put myself into it." "I often felt I must be him." "I lived within him."[39]

Sherry continues, "If you are going to write about a man who is highly sexed, you can't change that. Besides, you can't help but admire him for having sex with everything in sight."[40] Sherry describes how his attempt to be honest to every aspect of his subject's life ruined his health and alienated his family. He got tropical diabetes in Liberia while recreating Greene's research for *Journey Without Maps.* He contracted dysentery in Mexico while tracing Greene's path for *The Power and the Glory.* He developed intestinal gangrene while in Paraguay researching the background of Greene's *The Honorary Consul;* "I almost destroyed myself. By the time I had finished my life had been taken from me."[41]

A few years before Sherry's confession to Dinitia Smith, Fred Kaplan, the biographer of Gore Vidal, nearly had his life taken from him by his subject. During 1999, when the attack on biography seemed an unstoppable trend, Kaplan's 890-page biography of Vidal became the standard by which archive fever was gauged. And it was another one of those unfortunate cases, when unexamined transference and archive fever fed off each other. Richard Eder's critique on the megalography of Kaplan's biography of Vidal in his *New York Times* review was echoed in Willaim Deresciewicz's *Sunday Times* review of that volume. They both also called attention to Kaplan's shameless idealization of Vidal.

When Gore Vidal first approached Fred Kaplan, the eminent biographer of Carlyle, Dickens, and Henry James, to be his official biographer, initially Kaplan observed that, "I prefer my subjects dead."[42] In his review Eder comments that Kaplan was "dead right in his preferring."[43] As Kaplan would discover as he neared the completion of the biography, Vidal had actually confused him with that other eminent biographer, Justin Kaplan. But still Kaplan confessed, without shame, "the inevitable happened: I grew fond of him."[44] Then, adding without a blush, "Had he grown fond of me? There was reason to think so."[45] But, as Kaplan must have already known before he made his confession, Gore had thoroughly rejected him, taking the side of those who attached the biography and wishing out loud that he should have gone with the other Kaplan.

In any event, Kaplan had some warnings about the social posturing that covered over the shallow depths of his subject. As he was reading Gore's semi-memoir *Palimpsest*, Kaplan recognized that it was "a non-introspective memoir without a center of consciousness."[46] Early on in their talks (presumably when Vidal still thought of Fred as Justin), Mr. Vidal told Mr. Kaplan, "I don't know how you are going to do this because there isn't anything there."[47] This was a "red flag"[48] comments Eder, "and biographers, particularly with the prospect of unlimited access to their subjects are bulls. It is Mr. Kaplan though, who has been gored."[49]

Here Richard Eder is making a convincing case for my hypothesis about the way biographers employ material reality to disguise the paucity of their insights into their subject's psychic reality. This, of course, does not mean that Gore Vidal has no psychic reality but rather that having unlimited access to a living author's life can be a disadvantage with a biographical subject like Vidal, whose superficiality and social posturing are devices that are designed to ward off access to his inner psychological world, his psychic reality.

Finally, because he was unable to "pierce Mr. Vidal's skillful mask making,"[50] Kaplan's biography is itself "a mask about a mask."[51] As Eder is quick to point out, "Mr. Vidal gives his biographer lots of surface and few openings."[52]

The review of Kaplan's book by William Deresiewicz, a professor of English at Yale University, entitled "His Cigar is Just a Cigar," goes right to the goring of Kaplan: "Kaplan allows himself to become too identified with his subject, dazzled by the brilliance of his fame, seduced by his charm or the illusion of intimacy. Its effect can be felt on every page. Everywhere Vidal's view of events is endorsed, his actions defended, his enemies belittled, his hypocrisies and cruelties explained away."[53]

Apparently Kaplan accepted Vidal's remarkable claim that he has no psychology. In support of this claim Kaplan quotes Judith Calvino, widow of Italo Calvino and a close friend of Vidal, "Gore is a man without an unconscious. . . . There are no bad things lurking somewhere in his mind or body."[54] As he comments on Kaplan's naïve acceptance of Vidal's claim of having no psychic life to speak of, the reviewer makes an inadvertent interpretation of the relationship between this purported paucity of psychic reality and the accumulation of material reality in the Vidal biography. "After a beautifully done opening chapter on Vidal's family history, Kaplan descends to a prose of depressing clumsiness, as if, having stuffed his word processor with seventy-four years' worth of date books and account ledgers, he had left the machine to write the damn book itself."[55]

As the number of biographies written and published increased, seemingly in harmony with the increasing size of the biographies, the anti-biographical forces rose up with renewed force and conviction. Railing against the biography genre at large, Stanley Fish, in his *New York Times* Op Ed page column

"Just published: Minutiae Without Meaning," went on an all-out attack of the biography genre. His article focuses on all of those "details unattached to a master narrative . . . details that don't mean anything at all, or can mean anything at all, the piling up of details, letters, medical records, the names of boyhood sleds in order to compensate for lack of meaning."[56] Most often biographers are left with "little more than a collection of random incidents the only truth being told is the truth of contingency, of events succeeding one another in a universe of accident and chance."[57]

In an essay in the *Sunday New York Times Book Review*, Ellen Willis spoke fervently against the "sheer heft" of contemporary biographies, "overloaded with details that show off the author's scholarship but fail to distinguish between the crucial and the trivial."[58]

The vehemence of the general attack on biography inspired a few writers to try to muster some arguments in its favor. With all good intentions, John Updike's defense, "One Cheer for Literary Biography," ends up sounding very much like another attack. The tone is set when Updike begins with an epigraph from F. Scott Fitzgerald's notebooks: "There never was a good biography of a good novelist. There couldn't be. He is too many people, if he's any good."[59] Updike then tries to counter Fitzgerald's pessimsim by giving a faint cheer. He argues that certain biographies, like George D. Painter's "splendid" two-volume biography of Marcel Proust, become a way of re-experiencing the novel, with a closeness, and a delight in seeing imagined details conjured back into real ones, "that only this particular writer and his vast autobiograhical masterpiece could provide."[60] Painter's biography, Updike comments, "is more of the same, mirrored back into reality."[61]

Along the way, however, most of what Updike says about literary biography is not accorded even the weak one cheer. And to compound matters, even this lonely champion of biography is caught up in the page-counting fad. "Although one rarely sees literary biography on the best-seller list, a prodigious amount of it is produced, some of it at prodigious length."[62] Beginning the tour in his library with Holroyd's three-volume biography of George Bernard Shaw and Edel's five-volume James, Updike then takes us out to his barn, where he begins a serious count-down.[63] Five-hundred pages for Edmund Wilson, Simone Weil, and Joyce Cary; six-hundred for Oscar Wilde and Ivy Compton Burnett; six-hundred-and fifty for Norman Mailer, seven-hundred each for Jean Genet and Samuel Beckett; eight-hundred for Zola; and the real heavyweight of twelve-hundred for the life of James Thurber. Updike then speculates that maybe length of biography has something to do with length of life. Sylvia Plath, dead at thirty, got only three-hundred-and-fifty pages. Anne Sexton, however, having lived a decade longer, got one-hundred pages more than Plath.

Acknowledging that "the life of a writer, which spins outside of itself a secondary life, offers an opportunity to study mind and body, or inside and outside, or dream and reality, together as one,"[64] Updike nevertheless prefaces his apparently reluctant, "one" cheer, "literary biography does perform useful work,"[65] with this personal statement: "As long as I am alive, I don't want somebody else playing on my jungle gym—disturbing my children, quizzing my ex-wife, bugging my present wife, seeking for Judases among my friends, rummaging through yellowing old clippings, quoting *in extenso* bad reviews I had rather forget, and getting everything slightly wrong."[66]

Finally, toward the end of the winter of 2000, the attack on biography could no longer be ignored by serious and committed biographers.

In his personal response to the attacks on long biographies, Fred Karl, biographer of Conrad, Faulkner, and Kafka, wrote an essay entitled, "The Long and the Short of It," where he counterattacked the critiques of long biographies by scorning the new series of brief biographies that were brought into existence purportedly to "revitalize an aging genre" and to introduce "a new generation of readers to this once popular genre."[67]

But, protests Karl, how can this new generation of readers get to appreciate biography through the easier, less demanding reading of brief biographies, "when there is so little biography at hand?"[68]

"In the brief forms of biography we find no notes or else notes that are very skimpy, no index, little or no bibliography; and most importantly, no new material or new archival research, no expert in the field—instead a well-known writer."[69] Blaming the publishers of this brief biography series for their cynical reliance on celebrity culture as an antidote to the literary and historical values that are the foundation of serious biographical studies, Karl goes on to review several of the misbegotten ventures into brief biography. Along the way, Karl tries to make the point that length is not the important point of argument but rather whether or not the person who presumes to write a biography possesses the proper knowledge of the traditions and skills and tools that make the writer of a biography into a "proper" biographer.

Despite the fervor of his counterattack, Karl, nevertheless, has the generosity of spirit to consider how two brief biographies written by celebrity writers, Mary Gordon's *Joan of Arc*[70] and Edna O'Brien's *James Joyce*,[71] though they suffer from all the problems associated with the "briefies"—details that are derivative of previous biographies, narratives that are devoid of deep analysis, text not edited, and full of undigested material—finally, do justice to their subjects anyhow. As he looks into these two good briefies, Karl discovers that each of these writers, even though she was not a proper biographer, was able to enlist personal feelings for her subject and was, in addition, passionately attuned to the cultural and social issues that her subject embodied. Apparently, a compelling portrait of a subject can result, even with brevity, and even without deep analysis, if the writer's "acknowledged" passion and identification with her subject is allowed to play a prominent role in the composition of the biography. In other words, although Karl does not use this language, if a consciousness of transference is brought into play, even a brief biography might be deserving of the term, *biography*.

In the conclusions to his counterattack, Karl takes a few shots at James Atlas, the founder and editor of the Penguin brief biography series he is disparaging. He recalls how Atlas, in his pre–brief biography days, used to give enthusiastic reviews for "full-fleshed," long biographies. He condemns Atlas' recent reviews and essays for hauling long biographies over the coals and bemoaning the state of biography "left in the hands of the long-winded set."[72] In this context, he calls attention to the fact that Atlas worked for nearly a decade on his inclusive and exhaustive life of Saul Bellow during the same years that he began his attacks on long biographies. Karl comments: "He is, indeed, a man caught between conflicting ideas, and he begins to sound as if all he has said is self-serving praise for the big boys when he was entering the arena, and then disdain for them when he edits the briefies, and finally positioning himself once again with the big boys when he publishes his Bellow life."[73]

Karl contends that it is the very quality of lengthy biography that gives Atlas' *Bellow* whatever positive value it does have. In the first half of the biography, before Atlas became the editor of the brief biography series, the material seems fresh, alive, and insightful. But in the second half, after he became an avid proponent of brevity, the biography deteriorates into an endless repetition of dates and events, some significant, some inconsequential.[74]

Whether the material is long or the material is brief, if it is employed in the service of murdering vitality, it can be considered a symptom that has been cultivated and nourished in a culture of fetishism. Either way, long or short, these days a biographical subject seems to end up with the choice of either being drowned by the too much or strangled by the too little of whatever has been evoked in order to bring him to life.

Karl's positive assessments of *Joan of Arc* and *James Joyce* make the crucial point. If the author allows her own passions to enter into the biography, it does not guarantee that the subject will come to life, but at least the subject stands a chance of beginning to breathe. While unexamined transferences collaborate with archive fevers of the long or the short kind, acknowledged transferences—that is, a knowledge of how one's own vitalies enter into the composition of a biography—stand, at least, a fighting chance of bringing vitality to the subject.

Brenda Wineapple, author of biographies of Janet Flanner, Gertrude and Leo Stein, and Nathaniel Hawthorne, was one of the dozen or so biographers who were invited to respond to the special issues of *American Imago* on "the transferences underlying biographical creation." By taking a stance that seemingly went against the grain of the assigned topic, Wineapple arrived at a truth about biography that manages to banish the futile longie/briefie debate to the dustbin. Paradoxically, she accomplishes this by demonstrating how the *anarchic, archiviolithic* drive, the death drive that Derrida speaks of in *Archive Fever*, can be transformed into a life-enhancing force. Let me remind you of Derrida's commentary:

> This impression of erogenous color draws a mask right on the skin. In other words the *archiviolithic* drive is never present in person, neither in itself nor in its effects. It leaves no monument, it bequeaths no document of its own. As inheritance, it leaves only its erotic simulacrum, its pseudonym in painting, its sexual idols, its masks of seduction: lovely impressions. These impressions

are perhaps the very origins of what is so obscurely called the beauty of the beautiful. Memories of death.[75]

Though Wineapple never mentions Derrida, her essay is about transforming the *archiviolithic* drive into memories of the lost one. Though she never mentions the word "transference," she tells us that "All of the subjects of my biographies have suffered loss. In retrospect, I realize I chose them for that reason."[76] As a result of her long experience of thinking about the perils of collecting and hoarding data, Wineapple's meditation on death and mourning sheds a new light on the archive fevers that haunt every biographical undertaking. By comparing the biographer's quest to the mourning process, Winneapple demonstrates how archives, with all their potential destructiveness, nevertheless are also an essential first step in bringing a dead subject back to life, or, for that matter, a still living subject into a biographical life.

She entitles her essay "Mourning Becomes Biography." At first, Wineapple focuses on the fevers of mourning. But Wineapple has no intention of lingering in the land of the dead. She does not want the archive to become a cocoon in which to hide from the trials of living a life. It soon becomes evident that her larger purpose is to depict the delicate process of transformation from the initial, feverish, phase of mourning the lost one, to the second phase of returning to life, carrying the lost one inside as an aspect of the self. "For biography, like mourning implies retrieval. It constructs an archive of the dead to bring the subject back to life."[77] In other words, mourning befits biography, but the mourning process must eventually metamorphose into a biography of a living person.

Initially the biographer behaves like a mourner, turning the subject "over and over in her mind, remembering details that no one else notices or cares for."[78] "The biographer marshals together all the detritus of a life once lived . . . photographs and letters, lockets of hair, frayed envelopes and dog-eared manuscripts, crinkled slips of paper stained with grease, even waistcoats and buttons smoothed by age and constant wear. Former houses, first editions, old lipsticks and rusty keys."[79]

Finally, biography must be transformed into something more than an inventory of artifacts and relics. The biographical subject must re-enter the life it once lived (or is still living) by entering the imagination of the biographer.[80]

As I said earlier, "Edel struggles with archives and he struggles with transferences, never perceiving the fearful symmetry that binds them." For the several decades that he wrote biographies and wrote about the writing of biographies, Edel would think about transferences and archives as demons. According to Edel, if a biographer wanted to write a successful biography, he had to avoid these monsters as he would avoid the perils of a plague. He was unable to see that they were both essential to the writing of a biography. They represent two phases in the complex process that Strachey described as "the most delicate and humane of all the branches of writing."

True, archives can be a potentially deadly illness, or, as Derrida said, a *Mal d'Archive*. In the first phase, however, the biographer has a need for archives; he is *En Mal d'Archive* and must, therefore, yield to the regressive tendency to bury himself in the detritus of the archive, risking its fevers, risking drowning in the sea of data. But, sooner or later, if he is to write a successful biography, he must emerge from the archive and, if he hasn't already done so, try to become conscious of his transference to his subject, or that transference might also, in one way or another, immolate the biography. On the other hand, a transference to the person he is writing about is not only unavoidable, it is necessary. The biographer's transference enables his subject to enter into his imagination and come to life.

When Edel gave his lecture to psychoanalysts in 1961, he started out by addressing the communalities in the tasks of the biographer and the psycho-analyst. He was trying to illuminate the "common ground" they shared. "Are we not all, really, biographers and historians, biographers of the human-spirit and the human soul . . .?"[81]

> you—so to speak—write and rewrite a man's life under his very nose. What is more, you make him write and rewrite it himself! This is doubtless one of the fascinations of your task; it is also the envy of your fellow biographers, who deal with a more silent kind of data. You talk to your subjects; you even listen to them! Our subjects neither talk nor answer back. They are as inanimate as their pocket diaries and their cheque stubs and all the personal memorabilia which they have left as record of their passage on this earth.[82]

Edel was right, but only up to a point. As we have learned, the subjects of biographies do talk and they do answer back, even the dead ones. And they are not inanimate. They can become as animate and confrontational as any still-living human being, that is, if they do not get buried alive under the mound of archival fragments that mark "their passage on this earth."[83]

The remainder of Edel's lecture is mostly about the differences between psychoanalysts and biographers. He felt that there had been too much "muddying of the waters,"[84] by obscuring these differences. Edel was candid with the psychoanalysts—and, at times was gently critical of some of their presumptions. As he neared the conclusion of his lecture, he referred to that then-popular psychoanalytic image of the human mind—the iceberg, seven-eighths submerged beneath the icy waters, with its tip showing one-eighth above the water line. "When psychoanalysts write papers on literary subjects and describe the mass below the water-line, is it any wonder that most readers find it unbelievable and 'far-fetched'?"[85]

With this keen analysis of one of the major pitfalls of psychoanalytic writing, Edel brings us to the subject of our next chapter, "Unfree Associations." I begin by addressing the various ways that the fetishism strategy infiltrates the training of psychoanalytic candidates. As I describe how this training squelches the candidate's creativity and independent spirit,

I am illustrating the second principle of the fetishism strategy. *Fetishism transforms ambiguity and uncertainty into something knowable and certain and in so doing snuffs out any sparks of creativity that might ignite the fires of rebellion.*

In his lecture, Edel reprimanded psychoanalysts for enjoying "their under-water snorkling to such an extent that they never once looked up to see the great glittering exposed mass of the iceberg."[86] I replace the surface-depth iceberg image with a foreground-background image. I suggest how a knowledge of the foreground-background principle of the fetishism strategy can help analysts to keep the flame of creativity alive in themselves and in their patients.

The "above the surface/beneath the surface model," the so-called *topographical** model of psychoanalysis, has been augmented by what is called the *structural* model—the dynamic relations between id-ego-superego and external world. Nevertheless, the ghost of the iceberg image above-conscious and below-unconscious, continues to haunt psychoanalysis. There are those who still cling to the notion that what lies beneath the surface is psychologically deeper and more profound than what is on the surface. "True," argues Edel, "the submerged part does have an immense and crucial influence on the part that is visible. Nevertheless, it is the visible shape that confronts the world and the light of day, and *it is the relationship between the submerged and the exposed which is all-important (itals. mine).*"[87]

These days, there are analysts who want to banish the topographical model altogether and replace it with the more fashionable structural model. This also is a symptom of the fetishism strategy. An appreciation of the relations between the two models of the human psyche is as crucial to psychoanalytic understanding as an appreciation of the relations between surface and depth.

I will be expressing these controversies in terms of the foreground-background principle of the fetishism strategy. Psychoanalysis is most creative and alive when it addresses the dynamic relations between foreground and background. Furthermore, psychoanalysis is a process of many constantly shifting surfaces, none of them essentially deeper or more profound than any other.

That said, we go now from the archive fevers of writing lives to some manifestations of the fetishism strategy in psychoanalysis.

---

* Freud's investigations made him aware that *accessibility to consciousness* is not a good enough criteria on which to base psychoanalytic theory. He therefore proposed (in The Ego and the Id, 1923) that his original *topographical* model, which divides the mind into conscious, preconscious, and unconscious, be replaced or, at least, drastically augmented by what has become known as *structural* model, the division of the mind into an instinctual part (id), a part that compriuses moral functions (superego), and a part (ego) that mediates among the first two parts and the outer world.

Seven

Unfree Associations
The Training of Psychoanalysts

Like Freud's "Fetishism," footbinding, the making of films, writing on the skin, and the writing of biographies, so also the training of psychoanalysts can be a culture that breeds and nutures the fetishism strategy. The training of psychoanalysts brings out vividly the irony that was implicit in previous chapters.

Until this point, we've seen how the sexual fetishist uses his fetish to tame and subdue the otherwise unpredictable erotic vitalities of his sexual partner. To the fetishist, the lifeless, or nearly lifeless body is far preferable to a desiring body that might assert its own ambiguous energies. Thus an object (the fetish) that presents itself as an emblem of erotic liberation turns out to be a servant of necrophilia. In the making of films, the vividly seductive body of a woman occupies the foreground of the visual field, so that the traumatic histories that created this icon of sexuality can be kept in the background, where they are barely visible, or only visible in the light of interpretation. Thus the body of a woman is the glaring white lie that covers over and masks the corruptions that created her. We've seen how writing on the skin can serve as a rebellion against the fetishism strategy or become a mirror and expression of that potentially murderous process. The writing of a biography is meant to bring to life the life story of a living or once-living subject. However, all too often the archive fevers that plague that noble enterprise succeed in squelching those vitalities. The biographical subject is crushed under the avalanche of the facts that were meant to bring him to life.

The fetishistic structure of the training of psychoanalytic candidates brings out the irony in a most dramatic way. For, if ever a cultural endeavor had been devised to augment and sustain life, and triumph over the forces of death, it is psychoanalysis. And yet, the training of psychoanalysts is conducted in an atmosphere designed to murder psychoanalytic creativity.

Rightly or wrongly, psychoanalysis is thought of as an orderly process. However, that process is also based on an ideal of free association. Can something that is meant to be free come to life in a process founded on the principles of law and order? According to the principles of the fetishism strategy, anything that threatens to be freely flowing and mobile must be bound. In addition, events and experiences that might otherwise disrupt what we presume to be an orderly and predictable process must be tamed and subdued. Therefore, free associations, often thought to be the heartbeat of the psychoanalytic situation, can also be construed as a threat to the psychoanalytic process.

How can this be so? Traditionally, a patient in psychoanalysis is encouraged to free associate, to say whatever comes to mind; to speak freely and to try not to censor her thoughts and fantasies. Admittedly, there is a mutual understanding between analyst and patient that it will not always be possible to free associate—the super-ego censor is always keeping a watchful eye, the patient's ego defenses are always on guard, ready to leap to the fore if things seem to be getting too free for comfort. Nevertheless, despite these inevitable obstacles, and recognizing that the expression of thoughts and fantasies can never be entirely free, free association remains an ideal of the psychoanalytic therapeutic process.

Of course, a patient is not cured of her symptoms merely because she has a talent for free associations. Free associations, however, provide *one* essential key to unlocking the unconscious conflicts, defenses, wishes, memories, thoughts, and fantasies that are the source of a patient's symptoms.

But what if the patient's free associations contain thoughts and wishes that represent a disruption of the psychoanalytic situation?—an urge to murder the analyst, a wish to throw the analyst's books on the floor, a need to peek into the analyst's closets; actions that are permissible in the realm of thought, but not encouraged as actual behaviors to be enacted in the analysts, office. Then there are those uncontrollable impulses that sometimes do get enacted; coming to sessions late, not coming at all for several weeks, not paying the analytic fees, belittling the analyst for his bourgeois clothing and stuffy moral attitudes, standing up from the couch or chair and stomping up and down around the room. Even though they come to be expressed in actual behavior, these enacted impulses, wishes, and fantasies are also part of the free association process. As with any other free association, the analyst undertakes to understand the unconscious significance of these rebellious gestures that disrupt the law and order of the analytic process. Nevertheless, they can be experienced by some analysts as threats to his or her self-esteem and authority. And if the analyst is not aware of the source of his or her countertransferences, he or she will respond, consciously or unconsciously, with an authoritarian attitude that effectively stifles the heartbeat of the analytic process. The message gets communicated, "Free associations can be free, but only up to a point."

There is another irony, and this irony is the central focus of this chapter. It has to do with the training of psychoanalysts, and only indirectly on how that training goes on to affect the psychoanalyst's behavior with her patients. Is the analytic candidate, the young man or woman in training to be an analyst, encouraged to express his or her free associations? Well, yes. But only sometimes. Only with certain qualifications and under certain conditions. How does the psychoanalytic candidate get to experience and appreciate the heartbeat of the psychoanalytic process, if the entire course of her training takes place in a psychoanalytic association that is the embodiment of an unfree association?

A prominent member of one of the training institutes I am referring to was a foremost defender of free association. However, he was frightened of modifications of already established psychoanalytic principles. "We should try to keep what we already have—cultivate the land that has been cleared and guard it against *the return of the jungle and against corrosion*."[1] (*itals.* mine). According to this analyst, free associations are o.k., even essential to the psychoanalytic method. On the other hand, thoughts that might corrode the purity of the psychoanalytic situation should be outlawed.

The phrase "*unfree* associations" was first used by Douglas Kirsner, an energetic and persistent senior lecturer who teaches philosophy and psychoanalytic studies at Deakin University, Australia, where twenty years ago he founded the Annual Freud Conference. In the late 1980s, Kirsner set out to examine the role played by psychoanalysts in generating and perpetuating what was then and still is the ongoing decline and crisis of psychoanalysis. His detailed investigations of the four major American psychoanalytic institutes (in New York, Boston, Chicago, and Los Angeles),* revealed how the institutes that train psychoanalytic candidates had arrested free speech and free inquiry, and by extension the free association process and "saying whatever comes to mind." As Kirsner says in the introduction to his book *Unfree Associations:* "Psychoanalytic institutes have been notable as closed shops. Their solid walls have kept them sealed off and mysterious to the outside world, including the mental health professions and the academy. Authoritarian cliques, power struggles and intrigues have predominated inside the institutes."[2]

The question of psychoanalytic free expression has caught the attention of numerous scholars. In his introduction to *Archive Fever*, Derrida spoke of the principle of commandment, that is to say, the principle according to the law, or the place where the authority, of man or god, is exercised.[3] To put his complex thoughts in plain terms, there is a tension between the analyst's investment in the "mercurial and flowing" energies of the analytic situation,

* Since I live and practice in New York City, I am most familiar with the politics of the New York Psychoanalytic Institute. Although this chapter focuses almost exclusively on the authoritarian cliques and power struggles within that training institute, the dynamics apply to the dozens of other institutes in the New York City area, as well as to those in Boston, Los Angeles, Chicago and the rest of the United States and the rest of the world; in other words, wherever psychoanalytic institutes exist. As Douglas Kirsner says in *Unfree Associations,* "Psychoanalytic institutes have been troubled everywhere and always. Whether they are medical, nonmedical, Freudian, Jungian, Kleinian, Kohutian or Lacanian,' whether they are in New York, Chicago, Paris, London or Sydney, psychoanalytic institutes behave in strikingly similar ways."

which allow the unforeseen, unknown, and possibly errant vitalities of the patient's innermost psychic reality to emerge, and the principles of law and authority that are perpetuated in the psychoanalytic training institutes. Any potentially free expression can only be expressed if it is first domesticated and brought under the subjugation of a training institute—a phenomenon that Derrida refers to as "house arrest."[4]

Otto Kernberg's 1996 commentary, "Thirty methods to destroy the creativity of psychoanalytic candidates," published a few years before he became president of the International Psychoanalytic Association, deals specifically with the rigid structures and inflexible educational organization of the official institutes that are responsible for the training of psychoanalysts. "Thirty methods" was one of the documents that informed Kirsner's investigation. Furthermore, I assume that Kernberg is suggesting that the rigidity and inflexibility of psychoanalytic training, which invariably stifles the creativity of the potential analyst, will create a ripple effect of deadening the interactions between analyst and patient.

What is it about the creative vitalities of the clinical situation that might be so frightening to the senior analysts who are responsible for training future generations of analysts? The last two sentences of Kernberg's paper sum it up: "where there is a spark, there may develop a fire particularly when this spark appears in the middle of dead wood. Extinguish it before it is too late."[5] Usually candidates have been attracted to psychoanalytic training because they view psychoanalysis as a medium for expressing their own creative energies. They view it as a culture that breeds and nourishes aliveness and creativity. They are, at least in the beginning of their training, eager to express the fantasies, wishes, and thoughts that express their creativity. However, the authorities who keep the psychoanalytic enterprise under "house arrest" and have the responsibility of training these candidates have, in the course of their own training, been drained of their sap and turned into dead wood. Dead wood can all too easily ignite and then quickly turn to ashes when it is struck by a spark of creative energy.

Here, Kernberg was stating one of the fundamental principles of the fetishism strategy. Where there is an energy or force that is incessantly mobile and inaccessibly ambiguous, unpredictable, and uncontrollable, a source of vitality that "is as mercurial and as flowing, as compact of temperament and emotion as the human spirit,"[6] destroy it before it runs amok and creates havoc with the commandments and laws established by the authorities. Psychoanalysis is a source of human vitality, but when it is brought under the "house arrest" of a psychoanalytic training institute, it becomes a breeding ground for dead wood.

Before presenting a few of Kernberg's "Thirty methods," which have to do with the destruction of analytic creativity, I want to make a promise. Later on in this chapter I will show how analysts might employ an appreciation of the dynamics of the fetishism strategy to enable them to work more creatively with patients and keep the therapeutic process alive and flowing.

Of the thirty methods for destroying the creativity of psychoanalytic candidates that Kernberg ennumerated, I have selected only four, to convey the spirit of his remarks. The first of Kernberg's "Methods" depicts the tortuous pacing of the progress of the candidates' educational experience: "If long periods of waiting in uncertainty become a regular part of their progression experience, they will tend, in turn, to become slow to respond and to take initiatives."[7] This tried and true method of indoctrinating psychoanalytic candidates will later on infiltrate their consulting rooms, showing up in the subtle ways that the well-trained analyst unconsciously inhibits the patient's capacities for initiative.

A toleration for uncertainty is an essential aspect of an analyst's creative response to a patient. Like free association, this toleration for uncertainty contributes to the heartbeat of the psychoanalytic process. However, when "waiting in uncertainty" is employed as a method of intimidation and indoctrination it has the paradoxical effect of squelching an analytic candidate's toleration for uncertainty and ambiguity. Therefore, when she is finally anointed as a fully qualified psychoanalyst, she will be uneasy with ambiguities and try to bring her patients' free associations under house arrest.

Another method has to do with the use made of Freud's writings, the Freud archive, the commencement or origins of psychoanalysis:

> It is important for the instructor to keep in mind that it is the *conclusions* that Freud arrived at that have to be taught and memorized, not the *process of Freud's thinking*: in fact, if the students acquire a grasp of the methodology of Freud's thinking, which was unavoidably revolutionary, this may lead them to dangerous identifications with his originality and thus defeat the purpose of the isolated and exhaustive focus on his conclusions.[8]

In other words, the lulling repetition of Freud's writings is employed to dampen any excitement that a candidate might feel about the revolutionary spirit of the mobile *process* of psychoanalytic thinking.

Quite a number of the methods Kernberg listed are directly concerned with upholding the authority of the institute. Since paranoid fear would discourage analytic candidates from advancing courageous initiatives or asking challenging questions, those analysts permitted to engage in the psychoanalysis of candidates, traditionally called "training-analysts," should be instructed to report regularly on the therapeutic progress of the candidate.[9]

By the time Kernberg drew up his thirty methods, this sort of scare tactic had been eliminated and declared unethical by most psychoanalytic institutes. However, Kernberg contended that the long-standing habit of instilling paranoid fear in candidates continues to remain alive "in the irrepressible tendencies of some training analysts to indicate, sometimes openly, sometimes indirectly and surreptitiously, their feelings about the candidates entrusted to their care for a training analysis."[10]

Kernberg also cautions that if the teaching faculty were imbued with a spirit of creativity, even all these other measures combined would not suffice to murder the creativity of candidates. The best guarantee for inhibiting the creativity of the teaching faculty is "the hierarchical extension of the educational process into the social structure of the psychoanalytic society."[11] The most reliable tool for keeping candidates, and the entire faculty, and the entire society in line is for the training analysts to hold themselves apart from the general membership as the only ones who have authority and control.

And, in conclusion, after listing all thirty methods, to insure that there would be no opportunities for dilution, distortion, deterioration, erosion, and misuse of psychoanalysis, Kernberg offers the following piece of advice, which I called attention to at the outset. "Always keep in mind: where there is a spark there may develop a fire."

When writing particularly about the New York Psychoanalytic Institute, Kirsner contends that the source of the murderous orthodoxy at that Institute has been misunderstood. "The real situation was quite contrary to the popular view that the institute was under the control of the most well known psychoanalytic theoreticians and clinicians—the founders of ego psychology."[12] According to Kirsner, these analysts may have exercised control over intellectual matters such as who got published in the major journals, but they did not have any real power over the training of candidates.

Kirsner's investigations led him to attribute the origin of these authoritarian trends in psychoanalysis to Otto Isakower, one of the dozen or so analysts who escaped the Nazi regime, found a home in the New York Psychoanalytic Institute, and set up what he and the group of emigre Viennese psychoanalysts under his command referred to as the "only genuine psychoanalysis," a brand of psychoanalysis unavailable to the vulgar and mechanistic Americans who, because of their cultural and intellectual limitations, were incapable of doing "real analysis."

Isakower justified his domination of the Institute by pointing to the overly intellectualized theorizing of the Americans. According to Isakower, the American analysts were afraid of the unconscious. They were more interested in cure than in encouraging the patient to express what was on her mind. They were more interested in theory and the applications of theory than in tuning into the patient's unconscious. When confronted with the power of the sexual and aggressive drives, they retreated to theoretical abstractions. Isakower believed that his concept of the "analyzing instrument" would help to counteract these Americanizations of psychoanalysis.

Basically the analyzing instrument describes an interaction between patient and analyst occurring in a dreamlike, regressed state in which images emerging in the patient evoke counterimages in the analyst. As she selectively communicates her counterimages to the patient, the analyst contributes to the unfolding of the patient's imagery.[13]

Though Freud never wrote about an analyzing instrument per se, he did recommend a procedure analogous to Isakower's analyzing instrument. He said that the analyst: "should surrender himself to his own unconscious activity, in a state of even and partial attention to avoid so far as possible reflection and the construction of conscious expectations, not to try to fix anything that he heard particularly in his memory, and by these means to catch the drift of the patient's unconscious with his own unconscious."[14]

Isakower would insist that he was not talking about the analyst's identification with her patient, but rather an identity between the states of mind of analyst and patient. When his colleagues requested that Isakower explain and elaborate this rather abstruse concept, he insisted that the analyzing instrument is not a permanent system within the psychic structure of the analyst. He said that one should think of this instrument only "in its activated state, when it is in rapport with the patient; or, better perhaps, to see it as a composite, consisting of two complementary halves."[15]

Isakower would argue that theory is antagonistic to the analyzing instrument. The theoretical insights that might sneak into the analyst's mind during the activation of the analyzing instrument should not be thought about, for they can only interfere with the emergence of the analyst's counterimages. Such theoretical uprisings are in all probability defensive; resistances to the unconscious material that is about to emerge through the activation of the analyzing instrument.

Isakower had introduced his idea of the analyzing instrument in order to free analysts from being burdened by theory in their work His analyzing instrument has all the external markings of freedom of expression. However, several of Isakower's colleagues have pointed to the authoritarian spirit of Isakower's recommendation that it is better not to think theoretical thoughts. William Grossman, a training analyst at the New York Psychoanalytic Institute, said that the recommendation "seems to introduce criticism, constraints and rules into 'free' association . . . there is a kind of irony that this should be so when the goal is the free flow of thought."[16] Isakower's analyzing instrument began to assume the form of a binding of free-flowing analytic listening, the very binding and constraining effect it had been designed to counteract. As Grossman pointed out, "It gradually changed— I think inevitably—into a set of prescriptive and restrictive injunctions aimed to exclude 'inappropriate thoughts.' "[17]

The restraints on free associations come in various guises, many of them, such as Isakower's analyzing instrument, masquerading as the sine qua non of freedom.

Moreover, since only analysts gifted with a special kind of empathy could communicate with patients in this way, Isakower's analyzing instrument became a method of restricting analytic anointment to the gifted. Those who had this gift were in. Those who lacked this gift were out.

Jacob Arlow, who after the Isakower Age became one of the new leaders of the New York Psychoanalytic Institute, claimed that the holy status accorded to the Isakower analyzing instrument was reminiscent of Jewish mysticism, or Caballah. The ability to understand "the true essence of existence, which was granted only to very special people" corresponded to "feelings of a special endowment which came from the possession of secret knowledge."[18]

Isakower's ideological platform for making the unconscious conscious through the encouragement of a regressed configuration of analysand-analyst communication, was seen by some of his detractors as a shabby remnant of

Freud's outmoded topographical model, a supposedly "archaic" version of psychoanalysis, where associations were free to bypass the strictures and restrictions of the conscious mind. At other times, the era was depicted as a hot-bed of rampant instinctual expression, of sexual and aggressive drives. Isakower's analyzing instrument was said to be symptomatic of a breakdown of structural restraints, a demonic Id Psychology that ran roughshod over the ego and the superego. While these are crude distortions of Isakower's position, they represent what some analysts thought about him and his analyzing instrument, either publically or privately, and helps to explain why many of them might have been fearful of both the inventor and the cabalistic instrument he invented.

On the other hand, many present-day analysts, both older generation standard bearers and the so-called younger generation, assert that Kirsner's story of Isakower's sway over the New York Psychoanalytic Institute may have been an exaggeration. They barely acknowledge the influence of Isakower and his analyzing instrument, and instead trace the authoritarian regimes back to another analyst, Heinz Hartmann, the champion of Ego Psychology, who is said to be representative of all that went wrong with American psychoanalysis during its halcyon days—the '40s, '50s, and '60s.

In contrast to Isakower's alleged Id Psychology, Hartmann is said to be guilty of promulgating a narrow version of Ego Psychology that advanced such idealistic notions as "conflict free" areas of functioning, adaptation, and ego autonomy. It was the religion of Hartmann's Ego Psychology that is said to have permeated the New York Psychoanalytic. He and his followers claimed as their banner Freud's dictum "where id was, there ego shall be," which many other analysts believe to be a mistranslated and therefore misunderstood phrase that misrepresents the ego as dominating the id, when in fact it is the other way around, with the forces of the id shaping the ways in which the ego may respond; "ego shall be where id is."

A few of the present-day advocates of Hartmann's Ego Psychology like to claim that Hartmann's status as president of the International Psychoanalytic Association from 1951 to 1957 meant that he and his theories had worldwide respect and analytic influence. However, this claim evokes passionate and vociferous opposition, particularly from analysts outside the United States. The objection is not only about Hartmann's purported worldwide influence but also about the validity of his proclamations on Ego Psychology. As French analyst Andre Green insisted, there was no "Hartmann era;" the very phrase is a symptom of the arrogance of the analysts who believe it to be true. Ego Psychology is now, and was then, totally absent "in Latin America, and in Europe its influence was limited to the agreement of Anna Freud and her group."[19] Furthermore, and even more seriously, "To say that we can put the ego on a par with the id is inconsistent because it is a major hypothesis of Freud that the id dominates the ego. . . . The whole construction of the psychic apparatus is built on the foundation of the id. If you disagree with this principle, then you disagree with the whole description of Freud's psychic apparatus."[20]

Obviously, Green has his own authoritarian attitude. Anyone who disagrees with him is not a "real analyst." Yet, there are many analysts throughout the world who applaud Green's belittling portrayal of Ego Psychology. The considered opinion is that the phenomena of Ego Psychology was a temporary local manifestation, primarily in New York with a few pockets of Hartmania in New Haven and London.

Nevertheless, even though physically localized, Hartmann's adherents did control the editorial policies of three of the major psychoanalytic journals in the United States, and these reflected the ego psychological thinking of the Hartmann "group." In this sense, they did have some limited, but influential, power over the intellectual domains of psychoanalysis, at least on the Northeast coast of the United States. They were also sufficiently powerful to perpetrate some rather extraordinary abuses of power within the narrow limits of The New York Psychoanalytic Training Institute.

The Hartmann group had a doctrine, an intellectual agenda that became more and more out-of-step with the international psychoanalytic movement. This agenda entailed a major shift in focus from the unknowable;—the Id and concurrently the sexual and aggressive drives—to an emphasis on rationality, the conflict-free sphere, adaptation, a de-instinctualization or so-called neutralization of drive energies.[21] Hartmann's doctrine implied that there is an entire sphere of human existence that is free of instinctual demands, contradiction, irrationality.

In *The Hartmann Era*, a collection of essays published in 2000, the editor Martin Bergmann explained that Hartmann's utopian version of the ego was "a reaction against Freud's pessimism about the role of the ego in the process of cure."[22] Hartmann's optimistic doctrine generated enormous conflict, despair, and paranoid fear among candidates. Ego Psychology could be viewed as a thirty first method for destroying psychoanalytic creativity. During the Hartmann era, there was a reification of ego psychological concepts and a party line that had to be followed if a candidate wanted to graduate or be published. As Anton Kris, the son of two Hartmann-era analysts, Marianna and Ernst Kris, recounts: "the astonishing number of casualties in our field, among our own colleagues, at the hands of their teachers and their Institutes (or the Institutes that would not have them or would have them only under demeaning conditions), has been a powerful influence on my development as an analyst and teacher."[23]

Kernberg claimed that "The authoritarian quality of Hartmann and his group was enormous."[24] Or as Mortimer Ostow, who was a student during that era, reports, "the authoritarianism [of the Hartmann group] was really quite devastating."[25] "We were trained to be completely orthodox, completely compliant. If any student asked any question whatever, he was put down and told that he was resistant. It was really a religious orthodoxy complete with a scripture. And with ideas of heresy."[26]

By the mid-sixties, the struggles and fights between those in the New York Psychoanalytic Institute who wanted reform and the Hartmann in-group could sometimes be emotionally violent and scary to those who witnessed them.

In 1963, Charles Brenner, an analyst who had once sought to ameliorate the authoritarian structure of the New York Psychoanalytic Institute, co-authored with Jacob Arlow, *Psychoanalytic Concepts and the Structural Theory*, a monograph whose principles would soon become the foundation of a new orthodoxy, a new way of bringing psychoanalysis under house arrest. While the monograph was a more or less straightforward explication of the superiority of Freud's later structural model, a dividing of the mind into the mental structures of id-ego-superego, over Freud's earlier topographical model that divided the mind into unconscious, pre-conscious, and conscious, the principles enunciated in that monograph evolved into the next orthodoxy of American psychoanalysis, at least in the New York Psychoanalytic. As the editors of the structural theory monograph stated:

> the authors [Arlow and Brenner] certainly leave no room for any misunderstanding of their unequivocal statement that, since the topographic and structural models are incompatible with each other, the former should be discarded. They treat the models as forthright dichotomies and, in detailing the inconsistencies between them, have no trouble in deciding in favor of the structural model. They do not feel that much is to be gained by an attempt to integrate the two.[27]

In other words, anyone who still believes in the topographical model, or even thinks they might integrate it with the structural model, is not a "real analyst." And, since the effects of this change in theory has had enormous impact on psychoanalytic treatment techniques, the problem of not being a "real analyst" could have real and serious consequences for candidates. Brenner claimed he was upholding the Freudian tradition.

At first, it seemed that Brenner was following, almost to the letter, the principles that Freud had laid out in *The Ego and the Id*. However, in Brenner's later writings, he made it clear that his version of structural theory represented a revision of some of the fundamental premises of Freud's theory, principally his convictions about the biological underpinnings of the libidinal and aggressive drives. For Brenner, however, everything in human psychology, whether normal or pathological, is the result of *mental* (itals. mine) activity; a mind never free of conflict, a mind always bent on achieving a compromise between all parties in the conflict—id, ego and superego. Most significantly, both mental conflict and the efforts of the mind toward compromise give rise to unpleasant affects such as guilt, depression and anxiety, which means that these affects are also the outcome of mental activity.

Paradoxically, over the years, as the Brenner doctrine became more and more formulaic and uncompromising, it came to be known as the theory of "compromise formation." Nowadays most recent graduates and younger generation members of the New York Psychoanalytic have been indoctrinated into compromise formation theory, which purports to be all one needs to know to be anointed as a "real psychoanalyst." Indeed, if a candidate or member analyst questions the centrality of compromise formation or tries to introduce an idea generated by the "fancy" new designer imports from England, France, or South America or even suggests the idea of integrating *one or two* of the basic notions from Freud's earlier topographical model, the challenger will run up against the minimalist dogmas of the compromise formation bible, Brenner's 1982 *The Mind in Conflict*, which he and his followers can recite and re-iterate on command and in exacting detail whenever one of its premises is challenged.

The Mind in Conflict argues that, "The very fabric of psychic life is woven"[28] of derivatives of our childhood impulses and wishes, of the conflicts they give rise to, of the anxiety and depressive affects connected with these conflicts, of the defenses erected to control, direct, and divert these derivatives, and of the manifestations of the superego—(itself a compromise formation), that are reflective of these drives and conflicts that arouse guilt and other painful affects. Nothing that anyone thinks or says is ever free from repression and other defenses. Every thought, every "association" is necessarily a compromise formation among the various tendencies of the mind. All of human life, and every human undertaking, is an outcome of one compromise formation or another.[29]

The problems with compromise formation theory are not that it is lacking in psychoanalytic wisdom. The problems are the narrowness of its focus; the arrogant tone of its proclamations; the authoritarian manner of limiting and excluding any other approach to understanding psychic life. By implication anyone who does not heed the strictures of compromise formation theory is not a "real analyst."

The minimalist design of Brenner's compromise formation version of structural theory has created an architecture that has the effect of erecting an unassailable wall around itself, as if to ward off those potentially contaminating thoughts, fantasies, or ideas that might disrupt and complicate things. I am not opposed to compromise formation theory, but to the fetishistic quality of the intellectual edifice that enshrouds it.

A long time ago, nearly three decades before Kernberg drew up his thirty methods for killing creativity, Wilfred Bion, a British analyst with a international reputation as a champion of therapeutic creativity, famously declared that the psychoanalyst should come to the clinical situation in a state of ignorance, "free of memory and desire."[30] In other words, we should approach each clinical encounter as a more or less blank slate that can be written on without the impediments of previous associations or past and present strivings and longings. If we are aware of our temptations to express such associations, strivings, and longings by prematurely interpreting, impulsively acting, or compulsively not-acting, or knowing too much too soon, we should be alert to the possibility of a (fetishistic) need to smother the creative sparks that might otherwise disrupt and question our analytic certainties.

Does this mean that analysts should never interpret? Does it mean that analysts should suppress all desires and longings? Or, that we never should employ the memories of past sessions to guide us in the present? Of course, these suppressions would simply be another version of stifling, this time of the analyst's freely ranging free associations that allow for creative under-standings of what is transpiring in the therapeutic situation. One way or another, it seems that an analyst's creative potentials are always in danger of being bound by the fetishism strategy. The unpredictable, the unknowables that transpire between analyst and patient seem to be a minefield of potential conflagration and explosion.

Perhaps this fear of conflagration helps to explain Charles Brenner's firm and insistently re-iterated claim that there is no such thing as "free" associa-tions. "Nothing that anyone thinks or says is ever free from repression or other defenses. Every thought, every 'association' is necessarily a compro-mise formation among the various tendencies of the mind."[31] While there is merit to Brenner's idea that no human activity, not sexuality, not parenting, not friendship, not artistic creativity, not culture, can be entirely "free," his descriptions of compromise formation do sometimes sound like an instru-ment for capturing and binding the ambiguities of the human spirit.

It was all of this *certainty* of structures and compromises and diagnoses and other mentalized containers that boxed in the creative energies of the patient and the analyst that Bion objected to. Although we can no more be free of memory and desire than we are able to freely, free associate, we should at least try to be free of *certainty*.

Maybe "Certainty" should be declared the motto of the fetishism strategy.

In 1818, in a letter to his brothers, John Keats came up with a motto that could be enlisted to enable present-day analysts to oppose and undermine the fetishism strategy. To preserve a patient's freedom of expression, the psychoan-alyst must be able to sustain a dialogue based on *negative capability*. When John Keats first formulated the idea of negative capability, he was not referring specifically to a quality of the poetic imagination, but more generally to the powers of a flexible mind and a certain way of approaching the ineffable complexities of life. Keats said that a person, "who is capable of being in uncer-tainties, Mysteries, doubts, without any irritable reaching after fact and rea-son"[32] will arrive at truth. On the other hand, "a man who cannot feel that he has a personal identity unless he has made up his mind about everything . . . will never come to truth so long as he lives, because he is always trying at it."[33]

Some thirty years after his famous pronouncement on memory and desire, Bion gave a talk that seemed to be re-iterating Keats' lines on negative capa-bility. He had been invited to speak at the 1997 conference on so-called bor-derline phenomena held under the auspices of the Menninger Foundation.

Bion introduced his remarks with a joke in French that set off a ripple of bewildered curiosity—that is, until he translated his joke into English. "*La reponse est le malheur de la question.*" "The response is the illness of the question,"[34] adding that the sentence had been loaned to him by the French analyst Andre Green, but that the tilted pronunciation of illness as Mahler rather than *malheur* was "my own original contribution."[35]

Bion's *malheur* quip referred to Margaret Mahler, the famous child psychoanalyst, and more specifically to the ways in which her work was representative of the United States brand of Ego Psychology—answering questions best left unanswerable, regulating and organizing behavior, and dividing up the inconsistencies and irregularities of human development into coherent stages and phases, and, of course, stifling "free" associations and creativity. Though I was one of Mahler's close colleagues, I agreed with the drift of Bion's commentary. From my clinical practice and from my research into child and adolescent development, I had come to understand that fruitful questions and uncertainties wither into stale conformities when sealed off into compartmentalized answers. Within recent years, moreover, I have come to recognize that Bion was unknowingly referring to one of the primary ways that the fetishism strategy infiltrates the clinical situation.

Shortly after the *malheur*-Mahler sequence, he announced that he was going to say the first thing that came into his mind. A free association, if you will. He said that he didn't know what that would be, but he wanted to say it anyway. And then he did say it. "Bloody vagina," "bloody cunt." And then he proceeded to light off on a five-minute diatribe on the sacred and profane meanings of "cunt," and "bloody cunt."[36]

Ostensibly he was making the point that when you are very angry with someone or something, the anger can be given a more genuine expression if you can be in touch with archaic and primitive language. Though his nasty chauvinism had many of the women bristling and a few of us doing a wild analysis of his association that slid so freely from Mahler to Cunt, most of the audience ended up agreeing with the overall intentions of Bion's remarks. After Bion concluded his speech, Andre Green, one the most vociferous of the anti–Ego Psychology analysts, who had loaned Bion "*la reponse est le malheur de la question*," walked up to the podium to give him a big hug.

Bion was furious with the fundamental goals of the conference, which were to answer all questions about that over-used and much misunderstood diagnosis "borderline" and to give precise definition to that term and to set up borders of inclusion and exclusion and to pin down the borderline diagnosis and thereby rob so-called borderline patients of their uniqueness and vitality. More generally Bion was out to stir up in the audience the emotional turbulence that lies beneath, "the superficial and beautiful calm that pervades our various consulting rooms and institutes."[37] Without intending it, Bion was making a plea for *uncertainty* and *negative capability*.

In 1998, Jonathan Lear, a philosopher with psychoanalytic training, put these matters in a somewhat different context. He spoke before a group of analysts, making a plea for *unknowingness*. He began by offering his general thesis that "our end of the century American culture, like Oedipus Tyrannus, has been suffering from an overemphasis on knowingness,"[38] an intense and directed need to know, which serves as a defense against anxiety. He then argued that knowingness is pervasive in our lives, that it is readily observed in the media's coverage of public life. Moreover, in psychoanalysis it is manifested in premature attempts to reach closure due to the inability of both analyst and analysand to tolerate the anxiety of not-knowing. This preoccupation, which entails an all-consuming focusing of our energies on what we know, may in turn rob us of the opportunity to learn something more profound about our patients, our analytic thoughts and attitudes, ourselves and the world around us.[39]

In 2003, Muriel Dimen, an anthropologist with psychoanalytic training, brought her feminist perspectives to bear on the issue of knowingness. Dimen invites her readers to "stay in the knot of not knowing,"[40] to transcend either/or certainties and to think instead in the language of multiplicities and ambiguities. She proposes that "the mobile, dynamic space between dualities yields resolutions that in turn give on to new complexity . . ."[41] In other words, resolutions are temporary waysides, not permanent structures. They are not meant to halt the procession of ongoing new solutions. They are meant to invigorate new ways of looking at issues that had seemed to have settled into a state of quiescence.

According to Dimen, Desire is a site of uncertainty and multiplicity. Unfortunately, American culture is so saturated with ideals of independence, fortitude, and self-realization that many American psychoanalysts have no room for desire, which evokes feelings of absence, lack, and longing. Desire is discontinuous and enigmatic; "like invisible ink: it won't show up until it gets wet."[42] Desire is about suspended excitement and a longing for something not yet there. Desire does not settle into a state of amiable quiescence. Psychoanalytic practice comes to life when it opens up a space for the passionate, elusive, and unpredictable complexities of desire. Unlike traditional psychoanalytic practice, where the focus has been on cleansing the patient of the symptomatic excesses of her sexual desires, the principle of staying in "the knot of not knowing" allows the analyst to help the patient to bring back to life a desire that has been lost. "The knot of not knowing" keeps alive the aliveness of desire.

Knowingness, a variant of certainty, inevitably deadens the vitality of the clinical situation. It is the core of the fetishism strategy in psychoanalysis. Still another attempt to address the issue of knowingness that Lear and Dimen observed, and the certainty that I have been referring to as the motto of the fetishism strategy, was a 2004 essay by Ralf Zweibel, a German medical doctor who had been trained as a psychoanalyst. Alluding to his long-time collaboration with Hans Morganthaler, a German analyst who has yet to be translated into English, Zweibel asserted a principle that sounds very much like Bion: "When we initiate an analytic process with an analysand, we are confronted from the very first session with the emotional undercurrents of the unruly id. . . . We should not believe that we can figure out or control this emotional movement."[43] Citing Morganthaler's work, Zweibel defines this emotional movement as "an expression of aliveness."[44] He adds that the analyst must be able to tolerate the anxiety, uncertainty, and doubt that arise in connection with this expression[45] of aliveness. John Keats might have been put off by the elaborate diagrams that Zweibel drew up to "capture" his theory of aliveness; but I imagine he would have been immensely gratified that his ideas on negative capability were still alive.

I shall now keep the promise I made at the outset of this exploration. I will demonstrate how a knowledge of the foreground-background principle of the fetishism strategy might enlighten psychoanalysts about their daily clinical experience with patients.

Let us start at the beginning. In the early days of topographical theory, Freud postulated a consciousness above that censored an unconscious below, and the early followers of Freud spoke confidently of higher modes of mental activity inhibiting the lower levels. Psychoanalysis was construed as a technique for detecting the unconscious latent meanings that lay *beneath* a conscious manifest content. The dream was taken as the royal road to knowledge of the workings of the unconscious.

While dream interpretations are still crucial to our reflections on the patient's psychic reality, most present-day analysts focus on the ways in which we articulate dreams with other features of the psychoanalytic situation. We now appreciate that a dream, usually thought to be the dwelling place of the latent, can itself be a manifest content. For example, a patient might introduce a dream in order to obscure and marginalize the painful latent affects and thoughts that are threatening to emerge in the transference-countertransference interaction.

As one outcome of these shifts in our spatial metaphors, we have moved from a static to a constantly shifting *dynamic* perspective on the relations between manifest and latent contents. Instead of regarding the clinical situation as composed of upper surfaces and lower depths, we employ to our advantage (knowingly or unknowingly) one of the principles of the fetishism strategy—the foreground-background relationship. We focus our attention on the *shifting surfaces* of foreground and background. We do not accept one surface or the other as the true and only meaning.

When latent was presumed to lie *beneath* manifest, the latent content was frequently identified with truth or true meaning, while manifest content was presumed to be a species of sham or untruth, or at best a symbolic defensive structure designed to conceal some true latent meaning that lay beneath. This notion has persisted in other forms; for example, in the spatial metaphor favored by some present-day ego psychologists. These psychoanalysts issue a directive that psychoanalytic interpretations should proceed from surface to depth—as if the surface could not itself be psychologically deeper than what lies beneath it; as if one surface did not always contend with another; as if depth might not be a screen for what is a painful or frightening psychic reality of the manifest present.

Similarly, clinical experience has taught us to observe developmental sequences from the perspective of a patient's current psychic reality, which includes transference-countertransference sequences evoked by the present psychoanalytic situation. Unlike physical maturation (material reality), which tends to be progressive, psychological development (psychic reality) is not linear or progressive. Consequently, as I have often maintained, "earlier is not necessarily deeper or even more influential than later." For example, from the perspective of the manifest-latent interplay that characterizes psychic reality, memories of childhood trauma that emerge in the present clinical situation might be, and often are, retroactive memories constructed in the present in order to screen out the traumatic elements that might otherwise emerge as an outcome of the immediate transference-countertransference interaction.

In the analytic situation, as in the patient's life outside the analysis, whenever a symptom preoccupies the foreground, its vivid presence signals the possibility of an absence, and may be an indication of an effort to screen out, marginalize, or background another history of desire.

This spatial metaphor of shifting surfaces, each as psychologically deep as any other, has been derived from my understandings of the fetishism strategy. In contrast to the neurotic strategy whereby a symptom represents a compromise formation between desire and authority, between id and ego and superego, and the anxiety and depressive affects elicited by these conflicts, the fetishism strategy, based on disavowal rather than repression, encourages a collaboration and simultaneity of manifestly antithetical forces that can coexist in a play of shifting surfaces. One fantasy or thought is brought to the foreground while another fantasy or thought is temporarily relegated to the background. In some instances one aspect of the sexual life preoccupies the foreground of a patient's life, while another is relegated to the margins. Or, a neurotic symptom preoccupies the foreground while the intrapsychic conflicts and internalized personal relationships that are encapsulated in the symptom are in the background and must be deciphered or interpreted. Or, a shameful, infantile self-representation assumes a commanding presence both in a patient's everyday life and in her analysis so that adult self and object representations that would otherwise arouse guilt and anxiety may remain in the shadows.

Analogous to my discussion of the foreground-background dynamics of films, in psychoanalysis, our aim is not to eliminate the central or manifest, symptom, conflict, fantasy, or dream, but rather to comprehend how this conspicuously foregrounded narrative is systematically related to the discordant or latent elements that have been cast into the shadows, margins, and background.

It is one thing to be aware of the screening function of a dominating manifest text and to analyze it in order to approach the latent marginal texts. It is something else to eliminate the manifest. The purpose of animating the shadows and background of a manifest clinical narrative is not to discover "the real and true meaning" in the background but to arrive at an articulation between manifest and latent, the center and its margins, the foreground and the background. We protect the patient's psychic reality by creating an atmosphere that gives free rein and expression to the interplay between manifest and latent. On the other hand, we analysts sometimes revel in the tantalizing ambiguities of psychic reality in order to avoid acknowledging the ordinary and comparatively dull material realities that comprise the patient's everyday life.

Money is one of those supposedly ordinary and dull material realities. As in every analysis—indeed, as in every life—the consideration of money and other financial concerns that tend to get represented as objective, material realities are always bound up with the dynamics of the patient's inner psychic reality. How a patient earns or does not earn money, how she saves it, squanders it, hoards it, spends it, what she spends it on, is always symptomatic of conflicts within the patient. When money issues come up, analysts may enter into a collaboration with the patient's defensive strategies. However, when an apparent and seemingly evident material reality such as debt, credit card debt, compulsive shopping, or the injustices of financial distributions is subjected to analytic scrutiny, the patient is helped to acknowledge the various ways that she enlists material realities as defensive strategies that serve to protect her psychic reality—the psychic reality she does not want to acknowledge, examine, or change.

In his 2003 paper, "Full Pockets, Empty Lives," Paul Wachtel, a clinical psychologist trained as a psychoanalyst, presents a case vignette of Stanley as an introduction to his ideas about the psychological perils of living in culture where consumerism and commodity fetishism are the reigning values.

Briefly, Stanley, an immensely successful corporate executive, could not enjoy his financial success in a sustained way. He had grown up in a home where his mother habitually denigrated and disparaged his father. His success therefore was a forbidden triumph. "Stanley alternated between taking pleasure in success, relishing images of himself as a dashing man about town and seeing himself as a dull, mediocre, pathetic man."[46]

> The simple dichotomy that had dominated Stanley's understanding of his childhood years—disparaged father and cherished son—eventually gave way to a more complex configuration. The guilt of the Oedipal winner was only one part of his struggle. At another level he, too, was disparaged by his mother, but disparaged in a very particular way. Stanley suffered from a particular fantasy that he had internalized from his mother, a fantasy of himself as slothful, needing to be pushed and prodded, having as his natural state one of inactivity that he had constantly to counter.[47]

Since he saw himself as naturally inert, he imagined that he had to be always vigilant or he would end up doing nothing at all. Yet he were to experience himself as self-motivated, as a person who did not need to crack the whip to "keep himself from being mired in sloth," this self experience would be a betrayal of his mother, "whose opposition to his imagined inertia was experienced as essential to his psychic equilibrium."[48]

Wachtel employs the dynamics of Stanley's conflicts to illuminate a cultural phenomenon that he believes to be especially characteristic of the United States and other similar societies. If Stanley had been born into a different kind of society, he might still have had an inner world with a disparaging mother and a disparaged father. But, Wachtel stresses: "it would have been a *different* world. That difference itself should tell us that the inner world is not quite as 'inner' as some of our theoretical language seems to imply, not as hermetically sealed off from the influence of large social forces or the circumstances and experiences of daily life."[49]

Wachtel believes, and I agree with him, that the psychoanalytic habit of distinguishing between "deep" inner sources and the "surface" influences of the external environment implicitly downgrades the role of social forces on the structuring of a person's inner life. His words reminded me of Leon Edel's comment on the tendency of psychoanalysts to enjoy "their underwater snorkeling to such an extent that they never once looked up to see the great glittering exposed mass of the iceberg."[50]

In fact what goes on above the water-line has a profound impact on what lies below the surface. Wachtel insists, "Living in a consumer culture that converts our needs into commodities . . . shapes the very core of our being."[51] Finally, Wachtel criticizes the narrowness of the psychoanalytic focus on the inner life of patients. "Constructing a moat that seals off the inner world from the world of everyday life and society, defeats the central aim of psychoanalysis—of restoring intimacy and authentic selfhood to our patients."[52]

Wachtel's discussions of the profound relationships between a patient's inner world and the social world "outside" confirm my idea of psychoanalysis as a process of "shifting surfaces," and of an inside and outside that operate in tandem to produce an experience of self. Foreground and background are eternally in a state of mobility with dynamic tensions beween them. A "sort of" Mobius strip model of the human mind. We analysts make a serious mistake if we think of background as synonomous with the real, true inner life, and foreground as a merely defensive measure based on external realities. In fact, we seem to pride ourselves on our ability to keep focusing on the "deep" psychic realities of our patients and not be distracted by the "surface" material realities that the patient sometimes brings into the foreground of her analysis. We think of the patient's preoccupation with the manifest daily realities of her life as a mask for the life of Desire—with its absences, ellipses, uncertainties, ambiguities. And, yes, this is often what is going on during an analytic session. Surely, though, the ideal of analytic neutrality is not to glorify the life that lies beneath the surface, but to ameliorate the patient's sufferings and enable her to participate more fully in daily life and in society. Though these old-fashioned prosaic notions may offend our holy aesthetic of analytic neutrality, we and our patients are better off when we can name and identify the social forces that have given shape and direction to their inner lives. In fact, neutrality means to keep our attention evenly divided between the inner world and the outer world.

If the material reality of the patient's existence, the culture that surrounds him and contours the minutes, days, hours, and years of his everyday existence, is a culture that breeds a sense of personal alienation, which in its turn nurtures a desperate longing for consumer goods that might fill the emptiness of his life, what, if anything, can the analyst do to enable the patient to resist and prevail? To assert these social dilemmas and intrude them into the patient's analysis would amount to a betrayal of the free association process. However, we should be aware of and take into account the ways in which these material realities have contributed and continue to contribute to shaping "the core of the patient's being."

Perhaps, though, we analysts are too impacted by the cultures of fetishism that infiltrate our daily lives to even notice, much less understand how they impact on the psychic life of our patients. Perhaps, most of the time, we inure ourselves to the pernicious psychological fallout of consumerism and commodity fetishism by walking about with our "eyes wide shut."

EIGHT

THE FETISHISM OF COMMODITIES

The ghostly presence of Karl Marx has been haunting these pages. So, as we now enter into the mystifying territory that he identified as "commodity fetishism," it seems fitting that I should once again summon up his words. "All our inventions and progress seem to result in endowing material forces with intellectual life and stultifying human life with a material force."[1] This statement served as a background for several of my previous discussions of the fetishism strategy. Now I will be bringing Marx's words into the foreground, linking them with his meditation on "The Fetishism of the Commodity and its Secret" the title of the fourth section of Chapter One of his magnum opus, *Capital*.[2]

Though commodity fetishism represents only one small corner of Marx's voluminous writings, it is the cornerstone of his theories on the social relations that are embedded in the production of commodities. Briefly, commodity fetishism arises out of the twisted relationship between the worker whose labor produces the commodity and the capitalist who feeds on that labor to maximize his profit from the sale of the commodity The "Secret" of commodity fetishism is the *surplus labor* produced by the worker the crucial factor that enables the capitalist to make the biggest profit possible from the goods he produces. Surplus labor and the commodity fetishism it represents are still around as major characteristics of the twenty-first-century global economy. It is also represented in the commodification of human beings, as exemplified by Reality TV.

The first principle of the fetishism strategy is given consummate expression in Marx's concept of *surplus labor*. In the first chapter, when I listed the five principles of the fetishism strategy, I mentioned that Marx's concept of surplus labor is *nearly* identical with the first principle of the fetishism strategy— "*a mental strategy or defense that enables a human being to transform something or someone with its own enigmatic energy and immaterial essence into something or someone that is material and tangibly real.*" When the surplus labor of a worker is transformed into the profits of the capitalist, the worker is transmographied into a commodity—a nonliving thing like a shoe or a diamond or a table, a material thing that can be exchanged for other material things, a thing that can be manipulated and controlled.

As Otto Fenichel, a psychoanalyst who was also a Marxist, explained in "The Drive to Amass Wealth," "Our system of production [Capitalism] is an economy of commodities which does not produce in order to satisfy the needs of the producer directly but in order to create products for sale, bene-fiting the producer only indirectly and in such an economic system a certain commodity *labor*, has the characteristic of producing greater value than its own market price."[3]

This value that is greater than its own market price is surplus labor or surplus labor value.

Surplus labor is a guiding theme of this chapter. As I mentioned, it embodies the first principle of the fetishism strategy. Of course, the principles of the fetishism strategy cannot be separated into neat and orderly categories. They are not distinct entities. They are shades and reflections of one another. They overlap and usually operate in tandem. So, as we bring out the various expressions of surplus labor value, other principles of the fetishism strategy will come into focus, now and then, here and there.

The fetishism strategy is also represented in some personality traits of Marx himself. For example, Marx's endless ruminations, gathering of data, and writing and re-writing endless drafts of his theories are symptomatic of archive fever. And, yet, because these "symptoms" also had the effect of leaving his theory open, uncertain, and flowing with energy, they paradoxi-cally oppose and challenge the fetishism strategy. We shall be encountering Marx's intellectual grandiosity, his preoccupations with financial manipula-tion and theories of money, his voracious need to know everything about everything, his compulsion to counterpose a dissolution for every solution. And each of these personal "idiosyncrasies" could be regarded as a way of smothering the vitalities of the subjects he was exploring, but also as a way of keeping them alive and vibrant by allowing them to emerge and materialize in their own time, according to their own uncertain and unpredictable destinies.

Marx was a genius, whose far-reaching mind grappled with the major philosophical ideas of his time, and then went beyond them to arrive at a form of philosophical inquiry that was powerful enough to challenge the economic and political forces that kept most of the workers of the world enslaved. These forces, previously hidden away in the folds of apparent political and economic normalities, were devious, disguising themselves in forms that constantly shifted, presenting themselves as more powerful than the human rationalities and passions that might be enlisted to oppose them. Marx was often overwhelmed by the elusive and ever-changing appearance of the demonic forces he was observing. But despite the enormous anxiety such ambiguity must have evoked, Marx stood fast and did not yield to the temp-tation of premature certainty. Marx stared long and hard at these bats that sometimes looked like birds and sometimes looked like mice, refusing to pin them down to a permanent, easily identifiable form.[4] In this sense, he was opposing the fetishism strategy. By keeping those uncertain forms open to further interpretations, he discovered that some of the bats were vampires. "Capital is dead labor which vampire-like, lives only by sucking living labour and lives the more, the more labour he sucks."[5]

Many of Marx's convoluted economic theories changed from one moment to the next, eluding and baffling him until the day he died. But his theory of commodity fetishism achieved a permanence that is as wise today as it was in Marx's day. The essential components of Marx's mature formulations of commodity fetishism were already laid out in his earliest works on fetishism, money, and alienation.

In an 1842 paper on fetishism, the seed of Marx's theory of commodity fetishism took root.[6] Taking a vigorous stand against a contemporary philosopher's view that religious fetishism raises man above his sensuous desires, Marx insisted that the worship of inanimate idols *is* the religion of sensuous desire. The material object that the fetishist worships does not possess magical powers. It cannot gratify his desires. It cannot protect him from danger. In fact, by endowing the material object with magical, life-giving properties, the fetishist deprives himself of the real powers of his own living desires.

Two years later, in "On the Power of Money in Bourgeois Society," Marx asserted that the lust for money turns imagination into reality and reality into imagination.[7] That is, real human faculties are transformed into imaginary abstractions while, at the same time, imaginary abstractions are transformed into material and actual powers. What is human becomes unreal and imaginary. What is imaginary becomes real and tangible. Unknowingly, Marx was writing about the fetishism strategy. The paper expresses the central tendencies of the fetishism strategy, in which material things substitute for living vitalities, and living vitalities are subdued, tamed, and even murdered, if necessary.

"Alienated Labour," also published in 1844, describes how the exploitations and dehumanizations endured by the worker in the production of commodities lead to his feeling alienated from his own self and from other human beings. When Marx writes that "The product of labor is labor embodied and made material in a thing, it is the *objectification* of labor"[8] he is already alluding to the secret of commodity fetishism, what he will later refer to as *surplus labor.*[9]* The varieties of human alienation that Marx describes in that seminal paper become a leitmotif that runs through many of Marx's writings. Commodity fetishism is stamped on one side of the coin. Turn it over and we see the stamp of Alienation.

Unlike many of Marx's writings, which remained buried under the rubble of incomprehensible thoughts and unreadable words, at least "The Fetishism

* In Volume III, put together by Engels from Marx's scribbled notes, the relationship between surplus labor value and profit is re-examined. As with so many other things that were revised in the transition from Volume I to Volumes II and III, value and profit were given different interpretations. However, because of the consistency of Marx's theory of commodity fetishism, his ideas on the fetishistic structure of surplus labor value remain constant.

of the Commodity and its Secret" was brought to life. Marx's scrawling notations on commodity fetishism were not only transcribed into a legible, readable form, they were published. In contrast, many of the words Marx wrote never left his copy books. Some other published words, like many sections of *Capital*, are so dense and incomprehensible that most people give up trying to understand them. They never finish reading the first volume, much less the other, eternally proliferating ensuing volumes. There is an ambiguity here, which I will clarify later when I describe the term "dialectics" as a process of continually materializing reality. At first, I will suggest that this process can, and often does, resemble the archive fevers of biographers. However, as I go on to explain, by enabling a toleration of ambiguity and leaving ideas open to change Marx's dialectics generate vitality.

It is hard to imagine Marx's early theories of fetishism, money, and alienation attaining their mature formulations, if it had not been for the presence in his life of another German writer, Friedrich Engels. Early in 1844, Marx read Engels' essay on the "political economy" of the British and recognized a kindred soul. When Engels came to Paris later that year, he looked up Marx. "They had so much to say to one another that they spent ten days together."[10] It was the beginning of their lifelong collaboration. Engels, three years younger than Marx, brought a down-to-earth practicality to Marx's abstract theories.

The darkly brooding Marx tended to be stubborn, suspicious, and sedentary. It was generally agreed that he was arrogant, contentious, obstinate, condescending, self-absorbed, penny-pinching, and decidedly unkind and unwelcoming to everyone, except to his wife, his children, and Engels and at least in spirit to the anonymous mass of laboring workers whose terrible plight became the guiding passion of his life's work. Engels was light-hearted, lively, and physically active—fencing, riding horses, swimming, reading and re-reading Shelley, enjoying life's pleasures and the company of other men and women. He was generous, caring, yielding, humane, empathic, and open-minded—everything that Marx seemed not to be.

Not surprisingly these personality differences were reflected in the different ways that the two men wrote. Even their handwritings expressed these essential differences. Marx wrote in an illegible scrawl, a veritable scribble of letters and words that were made all the more unintelligible by their blotchy deletions and additions.[11] Engels' script was neat, precise, elegant, and pristinely legible.[12] Their differences were also manifest in the size of their manuscripts.

Early on in their collaboration Engels proposed to Marx that they co-author "Critique of Critical Criticism," a pamphlet on the theoretical absurdities of the philosophers *manque* Bruno Bauer and his two brothers. Sensing Marx's proclivities for endless ruminations, Engels firmly emphasized that the pamphlet should be no more than forty pages, and promptly sent Marx his own twenty-page contribution. He then took off for an extended visit to his family. Several months later, when he returned to Paris, Engels was horrified to learn that the pamphlet "was now a swollen monstrosity of more than 300 pages" and had been renamed *The Holy Family, or Critique of Critical Criticism:Against Bruno Bauer*.[13] Protesting that he had contributed very little to this work, Engels pleaded to disown his authorship. "The thing is too long," he wrote to Marx. "The supreme contempt we two evince towards Bauer's journal is in glaring contrast to the 352 pages we devote to it."[14]

Despite Engels' repeated experiences with Marx's inability to write concisely and finish his writings, he did not give up. He continued to prod him. In 1845 he was urging, "Do as I do, set yourself a date by which you will *definitely have finished*, and make sure it gets into print quickly."[15] In 1863 he was begging Marx to complete *Capital* and send it off to the publisher. Marx just couldn't simplify things. Moreover, his endless re-writings and emendations, his total immersion in the physical materiality of writing down endless words, kept him safely distanced from the horrors of the human realities he was writing about. These writing habits were fetishistic devices!

As Edmund Wilson states in *To the Finland Station*, his book on the intellectual history of the Russian Revolution, "Marx's thinking, though realistic in a moral sense and though sometimes enriched by a peculiar kind of imagery, always tends to state social processes in terms of abstract logical developments or to project mythological personifications, he almost never perceives ordinary human beings."[16] Engels, on the other hand, was sympathetic to the life around him. According to Wilson, he possessed an openness and simplicity of heart that allowed him to see into the lives of other people. It was Engels who took note of the conditions of the working class in Manchester, England, where he spent much of his adult life working as a sort of manager-bookkeeper, who kept an eye on conditions in his father's cotton mill, and conscientiously wrote up neat and legible reports on the financial and practical affairs of his father's business.

But Engels saw far more than his father had intended. Wilson describes how "He saw the working people living like rats in the wretched little dens of their dwellings."[17] He smelled the dank earth on which they slept without comfort of beds or blankets, among piles of their excrement and garbage. He could taste the flour mixed with gypsum and the cocoa mixed with dirt, which the workers ate and fed to their children. He saw children being fed into factories at the age of five or six. He observed with horror and trembling how men, women, and children expended the better part of their lives crawling underground in narrow tunnels. He took careful note of the breaking of the rotten ropes, the caving in of the overexcavated seams of the mines, the explosions that resulted from the carelessness of exhausted children, and the inadequate ventilation.

Marx's abstract theories on the social relations between worker and capitalist complimented the details of working-class wretchedness that Engels had witnessed and described in concrete detail. The two men recognized the compatibility underlying their differences and recognized how each of them might supplement the energies and thoughts of the other. Marx, as an outcome of reading Engels' 1845 *Conditions of the Working Class in England*, began to read factory reports on the conditions that prevailed in the laborers' work environments. He went on to include many citations to Engels' work in *Capital*, Vol I. Engels benefited from Marx's example by learning to write

more convincingly about theoretical issues. Engels knew that Marx was a
genius and felt that he, like all the other political writers he knew, was "talented at best."[18] His own love of life, of riding horses and spending evenings
with his spirited working-class Irish mistress, Mary Burns, were trivial compared to Marx's lofty philosophical truths. Engels, in his subservient idealization of Marx, sometimes handed over to him projects that originated in his
own mind, feeling certain that Marx, because he was an accomplished theoretician and philosopher, would do better with them than he could.

In 1847, on the eve of the revolutions that swept across Continental Europe
in 1848, Marx and Engels were commissioned by The Communist League to
draft a statement of principles for the upcoming Second Congress to be held in
London that November. Engels prepared a draft entitled "Principles of
Communism" but then, recognizing its limitations, suggested to Marx that he
should redraft, rearrange, and expand that initial draft. By then he knew that
Marx had a talent for expanding things. Marx drew on a few of Engels'
passages. But the final version of the "Manifesto of the Communist Party"
was written by Marx, whose revolutionary fervor gave force and vitality to his
descriptions of the class struggle between the proletariat and the bourgeois
capitalist.[19] "Let the ruling classes tremble at the prospect of a communist revolution. Proletarians have nothing to lose but their chains. They have a world
to win. PROLETARIANS OF ALL LANDS UNITE!"[20]

The 1848 revolutions in Europe proved to be monstrous failures. The
revolutionary ideals that Marx had proposed in the "Manifesto" had been
dashed by the economic upswing that followed the revolutions.

This defeat led to one of Marx's most brilliant papers, which in the process of
illuminating the reasons why humans are unable to succeed in their rebellions
against the powers that keep them in chains, evolved into an unintended commentary on the cultures that breed and nourish the fetishism strategy.

On this occasion, an idea that Engels freely lent to Marx came out in
Marx's writing as if it had originated in his own mind. Engels, in a wry commentary on the coup of December 2, 1851 by Napoleon's nephew Louis
Bonaparte (who soon afterward became Napoleon III) wrote to Marx the
next day, "It seems as if Hegel in his grave were acting as World Spirit and
directing history, ordaining most conscientiously that it should all be
unrolled twice, once as a great tragedy and once as a wretched farce."[21]

Whereupon, a year later, Marx in "The Eighteenth Brumaire of Louis
Bonaparte," while citing Hegel, actually echoed Engel. "Hegel observed
somewhere that all great incidents and individuals of world history occur, as
it were, twice. He forgot to add: the first time as tragedy, the second as
farce."[22] To the best of my knowledge, no scholar has ever discovered the
"somewhere" from Hegel. With few exceptions, most of them consistently
overlook the source from Engels.

Though Marx starts out "Eighteenth Brumaire" by echoing Engels, he
expanded his friend's words of wisdom into a memorable analysis of the
"repetition compulsion," later to be a central theme of Freud's *Beyond
the Pleasure Principle*.[23] Marx described how the living, as they make every effort

to create a form of human existence that does not yet exist, repeat the slogans and spirits of dead generations. It is as though "the past weighs on the living like an incubus"[24] that smothers their every good intention. Just as men appear to be engaged in a revolutionary transformation of themselves and their material surroundings, "they anxiously summon up the spirits of the past to their aid, borrowing from them names, rallying cries, costumes, in order to stage the new world historical drama in a time-honored disguise and borrowed speech."[25]

Marx's commentary on revolutionary repetitions expresses a principle of the fetishism strategy that we encountered in the preceding chapter on the training of psychoanalysts. It is safer to stick to what is known and certain, even if it means to suffer and re-suffer the traumas of the past, rather than to create something new and uncertain, with all its tempting ambiguities and challenging possibilities. Creativity is a danger. Where there is a spark, there may develop a fire. Extinguish it before it is too late.

There were many facets of human life in the bourgeois societies and capitalist economies that caught Marx's attention and clamored for written expression. He took elaborate notes on everything he saw. He filled up one notebook after another. And if the work, by chance or by Engels' urgings, managed to find its way to a receptive publisher, Marx would subject the edited publisher's proofs to endless re-writes.

If it were not for Engels' encouragement, we might never have seen *Capital*, Vol. I, which might very well have gone on and on, way beyond its nearly 1,000-page manuscript, and remained unpublished. Certainly, there would not have been the second volume, which Engels, in the last years of his own life, constructed out of four separate drafts, each of more than 1,000 pages. And finally, Engels, assisted by two professional editors, went on to publish the third volume, for which Marx had left only an incomplete first draft. The original plan for *Capital* was to have a fourth, fifth, and sixth volume. The fourth volume, extracted from twenty-three enormous notepads by Karl Kautsky, was finally transcribed and published as "Theories of Surplus Value."[26]

At Marx's graveside, Engels said, "Marx discovered the special law of motion governing the present-day capitalist mode of production and the bourgeois society that this mode of production has created."[27] Until recently, I had assumed that the special law of motion was the dialectical relationship between capitalism and the social relations that emerge from that mode of production.

But there is more to Engels' idea about "the special law of *motion*" than simple dialectics. Marx's dialectic* was different from the traditional thesis,

---

* Explanations of the meaning of dialectics in Marxist theory can be as off-putting and impenetrable as some of Marx's writings. My friend and colleague, the New York University Marxist scholar Bertell Ollman, wrote *Dialectical Investigations*. That volume begins with "An Introduction to Dialectics" and goes on to "Advanced Dialectics or the Role of Abstraction in Marx," and, finally, concludes with a discouraging note: "Not all of the important questions associated with dialectics have been dealt with in this essay. Missing or barely touched on are the place and/or role within dialectical method of reflection, perception, emotion, memory, conceptualization (language), appropriation, moral evaluation, verification and activity, particularly in production." In view of Ollman's cautionary tale, it would seem presumptuously un-Marxian to offer a *brief* definition of Marxian dialectics.

antithesis, and synthesis. The fundamental law of motion that Marx discovered is a dialectic that entails the *process* of materializing. Things do not exist from the start. They materialize and come into existence through evolving forms. As the eminent Marxist scholar Bertell Ollman says: "Dialectics restructures our thinking about reality, by replacing the common-sense notion of a 'thing' that *has* a history, with notions of 'process,' which *contains* its history and possible futures, and 'relation,' which *contains* as part of what it is its ties with other relations."[28]

I came to an understanding of the possible meaning of Marx's law of motion through my countertransference responses to Marx's archive fevers. As this chapter evolved, it expanded and underwent what seemed like endless revisions. I watched with amazement and some degree of horror as my ideas about Marx and his theories kept assuming different forms and contents as they materialized.

When I told Ollman about my identifications with Marx's archive fevers, he looked puzzled. I explained how some biographers, in their efforts to bring a subject to life, managed to smother the life energies of their subject under mountains of data. Didn't he agree that Marx's uncontrollable habit of writing mountains of words and theories could have the effect of draining his ideas of their life energies? Wasn't Marx practicing against his preaching by endowing material things with living faculties and thereby stultifying human life? Ollman thought for a few moments and then replied, "It depends what you mean by life."

He did not elaborate, and probably did not realize the effect his words would have on me. Naturally, I was defensive. I wanted to argue and defend my theory of Marx's archive fever. But I decided to consider Ollman's cryptic comment. He might not agree with the directions my considerations took me, nevertheless, soon after our conversation, I came to a new understanding of what Engels might have meant by Marx's special law of motion. Because Marx's theories were in a constant state of materializing and never settling down into precise meanings, they were perpetually mobile and alive. Perhaps the law of motion has to do with the living vitality of Marx's abstractions?

Thinking about "It depends what you mean by life?" enabled me to settle into this chapter on Marx's commodity fetishism. While I may have arrested the law of motion that had up until then allowed my ideas to achieve a certain degree of mobility and flexibility, I also cured my archive fever. I was able to focus on the central themes of this chapter commodity fetishism and surplus labor value and how they are both supreme expressions of the fetishism strategy.

In one way or another, Marx's theory of commodity fetishism is always addressing the inverted relation that exists between material things and sensuous human beings. As suggested in Marx's early papers on fetishism, money, and alienation, the deadening or reification of the human being goes hand-in-hand with attributions of life energy to material things.

By understanding the fetishism of commodities, we come to view the fetishism strategy from a new angle. For example, the necrophilic principle is here expressed as the vampire principle, in which dead capital grows rosy from feeding on the vitalities of the worker. A commodity, therefore, embodies within itself the life energies of the laborer who produced it.

How does a commodity differ from other material goods? Or, more to the point, we might ask, "Are all our material goods—our foods, our clothing, our homes, our household equipment, our beds and tables and chairs, our TV screens and computers and hi-fidelity set-ups, and so on—are these everyday, commonplace items inevitably and irrevocably commodities?" How could the essentials of food, clothing, and shelter, and all those objects that furnish and enliven our shelters, objects that are so practical and useful and necessary to our daily lives, be tainted by the fetishism of commodities?

Human beings, in the very process of producing objects in a capitalist system of buying and selling, are creating commodities. By the time we purchase the simple useful goods that we put on our tables and the objects that furnish our homes and gardens, these useful things have long since been transformed into the exchange values of commodities.

Here is where *surplus labor*—the vampire principle—enters the picture. If the capitalist paid every laborer involved in the production of his commodity the full value of their labor, he would have much smaller profits—or maybe, none at all. For example, if the worker works twelve hours, the capitalist will pay him a wage that is the equivalent of six hours of labor. The remainder, the *surplus*, or additional unpaid six hours, goes to plump up the voracious capitalist.

A commodity, by definition, is made up of the surplus labor of the worker. A commodity, by definition, is made up of the profits accumulated by the capitalist who underpaid for the labor that produced it. And it follows, therefore, that there is one commodity that has an opposite trajectory. In a capitalist economy, the laborer who produces the commodity is herself a commodity. Her value is not as a person with living desires but as an object that contributes to the exchange value of the product her labor has produced. A laborer and her work can be exchanged by the capitalist or the worker for a small quantity of diamonds, or one automobile or several pairs of Manolos.

The personal dehumanization involved in the production of a commodity goes on to produce alienation. Alienation creates a longing for something that can restore a sense of inner aliveness—a diamond bracelet, an SUV, a pair of shoes, the latest *Bushido* tattoo. The fetishism of commodities is *not* the same as the consumer fetishism that inspires us to buy more and more electronic equipment or the passionate longings that attach themselves to stilettos and other currently fashionable items. These familiar commercial products might legitimately be labeled as "fetishes" if the purchaser relates to them as if they embodied a living essence.

Of course, knowing what we now know about vampire mentality, we could say that the commodity, since it contains within it the congealed surplus labor of the worker, *does* in fact embody a living essence. But this is not what the woman is craving when she feels she must spend a week's salary on that pair of shoes. In fact, she probably would be horrified if she knew about the congealed labor that composed the shiny straps of her stilleto.

No, the woman who must purchase the latest shoe style is not a vampire or a werewolf. Her appetites have been fueled by a different sort of craving. The passionate longings for certain consumer goods is motivated by the alienations that are bred and nurtured in a social world dominated by commodity fetishism. A person who is alienated from her own inner life with all its wondrous range of human desires feels depleted and incomplete. She looks to the outer world to fill up her inner emptiness with things, with material objects, a pair of shoes, a fur coat, a hat, a chiffon scarf, an iPod, an SUV.

Marx's introduction to "The Fetishism of the Commodity and its Secret" is enlivened by a flourish of metaphorical animation as Marx creates visual images of a material object, a table, turning into a living thing imbued with human qualities. Wilson, who is often critical of Marx's writing habits, also refers to him as "the poet of commodities."[29] Marx captured the essential spirit of a commodity when he described an ordinary table, a functional piece of furniture that appears in many sizes and guises in most "civilized" homes, as a surface to dine on, as a desk to write on, as an accessory that we place next to our beds or armchairs to hold the candles that light up the books that we read. How could such a necessity, such a useful item as a table, be considered a commodity? Isn't a table sometimes just a table?

Marx would have agreed that a table, at first sight anyway, is a trivial thing, a useful thing intended simply to satisfy human needs and sensuous desires. However, Marx warned that when we stop to analyze the ordinary thing, we come upon a thing "that is a very strange thing, abounding in metaphysical subtleties and theological niceties."[30] An extraordinary statement with subtleties and niceties of its own.

Like Jonathan Swift, whose "modest proposal" became a model for some of Marx's more inventive writings,[31] Marx could be ironic about matters that were deadly serious. And when he was, he often brought his theoretical abstractions to life. He gives his readers a vivid demonstration of how a table materializes in the world as a living thing. "As soon as it [a table] steps out into the world as a commodity, it changes into a sensible and supersensible thing."[32] In other words, the table, as commodity, is no longer an immaterial substance made of wood, but a living thing made up of human parts and human sensibilities. "It not only *stands* with its *feet* on the ground, but, in relation to all other commodities, it stands on its *head*, and evolves out of its wooden *brain*, grotesque ideas far more wonderful than if it were to begin dancing of its own free will (*itals.* mine).[33]

The table comes to life as a human thing with human capacities because congealed within its essence is the worker's unpaid labor. The table is endowed with the life forces that the vampire drained away from the worker.

The vampire could never get its fangs into Marx. As a young man he proclaimed to his parents, "The writer must earn money in order to live and write, but he must by no means live and write to earn money."[34] Marx was a workaholic who toiled at his writing every day of his adult life but who, except for a stint as a paid journalist for the *Daily Tribune* in the 1850s, never as a wage earner. Even after he married "Baroness" Jenny von Westphalen in 1843 and they went on to have six children (two boys and one girl died in childhood) and were living in dire poverty, hounded by debtors, he would not consider working for a wage. For twenty years, until 1864 when Marx inherited the estate of Wilhelm Wolff,* one of his long-time admirers, he and Jenny were always pawning their coats and linens. The heirloom silver given to Jenny on her wedding day spent more time in the pawnshops than in the bare cupboards of the Marx household.[35] When it came to profiting from the labor of others, Marx could be something of a vampire himself. He thought nothing of borrowing money from a neighbor to pay for the funeral of his one-year-old daughter. When Jenny was seriously ill with smallpox he was unable to pay the doctor's bill. The neighbors, the doctor, the butcher, the baker, the tailor, the shoemaker could wait to be paid or never be paid while Marx gave himself the privilege of spending most of his days at the British Library studying books on money and credit. Marx even had the chutzpah to threaten to draw a banknote on his widowed mother's income, a desperate gesture that resulted in a further estrangement between the forever money-wheedling son and the tight-fisted mother.[36] In his mature years, his motto was, "I shall not let bourgeois society make me into a money making machine."[37]

Wilson was bewildered by Marx's reluctance to work for a wage: "It was one of the most striking contradictions of Marx's whole career that the man who had done more than any other to call attention to economic motivation should have been incapable of doing anything for gain."[38] Other German emigres had found work in London. "Yet on only one recorded occasion during the whole of Marx's thirty years' stay in London did he attempt to find regular employment."[39] Wilson is referring to Marx's attempt to apply for a job as a railway clerk. But he was saved from that ignominious fate by one of his other symptoms. His handwriting was so blotchy and illegible that his application had to be turned down.[40]

As with his patient and persistent oppositions to Marx's archive fevers, Engels would rescue Marx from the unfortunate outcomes of his aversion to wage labor. Time and time again, Engels used his own earnings from his job in his father's cotton mill in Manchester to pay off the debts of Karl and Jenny Marx.

It was in a general climate of roving in and out of desperate financial plights that Marx attempted to illuminate the horrendous working conditions endured by the working class. The "secret" of commodity fetishism, suggested in "Alienated Labour" and in earlier chapters of *Capital*, is not fully exposed until Chapter Ten, "The Working Day," when Marx confronts his readers with the vampirized bodies of the workers who produce commodities for the profit of the capitalist.

* Volume I of *Capital* was dedicated to Wolff.

However, Marx's head-on confrontations with the realities of the working day could not be sustained. His preoccupation with money seemed to take precedence over the working day of the worker. The gruesome and harrowing details of the working day are interspersed with monetary theories, algebraic equations, charts of labor time, and with long sections devoted to the scores of legal documents that had been drawn up to counteract the exploitations of the capitalists.

In order to extract the details of the working day from the massive mounds of monetary theory that entomb them, a reader might labor for several months. Fortunately, we can start out on a simpler footing.

Let us return for just a moment to "Alienated Labor." In that 1844 paper, Marx repeats the same theme in several different forms. Marx identifies the human characteristics set in motion by the economy—*greed* and the *war among the greedy*—competition.[41] But more importantly, Marx goes on to spell out the several other connections that evolve from that primary relationship, such as the intimate connections between economic value and the devaluation of men, the connections between "all this alienation and the system of money."[42] As he explains the principles of alienation, it is as if he is elaborating the first principle of the fetishism strategy. "The *externalization* of the worker into his product does not only mean that his work becomes an object, an external existence, but that it exists *outside him*, independently, as something alien to him, as confronting him as an autonomous power. It means that the life which he has given to the object confronts him as something hostile and alien."[43]

It follows that:

The more wealth the worker produces the poorer he becomes.

The more commodities the worker produces the cheaper a commodity he becomes.

The more value the laborer creates, the less value, the less dignity he has.

The better shaped his product, the more mis-shapen the worker.

The more civilized his object, the more barbaric the worker.[44]

When they assume their places in "The Working Day," the details of this early paper emerge as momentary flickers in a fiery dominion far worse than Hell. For his descriptions of the horrors of the working day, Marx very often relies on Engels' *Conditions of the Working Class in England.*

Here are some of the things we see:

Nine- and ten-year-old children are awakened from their beds before dawn and forced to work until nearly midnight, "their humanity absolutely sinking into a stone-like torpor, utterly horrible to contemplate."[45]

As a result of their working conditions, adult potters of both sexes become morally and physically degenerate. They grow old prematurely and die prematurely. They suffer from rheumatism, attacks of dyspepsia, and disorders of the liver and kidneys. "They are especially prone to chest disease, to pneumonia, phthisis, bronchitis and asthma."[46]

The production of matches, which requires applying phosphate to the tip of the matchstick, brought with it tetanus, a disease that haunted the makers of matches. The majority of match makers are children under 13 and young persons under 18. Furthermore, because of the unhealthiness of this occupation, "only the most miserable part of the working class, half-starved widows and so forth deliver up their children to it."[47]

In dressmaker establishments, working to death was the order of the day. But this was the situation in any place "where a thriving business" had to be done. Even the hearty blacksmith, when he comes to the city factory to ply his trade, "is made to strike so many more blows, to walk so many more steps, to breathe so many more breaths per day," and if he is able to fulfill these requirements, he dies at thirty seven rather than fifty.[48]

"The prolongation of the working day beyond the limits of the natural day, into the night . . . only slightly quenches the vampire thirst for the living blood of labour."[49] Capitalist production requires labor throughout every one of the twenty-four hours. And since the same person can't work for the entire twenty-four hours, the problem is solved by the "shift system"— twelve-hour day labor and twelve-hour night labor. However, instead of improving their work conditions, the shift system makes it necessary for nine- and ten-year-old children to work two or three twelve-hour shifts in a row.[50]

When the capitalist does agree to shorter hours, he works it out that the laborer works even harder: "what is lost by shortening the duration of labour is gained by increasing the degree of power exerted."[51] When the law decreed a shorter working day, the manufacturers instructed their "overlookers" to take good care "that the hands lost no time."[52]

Most manufacturers are fanatically opposed to additional devices to insure cleanliness, to provide adequate ventilation, or to the slight expenditures for appliances that would protect the arms and legs of their hired "hands." A certifying surgeon for the scutching mills (which are fed flax by rollers in the production of the linen that is used to make coats and other garments) reported that, "The serious accidents at the scutching mills are of the most fearful nature. In many cases a quarter of the body is torn from the trunk, and either involves death or a future of wretched incapacity and suffering."[53]

You might protest after "seeing" all these horrors of the working day, "these working conditions no longer exist. Almost everybody works an eight-hour day with an hour off for lunch and their evenings and weekends free for family time, leisure, and shopping. There are powerful labor unions that work to keep the excesses of dead capital under control. Children don't work in factories anymore. There are child labor laws and compulsory education until the age of eighteen." Yes, all of this seems true enough. But only if you've been keeping your "eyes wide shut."

As Andrew Stern, head of the Service Employees International Union, put it, "The age of automation and globalization with its race to the bottom among companies searching for lower wages overseas, has savaged the labor movement."[54] Barely one worker in ten is a card-carrying union member. Globalization has already cost millions of Americans their jobs and their pensions. Stern concludes, "I don't think workers in our country have a lot of time left if we don't change."[55] The unending race to the bottom was leaving American workers in the dust.

At the beginning of the twenty-first century, Central America beat out Mexico in "the race for the bottom" of the United States dressmaking industry.[56] Many of the factories and workshops that were supplying labor-discounted blouses, polo-shirts, dresses, gloves, jackets, and jeans to Wal-Mart, Gap, Sear, Banana Republic, Old Navy, and Strawberry were staffed by young women and working mothers from Guatemala, the Dominican Republic, Honduras, and San Salvador. However, by 2005, even those countries were finding themselves losing out in the race for the bottom. Each day it became more evident that the place in the world that was outperforming and underpricing all of these countries was China.[57]

Roger Williams, the president of the swimmer division of Warnaco, one of the world's largest apparel manufacturers, said, "We will always go to the least expensive places."[58] He predicted that Warnaco would soon be shifting to China.

Most of the garments the average American was wearing in the early years of the twenty-first century were "Made Elsewhere." If you wanted to know where the laborers from elsewhere came from, all you had to do was read the labels. This labeling from elsewhere applies to almost everything you purchase: umbrellas, watches, sunglasses, tableware, tables, chairs, and almost all of your clothing items. Chances are a great many of them will say, "Made in China." But if parts manufactured in United States are put into their final form in China the labels could say, "Made in United States. Assembled in China."

All this "racing to the bottom" is an expression of the *surplus labor* that breeds and nourishes commodity fetishism. It is also an expression of the fetishism strategy in which human beings are transformed into machines, and machines assume the vitalities of the human being. And since, these days, that race very often ends up in China, we have to wonder about the shapes that surplus labor might assume in a Communist nation.

In China, one of the latest surplus labor exploitations are gaming factories, where young men, called "gold farmers," are hired to play online computer games that revolve around warfare in distant galaxies or medieval kingdoms for twelve hours a day, seven days a week for $250 a month or less.[59] According to David Barboza's *New York Times* report "Ogre to Slay? Outsource it to the Chinese," the gaming factories "have come to resemble the thousands of textile mills and toy factories that have moved here from Taiwan, Hong Kong, and other parts of the world to take advantage of China's vast pool of cheap labor." It is estimated that there are about 100,000 youths "working as full-time gamers, in dark Internet cafes, abandoned warehouses, small offices and private homes."[60] Their job is to accumulate virtual gold coins or other virtual currency that is then purchased by players who don't have the time, inclination, or patience to plod through the earliest stages of World of Warcraft, Magic Land, Ever Quest, or similar online fantasy games. By paying a couple of hundred dollars or more, the more affluent can get into the games at the more exciting and usually more profitable, "max" levels. At these levels they can take on world-class dragons and demons by simply trading in the virtual gold coins earned by the gold farmers, who pounded on their computer boards for eighty-four hours a week, using their wits to fight off measly rats and koboids.

In the same month that Barboza described the gaming factory phenomenon, he and co-reporter Daniel Altman wrote, "That Blur? It's China, Moving Up In the Pack," a story about China's announcement that its economy was much bigger than they had previously estimated. Evidently, by the end of 2005, the "race for the bottom" was being accompanied by a "race for the top." The new financial figures implied that China's economy had already eclipsed that of France, Italy, and Britain, and was trailing only Japan, Germany, and the United States. It was the fourth-largest economy in the world. China's gross domestic product was estimated at $2 trillion.[61]

The Chinese Academy of Social Scientists has estimated that there are at least 10,000 businessmen in China whose assets exceed $10 million. Yet, despite the fact that China has the world's fastest-growing economy and a sizable number of multimillionaires, it is also one of the most unequal societies in the world. Each year the gap between the rural poor and the urban rich gets wider. According to a 2003 World Bank report, China ranked hundred and thirty fourth in income per person.[62]

By 2006, however, China was no longer the "bottom." The race for the top had created a labor shortage. Wages were pushed up. The ranks of the middle class were swelling. As David Barboza portrayed the situation in the *New York Times*, "On top of a strengthening Chinese currency, this is likely to mean that the cost of consumer goods shipped to the United States and Europe will rise." Manufacturers were already beginning to go to Vietnam, India, and Bangladesh to produce lower cost goods. A Goldman Sachs economist commented, "We are seeing the end of the golden period of extremely low cost labor in China." She further noted that though there was "still a lot of cheap labor, Chinese workers are getting skilled very quickly. They are moving up the value chain faster than people expected."[63]

In the early years of the twenty-first century, China, technically one of the poorest nations in the world, had become the largest, most populated, and most powerful Communist nation that had ever existed, while at the same time rapidly transforming itself into the epitome of a megacapitalist society that was capable of shaking up the economies of every Western Nation—especially the United States.

Haier, China's biggest appliance company, nearly snapped up Maytag. China National Offshore Oil Company made a 18.5 billion bid for Unacol Oil, which Chevron took seriously enough to make a serious counterbid.[64] The Chinese managed to make the financial markets nervous as they continued to grab fistfuls of U.S. Treasuries and thereby downgrade the value of the American dollar. Then in the middle of 2005, yielding to pressure from the United States, whose trade deficit with China was rising astronomically, the Chinese government decided to end its long-standing practice of tying the value of the yuan to the dollar and instead let it float "freely" by tying it to several other unspecified countries.[65] The financial pundits of the world disagreed about whether or not this move on the part of China would manage to restore the faith in the dollar. The one point of consensus was that China seemed to be on its way to supplanting the United States as the premier economic power. Some economists estimated that China could overtake the United States by 2035.

While all this financial hanky-panky was going on, the Chinese went on a frantic shopping mall spree and established their reputation as Land of Giant Megamalls. In a blink of the eye, they had produced half of the ten biggest malls in the world. And then, a nanosecond later, they already had built the two *very* biggest. First came the 7.32 million square foot Golden Resources Mall—the length of six football fields and exceeding the floor space of the Pentagon, the largest office building in the world. A few years later they constructed the 9.58 million square foot South China Mall, which featured large-scale reproductions of the high spots of Western culture—with clever imitations of the piazzas and architecture of Venice, bridges, canals, gondolas and all; and the Champs Elysee of Paris with a full-size reproduction of the Arc de Triomphe at its center; and Southern California's Hollywood with a giant Imax theater and of course the requisite McDonalds and Pizza Hut food courts dotting the landscape, here, there and everywhere.[66]

In August of 2005, just a few months before Communist China became the fourth-largest economy in the world, it was announced that Donald Trump was developing a Chinese version of the Reality TV show, *The Apprentice*. At the same time, Trump's Chinese counterpart, Vincent Lo, was preparing a competing show, *Wise Man Takes All*, which Mr. Lo said "was in line with our longstanding commitment to the development of China" and "designed to foster healthy competition and entrepreneurship among the younger generation."[67] Here was Communist China about to produce two competing blueprints on how to become a dead labor, capitalist vampire.

At the beginning of the twenty-first century, Marx's theory of surplus labor value came to life in a shape that he could not have predicted. Marx had always been puzzled by the ambiguities inherent in the capitalist mode of production; those bats that sometimes looked like mice and at other times seemed to be birds. Finally, he realized that many of these ambiguous creatures were actually vampires. Even so, he would have been amazed and perhaps bewildered had he lived to see that a vast number of dead labor capitalist vampires were Chinese communists.

If we extend our vision of the surplus labor situation just a bit further, we will confront scenes of the cheapest labor of all in many parts of the world. Child labor is concentrated in Asia and Africa, which together account for more than 90 percent of child employment. Child labor is prevalent in Thailand, Sri-Lanka, Bangladesh, Pakistan, Iran, and in lesser known places like Chad. Coming closer to home, we see evidence of considerable child labor in Brazil, Paraguay, Peru, and Costa Rica.[68]

The commodification of children, transforming children into surplus labor, into objects that are valued far less than the material goods they produce, is one of the saddest and most telling illustrations of the first principle of the fetishism strategy: *Fetishism is a mental strategy that enables one human being to transform another living, breathing human with its own enigmatic energy and vitalities into something that is material—a commodity.* The image of the dead labor capitalist vampirizing the bodies and souls of helpless little children makes high-minded, good-thinking American citizens cry out with moral outrage.

Yet, child labor is an intrinsic component of survival in most newly developing countries. A country that is already developed, like the United States, Great Britain, France, or Germany does not depend on child labor for its survival and therefore can afford to raise objections to that form of labor. On the other hand, manufacturers and exporters in the still developing countries have a stake in perpetuating child labor. When addressing the do-gooders from the United Nations, they protest that measures to prohibit child labor would rob them of their biggest advantage in the world market— lower labor costs. Since these child labor measures come from the already developed countries, they are viewed as an attempt by the rich countries to wipe away the developing country's profit advantages. The manufacturers from underdeveloped countries argue that placing trade restrictions on countries who employ child labor is tantamount to unfair labor practices, because: (1) not all child labor is exploitative; (2) Poor countries cannot afford such measures; and (3) Levels of poverty would increase.[69]

Chances are that child labor will continue to be a fact of life in most countries of the world for some time to come. Chances are that a ten-year-old from Sri Lanka or India will have contributed labor time to the blue silk dress that you wear to a charity benefit. Chances are that a four-year-old tied to a weaving loom has participated in the manufacture of the elegant "Persian" carpet that covers your entire living room floor. Look at your labels. If your carpet doesn't say "Made with Adult Labor Only," chances are a child's labor contributed to its exotic pattern.

A 2005 report from Human Rights Watch: Child Labor sounds very much like some scenes from the working day in *Capital.*

> Working at rug looms, for example, has left children disabled with eye damage, lung disease, stunted growth and a susceptibility to arthritis as they grow older. Children making silk thread in India dip their hands into boiling water that burns and blisters them, breathe smoke and fumes from machinery, handle dead worms that cause infections and guide twisting threads that cut their fingers. Children harvesting sugar cane in El Salvador use machetes to cut cane for up to nine hours a day in the hot sun; injuries to their hands and legs are common and medical care is often not available.[70]

Marx's depictions of surplus labor value and commodity fetishism are not outdated. Nor do they apply only to underdeveloped countries. On the contrary, the labor-capital relations that reflect these "theoretical" entities are prevalent all over the world, including in our contemporary developed societies, where we abhor the abominations of child labor but still fail to see or to question the widespread commodification of human beings that takes place every day, every night, right in our own backyard.

A central feature of the fetishism of the commodity is the commodification of human beings. It's all there in Marx's prediction, "All our inventions and progress seem to result in endowing material forces with intellectual life and stultifying life with a material force." We need not visit an Iranian carpet factory, or an Indian silk factory, or a Salvadorian sugar cane plantation to "see" this aspect of commodity fetishism.

A good place to view our present-day commodifications of human beings is in the fictional realm of reality TV. Though the producers' claims that they are representing real human beings behaving naturally in real situations are falsifications, many of these so-called reality shows inadvertently present a real and accurate portrayal of the "secret" of how human beings are transformed into commodities. In that sense, reality TV, despite its carefully scripted, detailed planning and heavy duty editing of pre-taped situations, is all-too-real. What we see when we view reality TV is the ultimate personification of the reification of human beings.

As a brief preface to our look at reality TV, I shall now bring into the foreground an aspect of Marx's commodity fetishism that I have relegated to the background. You may have noticed that my renditions of the capitalist's vampirizations of the worker left out what happens to the body and soul of the worker who is vampirized. I *did* discuss, at some length, the alienation suffered by the worker, and also how the surplus labor that is sucked out from the worker's body is drained off into the profits of the capitalist. But I *did not* refer to the contagion that results from vampirization. Nevertheless, as we all know from watching vampire movies, the vampirized worker, of course, would be transformed into a vampire himself.

The commodification of the human being includes his frenzied competition to get more than his fellow workers and to get more faster than they do. So, in addition to his alienation from his own self, now that he has been vampirized, the worker is likely to become alienated from other human beings.

Let us begin with *Survivor*, the prototype of the reality TV genre that I am referring to.* Just a few weeks of viewing how the human beings on *Survivor* manage to outwit and defeat their fellow participants and you could become an expert in manipulation, back-stabbing, humiliation, conniving, defrauding,

---

* Other reality TV shows, such as *Wife Swap, Nanny, Queer Eye for the Straight Guy, Makeover, Extreme Makeover, American Idol, The Contender, Runway,* while they **do** encourage competition and **do** manipulate and commodify the "real" people chosen to participate, nevertheless, **do not** offer explicit instructions on how to become a successful vampire. My analysis of the commodification of human beings in reality TV will be limited to *Survivor, The Apprentice,* and *Fear Factor.* My concluding remarks address the notion of reality as it evolved in the first reality TV show, *The Real World,* and the commodification of the young men and women who agreed to participate.

and just plain cheating. Viewing a full season, right up to the moment that one of the sixteen participants manages to out-maneuver all his fellow tribes-people, and win all the money, and you will have been in a position to acquire all the mental agility you need to become a first-class vampire. If you had become addicted to *Survivor*, and stuck with it season after season, it is possible that your vampire dexterities would have become inherent aspects of the person you are. Should you ever want to engage in backstabbing and manipulation of your friends and coworkers, you won't even have to think about it. It will come to you automatically.

If you have been a faithful follower of *Survivor*-type reality TV, you may not require my descriptions of those shows. Nevertheless, very likely you have not viewed them with an eye to identifying the specific methods they employ to exploit and dehumanize the human beings who they select to participate.

The United States version of *Survivor*, produced by Mark Burnett and hosted by Jeff Probst, was first broadcast in May 2000 on CBS. *Survivor* was the first American reality show to pit one human being against another.

A group of "interesting" human beings are taken to an inhospitable environment—the jungles of the Amazon, the Pearl Islands off the coast of Panama, the Australian Outback, a desert in Kenya—and encouraged to compete with one another to see who will be the last to survive and win one million dollars. The series starts with sixteen players, who are divided into two eight-person "Tribes." On each episode one player is voted off the show by the other remaining tribespeople. The two tribes compete against each other in challenges entailing physical endurance, intelligence, teamwork, dexterity, courage, and willpower.

After several episodes, usually when there are only eight players left, the two tribes merge. The players must give a new name to the new tribe and create a new flag for it. From that point on, challenges are won on an individual basis. Throughout, Probst encourages the players to make factions, to plot against each other, to lie about their motives, to steal each other's supplies, and to betray one another. Probst's provocations intensify as the episode approaches the meeting of the Tribal Council, where each week one player is voted off the show, either by members of her own tribe or the newly merged tribe. Before the actual voting, Probst gathers the players together to whet their vampire appetites, by reminding them of earlier betrayals, backstab-bings, nasty gossip, disturbing personal interactions, stealing. He also asks them to publicly express their opinions about the other players. Obviously, each player must exercise an exquisite balance between currying favor and denigrating her competitors. The players then vote secretly and one of them is eliminated. Probst takes the torch from the losing player, extinguishes its flame and declares, "The tribe has spoken." The player who loses is last seen leaving the scene of her defeat. In most episodes, her final words describing how it felt to be voted off are played over the final credits of the episodes.

The Apprentice pits aspiring capitalists against each other and could be a primer on the fetishism of commodities.[71] Donald Trump, the real-life

megacapitalist, is the main host, along with his two henchmen, Carolyn
Kepcher and George Ross, who in "real" life are said to be Trump's "trusted
advisers." Following the example of Trump, Kepcher and Ross maintain a
stony-faced, bland expression throughout. Maybe that heartless, unemo-
tional pose is supposed to make them look like "real" capitalists. The earliest
episodes pitched women against men.

In the 2004/2005 season, the episodes followed the pattern originally
suggested for the show: those candidates with those with street smarts
against those with book smarts. The challenges were related to business ventures; who can buy gold at the cheapest rate on a certain day; who can design
and build the most lucrative miniature golf course; who can raise the most
money for a charity; who can design the best outdoor building mural for a
neighborhood center; who can create the best clothing line that combines
fashion and technology; who can create the best promotional brochures for a
limited edition automobile.

Other than the fact that the scenes take place in a civilized, hospitable
environment, in most other respects, the show is closely modeled on
Survivor. There are two teams, one composed of ambitious entrepreneur
types with only a high school diploma who, in one season, decided to call
their team Net Worth, and the other composed of MBAs, lawyers, and other
college-educated types who decided to call their team Magna. As in *Survivor*,
the two teams are merged when there are only eight people left. However, in
The Apprentice, the members of each team are pitted against each other by
having to chose the two people who they want to deport to the other team.

At the end of each episode, the two teams are called to the Boardroom
(*The Apprentice* version of the Tribal Council) to determine which player
should get fired by Trump. While the provocations to make factions and
betray one another are more subtle and "business-like" with Trump and his
two assistants as the hosts, there is a built-in *Survivor* quality of nasty business
practice, which can be detected in the way the competition is set up for each
episode to encourage bad-spirited qualities in the players. In order to help
himself to decide "fairly" which person to point his finger at and pronounce
"You're fired," Trump asks the players to express their opinions about the
other players' business know-how and to reveal the personality quirks that
they have noticed. Again, as in *Survivor*, there is this delicate balance
between currying favor with the teammates who have the power to induce
Trump to fire them, and doing whatever they can to reveal the faults and
fallibilities of their fellow teammates. Occasionally, Trump asks his two assistants for their opinions. Occasionally, either Carolyn or George express an
opinion all on their own—but, of course, these are carefully scripted.

Another Mark Burnett reality show is *Fear Factor*.[72] Here, there is much
more focus on the challenges and much less opportunity for the six contestants to hone their vampire aptitudes. However, one of the three challenges,
the centerpiece of each episode, brings out with vivid clarity the dehumanizing qualities that are inherent in commodity fetishism.

The series, which lasts for five episodes per season, starts out with six contestants who are challenged to succeed in the shortest amount of time at three tasks, all of them involving physical endurance and the courage to overcome fear (of heights, of water, of speed, of close quarters). The second challenge, which also involves performing certain activities in the shortest amount of time, consists of such gruesome and demeaning challenges as sucking the liquid out of a cow's eyeball, spitting the liquid into a glass, and then doing the same with another eyeball and then another until the glass is filled to the brim, and then guzzling down the eyeball cocktail; standing barefoot in a vat filled with live squirming earthworms and squeezing them into a liquid which flows out of a tube at the bottom of the vat into a glass and then drinking down the earthworm juice; standing before a conveyer belt covered with dishes of pig uterus, cow brains, earthworms, ground-up insects, and trying to grab up a mouthful of each "tidbit" before the conveyer belt tumbles the "food" onto the ground—then back to the head of the belt for more. All of these challenges are judged by the speed at which they are completed. The one who is fastest is the winner.

Fear Factor, though it imitates the challenge format of *Survivor*, is basically a version of a much older Japanese show called *Endurance*, in which participants would compete to determine who could go the longest without eating, or urinating, or who could stay put the longest when standing in a pit of snakes.[73]

If, for the moment, we put aside the spirit of cutthroat competitiveness in reality TV, there is still another lesson to be learned about the fetishism strategy. The whole notion of the so-called reality of reality TV raises up the specter of the twisted relationship between real material reality and actual human life. As the real world is endowed with living qualities, the actual human life is transformed into a material commodity.

The prototype for these "unscripted" TV shows appeared in 1992 with *The Real World*, which featured small groups of young men and women trying to live together in the same house for a full TV season. Each season begins in a new city with a new cast of characters. People can get thrown out of the house by the other members, but the emphasis in this prototype reality show was not competition per se but real people trying to act real. Since then a variety of reality shows have garnered impressive ratings while the producers garnered Emmy nominations and enormous profits, and introduced millions of Americans to this new TV genre, where, except for the one winner in the case of *Survivor*, who gets one million dollars, the labor doesn't have to be paid anything at all—the epitome of surplus labor value.

The Real World, or as its aficionados call it, RW, sheds a different light on commodity fetishism. Although the RW characters are not put into situations where they are expected to vampirize one another, the very fact of appearing on this show means that they would be submitting to having all the real life drained out of them. And all for no pay. And all for a millisecond of fame. And all for *maybe* being pointed out at Burger King.

Chuck Klosterman, who *USA Today* likened to pop culture's version of Michael Moore, wrote about *The Real World* in his "low culture manifesto," *Sex, Drugs and Cocoa Puffs*. He identifies himself as "an amateur *Real World* scholar."[74] He explains that he calls himself an "amateur" because he has not done a serious university study of the show, but a "scholar" nonetheless because he no longer watches the show as entertainment but "in the hopes of unlocking the questions that have haunted man since the dawn of civilization."[75] Klosterman discovers a few fascinating truths about the nonreality of reality TV. After reading Klosterman, I realized that his discoveries unlock one of the "secrets" of the fetishism strategy.

Klosterman has seen every episode of each of twelve seasons of *The Real World* at least three times. He believes that the secret of understanding the characters in RW is mindless repetition.[76] If you were to try to *learn* what the characters like or don't like, "that would make you a weirdo."[77] You would seem ridiculous. "This kind of knowledge is like a vivid dream you suddenly pull out of the cosmic ether, eight hours after waking up."[78] Long before the 2005 Austin, Texas, season, sometime between the RW1 in New York and RW3 in San Francisco, Klosterman had already discovered the essence of reality TV. Here are some of the things that Klosterman learned about the nature of reality in reality TV from his repetitive watching of RW. The original RW, in 1992, was supposed to be an unscripted accident where the show would be a seamless extension of reality. But then the relationship got reversed. "Theory was replaced by practice."[79] The late adolescents in the original RW were "malleable personalities" that were "edited into flat, twenty-something archetypes."[80] In turn, those archetypes became the normal way for people of Klosterman's generation to behave.

"Ironically," says Klosterman, "the reason RW flourished is because its telegenic humanoids became less complex with every passing season."[81] Future cast members figured this out. They better not be too complex. Only two types of personality mattered, and these "two archetypes would become cornerstones for late-twentieth-century youth: the educated automaton and the likable anti-intellectual."[82]

Many viewers of RW are younger than the participants. Perhaps they watch as a way to think about what it means to live on your own, away from your family? Perhaps they watch to learn what kind of personality you have to acquire to be able to get along with people of your own generation? But, finally, they are learning that becoming an automaton is the surest way make friends and influence people.

Klosterman concludes his meditation on "the questions that have haunted man since the beginning of civilization" by evaluating his own potential for being a RW character. Apparently, he is too multidimensional. Yet he fears he may have to become a real uni-person in his own real world because RW's "unipersonal approach will become so central to American life that I'll need a singular persona just to make conversation with whatever media-saturated robot I end up marrying."[83]

The Real World captures a special dimension of the fetishism strategy. There is a possibility that it even predicts the robotization of the human being; and if so, it materializes Marx's predictions about human beings becoming unreal and imaginary while, at the same time, imaginary things become real and tangible. Karl Marx never imagined this particular outcome of the commodification of the human being. But, as the philosopher who predicted "All our inventions and progress seem to result in endowing material forces with intellectual life and stultifying human life with a material force," it would not have surprised him.[84]

In the next chapter we will explore how human beings think and fantasize about the possibilities of humans being transformed into robots and robots becoming more and more human. In these thoughts and fantasies about the human-robot interchange, you will recognize reflections of Marx's prediction and also a few of the principles of the fetishism strategy.

NINE

ROBOTS AND HUMANS
SILICON AND CARBON

The prophet Jeremiah and his son, Ben Sira, decided to study The Book of Creation. At the end of three years, they created an artificial man. On its forehead was written EMET.*The man was so human it could speak. It said to Jeremiah and Ben Sira, "God created Adam and when God decided that Adam should die, He erased the first letter, Aleph, from the word EMET‡ and Adam died. I greatly desire you should do the same to me, and that you never again create an artificial man, so the world will never doubt that Man was created by God." It further said to them, "Change the letters on my head and erase the Aleph" And Jeremiah and Ben Sira obeyed. And the artificial man immediately turned into dust.

—From "The Alphabet of Ben Sira," a medieval biblical text.[1]

These days the artificial man created by Jeremiah and Ben Sira would be called a robot, or more accurately, an android—a robot in human form. The word *android* has been around for a few centuries, a lot longer than the word *robot*. During the eighteenth century, when the craze for mechanical human figures that could draw pictures, sing, and play musical instruments was at its height, *android* was defined as an "automaton with a human face."[2] Two centuries later, in 1920, the Czech playwright Karel Capek coined the word "robot" from the Czech "rabota" meaning servile worker or serf.[3] The factory workers in his play *RUR (Rossum's Universal Robots)* are satisfied with their servile roles, until they are reprogrammed to think for themselves.[4] They rise up against their oppressors, take over the factory, and kill all the humans, except for the one who was "still working with his hands."[5] After the uprising, the rebel leader declares, "The power of man has been annihilated. A new world is born. The time of the robots has come."[6] *RUR* was

---

* EMET means Truth.
‡ The word MET (EMET minus the Aleph) means Dead.

said to have started a trend for mistrusting and fearing robots, especially those with humanlike characteristics—androids.

Coming to the rescue of the much-maligned robots and also of the humans they might possibly destroy, Isaac Asimov wrote a series of short stories and novels that portray android robots as programmed with an ethical system designed to assure they would never harm humans. In his collection of short stories, *I, Robot*, Asimov constructs intricate ethical situations in which robots have to figure out how to behave within the complex constraints of the three basic rules of Asimov's robotic ethics. While Asimov is generally credited with the invention of the three rules, in his autobiography, *I, Asimov*, he readily acknowledges that John W. Campbell,[7] the editor of the science fiction review *Astounding Stories*, was the originator of that now-famous formulation.[8]

Asimov employs the three laws to heighten the illusion that his fictional androids are alive enough and intelligent enough to remember, decipher, and obey Campbell's ethical brain-teaser:

1. A robot may not injure a human being or, through inaction, allow a human being to come to harm.
2. A robot must obey the orders given it by human beings except where such orders would conflict with the First Law.
3. A robot must protect its own existence as long as such protection does not conflict with the First or Second Law.

These laws do not apply to the millions of robots now obediently at work assembling automobiles, packaging food products, stacking prepackaged foods, assisting doctors in long-distance surgery and minimally invasive surgery, and performing tasks that would be hazardous for human beings, such as; exploring the deepest of deep seas, studying whales close-up and mapping coral reefs, drilling far beneath the earth where humans have never been, rescuing miners trapped underground, dismantling and cleaning toxic waste, exploring the surface of Mars, doing repairwork on the outer surfaces of spacecraft, acting in warfare zones as minesweepers and booby-trap searchers. These robots do not pretend to be human. They are constructed, activated, and carefully controlled by humans and thus do not require robotic ethical laws.

The three laws apply only to androids, those robots that look and act as if they are flesh-and-blood human beings. Whether androids come into existence in science fiction or in a research laboratory or in a factory that designs, manufactures, and sells them to the public, they are "creatures" that reside in that uncertain realm between living and nonliving matter. Because these artificial humans are intentionally designed to simulate living matter and to behave as if they have human capacities, they cast a special light on the principles of the fetishism strategy.

As we encounter some of the humans who design robots, study them, write about them, or manufacture them, we will have ample occasion to look at some of the fantasies humans have about robots. Until now I have been illuminating the fetishism strategy by focusing on how the principles of that strategy emerge in the cultures that breed and nourish them, such as, personal catastrophes, footbinding, filmmaking, biography, psychoanalytic training, the production of commodities. Indirectly, but sometimes directly, I called attention to some of the fantasies that inspire people to employ the fetishism strategy.

Now, with the subject of robots, creatures that spring forth from fantasies, I am going to be approaching the fetishism strategy by way of a direct engagement with the personal fantasies that evoke it. Though each of the principles of the fetishism strategy are subtly different from one another, taken together they express a central, dominating theme. Human desires, intellectual powers, emotional forces, and creative energies are, by their very nature, enigmatic and unpredictable. When they begin to assert themselves, the fetishism strategy is enlisted to tame and subdue them. The fantasy is that if these elusive energies were to be set loose, they would run amok, take over the social order, and then demolish the very universe that God and Nature had created.

The necrophilic principle of the fetishism strategy is evoked by the fantasy that living, animate beings are unpredictable and potentially dangerous. They can only be contained by extinguishing their life energies or by transforming them into something dead or inanimate. When the full identity of the sexual object is alive, with all manner of threateningly, dangerously unpredictable vitalities, the desire that he or she arouses must be invested in an object that is knowable and predictable.

The fantasy of machines acquiring humanlike capacities very often evokes the counterfantasy that humans might be transformed into machines. Paraphrasing Karl Marx, we ask "if we endow material things (like androids) with intellectual and emotional life, does it imply that human beings will be deprived of their intellectual and emotional vitalities?" Rodney Brooks, author of *Flesh and Machines*, head of the Artificial Intelligence Lab at MIT, a foremost inventor of robots, owner of the iRobot factory that produces commercially viable robotic products, has answered this question with a prophecy befitting a modern-day Jeremiah. He predicts that when the robotic revolution catches up with the biotechnology revolution, "It will transform the technology not just of our own bodies, but also that of our machines. *Our machines will become much more like us, and we will become much more like our machines*" (*itals*. mine).[9]

Brook's provocative prophecy, which refers to all robots and not just androids, is already a fact of life, a down-to-earth reality. With the advent of cochlea implants, biometric chips, digitized vocal chords, pacemakers, artificial organs, prosthetic limbs, and chemicals that fine-tune brain functioning and emotions, we are witnessing a progressive infiltration of the mechanical into human flesh. At the very moment that we humans are incorporating machines into our bodies, engineers and technicians are constructing androids that are more and more like living, breathing humans. There is a blurring of

the borders between the artificial and the organic. In this sense, Brooks'
prophecy has merit. Nevertheless, the idea of machines becoming human and
humans becoming machines is also a fantasy originating in the mind of
Rodney Brooks, and eagerly adopted by many other humans.

Many scientists are not troubled by the machine-human interchange—for
a simple reason. Their clear-eyed, hard-nosed, engineering approach to
robotic research endows them with an engineering-style of thinking about
these issues. Their basic premise is that humans are machines to begin with.
So as humans become more like machines, the resulting changeover from the
carbon-based life of humans to the silicon-based life of robots would not be
all that drastic.

When humans think about robots, they usually are thinking about
androids and not those little helpers who act as surgical assistants, spacecraft
technicians, and mine sweepers. It is often difficult for us to distinguish
between androids as they exist in the actual world and those that exist in
science fiction fantasy. One thing is certain: androids, whether actual or fantastical, are creatures of human imagination—reflections of our fantasies.
Therefore, the questions that arise in connection with the robotic revolution
are multilayered. The top layer has to do with the territory of Rodney
Brooks, the solid, hard facts of how androids and other robots are engineered
and constructed. The next layer entails the potential impact of androids on
the lives of the human beings who might purchase and use them.

A third layer concerns the propensities of some human beings to de-animate
other human beings in order to transform them into machines that will
submit to their desires, wishes, and fantasies. Closely allied is the tendency for
some human beings to de-animate themselves so they will no longer be troubled by their desires, wishes, and fantasies. For example, Chuck Klosterman
has called our attention to those confused young people who model their
own identities on the telegenic humanoids on *The Real World* and then begin
to behave as if they were one or another RW character.

Once upon a time, in the middle of the twentieth century, some American
psychoanalysts decided that "As-If Character" should became a diagnostic
label. These psychoanalysts affixed the "As-If" label to grown men and
women who, because they had not developed a secure sense of self during
infancy and early childhood, managed to salvage some remnants of a human
identity by becoming adept at imitating the thoughts, feelings, and behaviors
of other human beings.[10] The diagnosis also referred to the way an As-If uses
other people as if they were machines. For the most part these "others" exist
for the As-If only insofar as they are willing to do the bidding of the As-If. In
a kind of Aladdin-genie arrangement, the Aladdin As-If summons up the
genie "other" whenever he needs some emotional supplies. After he gets them,
Aladdin dismisses the genie until next time he needs love, affection, cuddling,
feeding, sex, adoration, or immediate relief from painful emotions like anxiety and depression.[11] Depending on who he needs for which need, an As-If
can have one personality on Monday and another on Tuesday. Some of the

psychoanalysts who believed in the merit of the As-If diagnosis would say that it applied mainly to actors and actresses and other glamorous and charismatic people.

Nowadays the term is rarely used—officially. Most As-If characters don't seek psychotherapy or psychoanalysis. They are content as long as they can find people who are willing to supply them with what they need. Nevertheless, even though psychoanalysts have little therapeutic experience with a full-blown As-If, every now and then, you might still hear a psychoanalyst saying that one of her patients was behaving in an "As-If" manner. It has been suggested that the "As-If" refers to a wide spectrum of personality disorders. It is also widely agreed that adolescents, who are trying out different personality styles on their way to becoming adults, are prone to imitating others, and behaving in an As-If manner. When they finally settle on who or what they are, they settle into their own skins.

One analyst told me that she thought of the As-If as the new hysteric, suggesting that something in twentieth-century culture had been breeding and nourishing As-If forms of personality, in the same way that the nineteenth century bred hysterical personalities.[12] Perhaps Klosterman has the best formulation. The Real World, a kind of As-If culture, breeds and nourishes As-If personalities—telegenic humanoids for other potential humanoids to mimic. And since most of the characters chosen to be in this reality show are themselves putting off choosing a permanent adult personality, maybe some of the young people who imitate them are also going through a prolonged adolescence? Maybe their imitative behavior is just a step on the way to choosing a final shape? Or, maybe it is a permanent state of being? No doubt about it, though, androids who can never change their shape once they are constructed and set in motion are permanent As-If humans.

The dehumanization of human beings on Survivor, The Apprentice, Fear Factor, and other reality TV shows is only distantly related to the fabrication of androids in science fiction, robotic factories, and research laboratories. We cannot blame androids for the sorry fates of commodified, As-If humans. Nevertheless, for androids who are becoming more and more human and for humans who are becoming more and more like androids, the identical principles of the fetishism strategy come into play. Indeed, these As-If humans who model themselves on TV humanoids are probably the kinds of people who would prefer to have intimate relationships with cellphones, iPods, computers, and other robotic equipment than with living, breathing human beings who might threaten them with all the ambiguities and uncertainties of their all-too-human desires.

In 2001 eighteen eminent scientists and religious leaders, and one robot, were given an opportunity to express their opinions, fears, and fantasies about these machine-human, silicon-carbon interchanges in Dolly, the third segment of Beryl Korot and Steve Reich's Three Tales, a video-concert performance about three of the technological follies of the twentieth century.

The first tale, *Hindenberg*, is about the invention and explosion of the dirigible "Hindenberg," named after the German president who appointed Adolph Hitler as chancellor of Germany. The second, *Bikini*, is about the scientifically planned atomic bombing of the Bikini atoll, which entailed the evacuation of all the men, women, and children of Bikini from the ancient homeland they had inhabited for centuries. The stated objective of this inhumane experiment in advancing the cause of Humanity was to study the effects of nuclear radiation on the living and nonliving forms that were not evacuated from the atoll.

Dolly begins with the cloning of the sheep named Dolly and then goes beyond the controversial issue of cloning to a more general debate about the wisdom of machines becoming human and humans becoming machines. Rodney Brooks participated in the *Dolly* segment, as did Cynthia Breazeal, his colleague at the MIT Artificial Intelligence Lab, where she was developing sociable robots—robots that could learn how to interact with humans. She was accompanied by Kismet, her prototype sociable robot, whose amazing humanlike responses had already made it into a media star. It was indeed amazing to watch the adorable Kismet upstaging the erudite men and women who participated in *Dolly*.

Breazeal thinks of Kismet as her baby. She expects no miracles from it. She wishes only that it might achieve the social behaviors of an average human toddler.

The closing scene of *Three Tales* is an interaction between Breazeal and her baby.[13] As mommy Breazeal asks baby Kismet how its day is going, it makes sounds that sound as if they might be gurgles and coos, and nods its head and spreads its huge red lips apart into a facial expression that could be interpreted as a smile. Breazeal then asks her baby what it plans to do with its day. But Kismet doesn't respond. Perhaps it couldn't process the question? So its mother asks if it would like to play with its yellow toy. Kismet's lips close together and its head turns away from Breazeal and her yellow toy. Were those body movements signs of wanting some other toy? Or, expressions of having been misunderstood? The last image of *Three Tales* is of mommy Breazeal and baby Kismet gazing at each other— with love?

Kismet doesn't get held in his mother's arms, and even if it did, "What would her body feel like to it?" "What would it make of her odors, her warmth, her body movements?" And then what about those times when a baby might just want to be by itself and look around at its world without having to be interacting with human beings? A human infant often wants to do that. If the people in his environment understand that desire, they let him play alone with his toes and his fingers. They let him try to reach out with his hands to touch the mobile that hangs over his crib. But Kismet does not have such desires, nor fingers nor toes, nor hands nor feet. Most importantly, it has not been equipped with a repertoire of things to do when it is not interacting with a human being—except to "fall asleep."

No matter how smart Kismet becomes, no matter how adept it becomes at responding to its "mother's" queries and instructions, it is after all a mechanical thing of metal parts, computer-regulated motors, and wires.

Kismet's most prominent features are his two large eyes with two foveal-front vision cameras set up behind their pupils. Two wide-angle, peripheral vision cameras are located behind the space where a nose would be. It has microphones in its ears. There is a gyroscope in the middle of its head. Aside from this basic sensory equipment, Kismet has several motors that control its eyelids and eyebrows, which can go up and down and sideways; four motors that guide the thick gray metal plates to move synergistically with the shiny red lips that can spread apart and open and close and bend to one side or another; and floppy doglike ears that can go up and down and forward and backward and sideways. It has built-in actuators that allow it to move its neck around three different axes and its eyes to scan left to right and up and down.[14]

Breazeal has created an ingenious robot, which, because it is designed to behave as if it has human thoughts and feelings, is technically an android even though it has no body or arms or legs and has a face that is a grotesque imitation of a human infant's face. Much of what Breazeal predicts about Kismet's future and the quality of its relationship to her is pure fantasy; a Pygmalion-Galatea fantasy translated into mommy-baby language.

As Breazeal explains in her book *Designing Sociable Robots*, Kismet was designed to have three basic "drives." Yes, drives—those innate energies and inner vitalities that have always eluded the grasp of human intelligence. Are such enigmatic "living" faculties possible in machines made of metal parts and energized by motors and computers? After I became more familiar with the energy sources activating Kismet's sensory equipment and motor responses, I could appreciate that an android, even one with a barely human face, could be fabricated to have artificially created drives, and that furthermore these so-called drives would also make the robot appear to be alive—expecially if the human who interacts with it wants to believe it is alive. If Kismet is to come to life, the human who chooses to interact with it has to bring a fantasy of robotic aliveness to the situation.

It seems that humans have a hubris drive that inspires them with the fantasy that they are able to breathe life into inanimate objects. Humans also have an anthropomorphic drive that motivates their fantasies that certain objects in the world around them are endowed with human characteristics. The most efficient social robot has features built into it that encourage humans to fulfill their fantasies by personifying it and believing that it is responding to them like a human being. As Breazeal readily admits, human beings who confront Kismet for the first time have to be trained to appreciate the meanings of Kismet's facial expressions and head movements. Only then are they able to elicit humanlike behaviors in Kismet.

Therefore the first of Kismet's drives,[15] an essential for designing sociable robots, is a *social* drive, a drive that motivates the robot to want to be in the presence of people who will interact with it. When Kismet is deprived of human interaction, it falls into a state that Breazeal has labeled "loneliness." The state of loneliness then motivates Kismet to behave in ways that help it to establish face-to-face contact with humans. On the other hand, if a human moves too close to Kismet or positions herself too close to its eyes, Kismet will feel overwhelmed and activate movements that allow it to avoid face-to-face contact.

The second drive, obviously tied to the first, is a stimulation drive.[16] This drive can be gratified if a human engages the robot's attention with a colorful toy. If Kismet is not stimulated over a period of time, it gets "bored," and displays this boredom by moving its eyes and mouth and ears into a posture of "please stimulate me." If Kismet is given too much stimulation, that is, more stimulation than its perceptual processes can tolerate, it will bring its eyelids down over its eyes, or turn its head away from the source of stimulation. The human is thereby encouraged to challenge the robot to engage in new activities; but not too much, and not too many all at one time. Humans learn to gauge and regulate their responses in ways that activate the social qualities of Kismet. As Breazeal puts it, "an ongoing dance between robot and human"[17] maintains the robot's drives.

Coming to the rescue from all this drive stimulation is Kismet's third drive, fatigue.[18] Eventually, as time passes and the fatigue drive approaches the exhausted level, Kismet "goes to sleep," and all drives return to homeostasis. The fatigue drive allows Kismet to shut out the external environment and to terminate any further responses.

When Kismet is awake, it is open to receiving repeated stimulations from the environment and able to respond to them with "emotions" such as anger and frustration, or joy and fear, which are accompanied by changes in facial expression that motivate the caregiver to modify her behavior.[19] For example, when Kismet displays a sorrowful facial expression (ears down, eyelids half over the eyes, eyebrows and lips turned slightly downward), it evokes sympathy and attention from the caregiver. Kismet shows its boredom by moving its head back and forth, lifting its ears, turning them outward and opening its eyes, in order to motivate humans to supply it with external stimulation.

Unlike the android child, David, in the science fiction film *Artificial Intelligence*, or the vast majority of androids that are being constructed these days, baby Kismet has not been programmed in advance by a set of rules that require it to respond in specific ways to specific environmental stimuli. Like most of the other robots in Brooks' lab, many of which have been constructed in the shape of insects, Kismet is designed so it can learn how to act and react from its interactions with the environment and thereby acquire or learn new responses. Rather than having an intelligence that is pre-set and automatic, its intelligence emerges as it interacts. Technically, it is called "emergent Artificial Intelligence."

On the surface, at least, this is similar to the way human intelligence develops. We come into the world with certain response capabilities. But soon after birth we begin to learn through our interactions with our environment. Intelligence can only come into existence in an environment that encourages interaction with it. However, unlike the human baby who also learns by interacting with his environment, Kismet does not have a central controlling apparatus—a primed-to-respond cognitive system or brainlike, nervous system mechanisms to guide and regulate its sensory-motor behaviors. Instead of being constructed with this kind of top-down arrangement, Kismet was designed to have many independent but closely connected visual and auditory systems that would add up to enabling Kismet to seem as if it could think. In artificial intelligence (AI) language, this is sometimes referred to as a bottom-up form of activation and control.

Brooks believes that this sort of bottom-up, embodied, situated-in-the-world type of intelligence will eventually bring robotic intelligence up to par with human intelligence.[20] Nevertheless, even he can appreciate the considerable limitations of Kismet's conversational style. "What Kismet cannot do is actually understand what is said to it. Nor can it say anything meaningful."[21]

For Breazeal, the ultimate, grand challenge of robotic life is the construction of "*anima machina.*"[22] This is a fantasy, an extension of Breazeal's Pygmalion-Galatea fantasy of bringing inanimate substances to life. Even the hard-nosed Brooks, who appreciates the limitations of Kismet and understands full well the provocative nature of his statement about machines becoming human and carbon-based human DNA "machines" that can one day cross the border into becoming silicon machines, sometimes succumbs to his own more elaborate Pygmalion fantasy of "living, breathing robots."[23]

Merely to begin to meet this challenge of imbuing robots with life energies, robot scientists would have to be able to construct an android that can manage its own daily physical existence without the assistance of humans. The android would have to have a synthetic nervous system that could "breathe the life" into the machine that is it. The android would have to have the ability to carry its own energy source wherever it goes and the ability to replenish this energy over time. Basically it would have to have access to batteries or electrical plugs and understand how to connect itself up with these sources of energy. To be entitled to the name "android," a robot would have to be more than a head, or a head and arms. It would have to be bipedal and capable of walking about in the world.

During the years that Brooks and Breazeal were working diligently to breathe real life into their mechanical robotic creations, other robot scientists had already taken a more practical approach to robotic intelligence. If they had any fantasies about breathing life into the machines they constructed, they did not let it interfere with their engineering ingenuities.

Within two decades, Japan, which had been losing out to the United States in the computer business, became Land of the Robots. After twelve years of experimentation by thirty dedicated research engineers, and many millions of dollars, and three preliminary prototypes, the Honda Motor company succeeded in building the first bipedal robot.[24] In 1993, they produced P1, the first prototype. Three years later, at a cost of $105 million more, they produced P2, which could walk like a human and "even climb up and down stairs."[25] P3, which arrived on the scene a year later, could also climb stairs and, in addition, could walk at the same speed as a human, kneel down and then stand up straight. When jostled it could regain its balance.[26]

And then in 2001, the bipedal android the world had been waiting for was introduced. It was given the name Asimo. Many people assumed Asimo had been named for Issac Asimov. However, Asimo, a Japanese android, was both the acronymn for Advanced Step in Innovative Mobility, and also the combination of *asi*, the Japanese word for feet, plus *mo*, the first two letters of the word for move. Asimo has feet that move.[27]

Unlike its predecessors, Asimo had been designed with interactive capacities. It could understand facial expressions and gestures and obey spoken orders. If somebody said, "Follow me," it would do so. If someone asked it to look for something, it would do so and also find it. It knew the names that went with different faces and could even go online to retrieve news and other information like the weather forecast.[28]

It will be quite some time before Asimo earns back what it cost Honda to invent and construct it. However, by 2004, there were thirty Asimos in the real world handling real jobs of various sorts. For the nifty price of $175,500, other industrial companies could lease an Asimo for a year. IBM, for example, rented an Asimo to act as an obedient and very prestigious high-tech receptionist.[29]

Sony, stimulated by Honda's successes, didn't lag far behind its mightiest competitor. Sony focused on money-making robots that could serve as companions in the home. One of their star robotic engineers, Toshida Doi, had once worked with Brooks at MIT. Said Doi of Brooks' emergent AI philosophy, "Brooks was too minimalist."[30] As a result there were limits on the possible practical applications of his emergent AI research methodology. Soon after breaking out of the Brooksian mold, Doi struck out on his own to create a recreational household pet—his famous robotic dog, Aibo [31] which means "friend" in Japanese. Doi, whose robotic ideals are different from those of Brooks, believes in programming robots from the top down and making sure their responses are well-controlled, so that they can appeal to the humans who will buy them and make them a part of their household. Although he designs his robots to behave in a "lifelike" manner, he is not interested in breathing actual life into his machines. He speaks of his creations as works of art. What his fantasies are about the robots he creates, he does not say. But I imagine they have something to do with "The Dreams that Money Can Buy."

By 1999 Sony was marketing Doi's robotic dog all over the world and raking in big bucks. In 2003, the Aibo upgrade, black pearl Aibo, appeared on the market. This entertaining robot dog could turn on CD's, collect e-mails, and act as a watchdog or an assistant who reminded its master of his daily work schedule. Sony sold hundreds of thousands within weeks.[32] When Doi, who by then had become president of Sony's Entertainment Robot Company, expressed a wish to build an android that could be an entertaining home companion, he received Sony's unqualified blessing and all the funding he requested. Near the end of 2003, Sony introduced Doi's tiny two-foot-tall Qrio, who could do all the things the four and half-foot Asimo did, such as interact with humans and hold conversations. But, Qrio could also move its arms and legs to the beat of music and throw a tiny football.[33] Despite its tiny dimensions, Qrio was more than an entertaining toy. Technically it could be considered an android. However, like Asimo, Kismet, and the vast majority of other As-If human robots, Qrio does not have a human face and does not look like any of the human-looking androids that we are used to seeing in science-fiction films.

NEC invented Pa Pe Ro, Partner Personal Robot, a home companion that was designed to seek out interaction with humans. It has a tiny, brightly colored body, an adorable chubby face with huge eyes that can light up. It dances, tells time, can switch on the TV, and go online to pick up and forward messages. If Pa Pe Ro is treated with affection it will be gentle and helpful. A harsh tone of voice will make it grumpy and lazy. It recognizes 50,000 Japanese words and can speak over 3,000 phrases.[34] But it does not look like a human being.

Waseda has designed a "converbot" named Robita, which is capable of carrying on a conversation at a cocktail party.[35] Robita, who is nearly human-looking, not only speaks, but can listen, understand what is said to it, and respond appropriately—in these respects behaving more intelligently than some humans do at cocktail parties.

At the 2005 Prototype Robot Exposition, Osaka University introduced Repliee Q1, a pretty, charming, well-dressed gynocoid with humanlike silicon skin who could flutter her eyelids, blink, speak, and even appear to breathe because of the subtle rising and falling of her breast.[36] Repliee looked exactly like a real-life human being. But people responded to this exact replication of humanlike qualities with an eerie feeling of being in the presence of the uncanny—something unfriendly and inhuman.[37]

The fantasy that robots can be equipped with human hearts, lungs, brains, stomachs, gall bladders, intestines, livers, and sexual organs was given expression in the film *Bicentennial Man*, where the android, Andrew (whose metal body and face resembled a human's right from the beginning), taught himself how to design replicas of these organs and figure out how to transplant them into his own body. Thus Andrew, the android, with the assistance of a flesh-and-blood human scientist accomplice, breathed life into himself.

No matter how close roboticists come to replicating human responses in androids, most of them admit that it will be quite some time before androids will be ready to take their place in the home. As of 2006, an insurmountable obstacle to building self-sufficient humanoid robots is their inability to produce their own energy. Asimo, for example, clever and charming as it is, runs out of battery power in 10 minutes.[38] It is perfectly fine as a receptionist who sits at a desk all day long, probably because that desk or the wall behind it is outfitted with an electric outlet that Asimo can be plugged into.

While they don't exactly believe that they will be able to breathe life into robots, some Pygmalions of the robotic industry do have fantasies about endowing robots with "As-If" lifelike capacities. They predict that they might eventually be able to program androids with the capacities to understand and implement instructions on how to repair and build themselves. For instance, androids could be shown android-building websites and learn how to read and implement these instructions. They might be able to go online to check out android repair sites. They might even learn to check out each other's bodily equipment and mend each other.[39]

In a joking mood, one roboticist suggested that androids be programmed to obey a variant of Asimov's three basic rules: [40]

1. A robot must protect its existence at all costs.
2. A robot must obtain and maintain access to a power source.
3. A robot must continually search for better power sources.

Journalists familiar with movies such as *I, Robot* and *Bicentennial Man*, in which the android is able to recite or otherwise demonstrate its knowledge of Asimov's three laws, often ask whether actual robots are endowed with a capacity to obey these laws. Rodney Brooks, in one of his less fantastical moods, says that "The simple answer is that they are not. And the reason is not that they are built to be malicious, but rather that we do not know how to build robots that are perceptive enough and smart enough to obey these three laws."[41]

As Brooks, Breazeal, and other emergent artifical intelligence researchers interact with researchers in artificial life, so-called ALife, they are hoping to incorporate lifelike evolutionary processes into the construction of their robots. Like many robot engineers, they are interested in what ALife research might contribute to the construction of robots, who thus far remain fixed into whatever form they were originally created. Kismet will always be a head with large movable eyes and ears and mouth. Perhaps its descendants will one day acquire a movable body with movable arms and legs. Breazeal's *anima machina* is a fantasy, but a fantasy that reaches out to the scientific world for verification and instrumentation.

A document sent to me by Breazeal's post-Kismet research team, the Robotic Life Group, led me to conjecture that they are considering how they might bring something resembling a life process into their future construction of robots.

The document refers to this process as autopoiesis, which means literally "self-production," from the Greek *auto* for self and *poiesis* for creation. The Chilean biologists Francisco Varela and Humberto Maturana are credited with the introduction of the term in 1973.[42]

According to Varela and Maturana, "An autopoietic machine is a machine organized (defined as a unity) as a network of processes of production (transformation and destruction) of components which (i) through their interactions and transformations continuously regenerate and realize the network of processes (relations) that produced them; and (ii) constitute it (the machine) as a concrete unity in space in which they (the components) exist by specifying the topological domain of its realization as such a network."[43]

One of the factors that motivated Varela and Maturana to apply autopoiesis to self-production in machines was their understanding of the functioning of the biological cell. The eukaryotic cell, for example, is made of various biochemical components such as nucleic acids and proteins and is organized into structures such as cell nucleus, organelles of various kinds, a cell membrane, and a cytoskeleton. These structures, *based on an external flow of molecultes and energy*, produce the components of the organized structure that gives rise to these components.[44] An autopoietic system can be contrasted with an allopoietic system (such as a car factory), which uses components (raw materials) to produce an organized structure (a car) which is something other than itself.

The key phrase in this autopoietic fantasy is "based on an external flow of molecules and energy." For without that flow of external supplies to "feed" a physical structure, that structure, no matter how well-organized, will not be able to produce the components that maintain the structure. And, vice-versa, if the structure cannot be maintained, it will be unable to produce the components. The automatic endlessly flowing circle of continuous creation cannot function without an external supply of "food," or "energy." Although the system is potentially internally autopoietic, insofar as it is dependent on external supplies it is still allopoietic. Perhaps one day, in the distant future, the energy sources on which robots depend might be more organically alive than the batteries, electrical switches, and computer programs that now keep them energized. But they would still be somewhat dependent on their environment for some kind of "nourishment."

Every now and then we are told about a possibility for making robots self-sufficient. One idea is to provide a robot with muscle fibers that can double as fuel cells. The robotic muscles would behave just like real muscles and power themselves instead of relying on batteries or electrical outlets. But even though these muscles have been created in the laboratory, no one has yet figured out how to introduce them into the body of a robot. Furthermore, these muscles still require fuel like ethanol or alcohol to get them going, and another unsolved problem is how to control the amount of fuel that goes into the muscles. People have a lot of interesting ideas about how to make robots self sufficient, but the practical problems of how to put these ideas into action are always put off to the future.

Therefore, our most serious immediate problem is not that robots will replace humans. It will be a long, long time before humans might be replaced by intelligent robots—which, at this point, even though they can do the tango, play a trombone, answer e-mails, drive a truck, and explore the deep-blue sea, still have the intellectual capacities of an infant or young child. Even those that play chess and beat human competitors must be programmed by very smart humans.

From my point of view, as a psychologist and psychoanalyst, the most difficult moral and ethical dilemmas concern the many ways in which humans are trying to develop the technology that would enable humans to become more like machines. As Natasha Vita-More, the founder and director of the Extropy Institute, describes how this could happen, her ideas sound very much like a bizarre conglomeration of all five principles of the fetishism strategy, with the necrophilic principle leading the pack. She proposes that the human body could be fused with machines by incorporating the metal- and silicon-based components that have been developed in the robotic and electronic technologies.[45]

To justify and rationalize her quirky proposal, Vita-More, whose surname has a fetching affinity to the philosophy underlying her Entropy Institute, introduces it by reciting all the usually cited benefits to the blind, the deaf, the mute, the paraplegic, the heart attack victims, the elderly, the mentally disabled, as well as to the nondisabled who have a full mouth of false teeth at seventy, who wear eyeglasses, who boast breast implants, who have faces enhanced by surgery, and skin made wrinkle-free and luminously youthful by deep chemical peels. But Vita-More's proposal goes far beyond these picayune, one-by-one enhancements of the human body.

> What I am proposing is to design a full body prototype that functions like a human body but is not 100 percent biological. Rather it is a whole body prosthetic that acts either as a spare body or an alternative body. This body "Primo" would house the brain and whatever organs and essential parts [that] would not be replaced. The other parts would be prosthetic, synthetic models working together; forming a system that acts to transport us just like our human body does today.[46]

When asked about the practicalities of a whole body prosthesis Vita-More again falls back on already existing robotic prostheses that turn out to look better and function better than the natural biological part. Such artificial bodies would be composed of "robotic computerized microchips, nanorobots, artificial intelligence and cosmetics."[47] She believes that after people see the advantages of something that can make life easier and better for them, they will want it. Most people want to live rather than die. If most of their body is no longer functioning properly, "I think most people will opt for Primo."[48]

Primo's simulation of flesh-and-blood life is the consummate illustration of "erogenous color drawing a mask on the skin." In Primo, inanimate parts masquerade as animate life. But the tint of erotic color masks what could turn out to be a deadly practice. When we think about the consequences of humans turning in their malfunctioning but still living, carbon-based body parts for silicon-based robotic body parts, we should remind ourselves of the necrophilic principle.

The necrophilic principle of the fetishism strategy is evoked by the fantasy that living, animate beings are potentially dangerous. Therefore, animate flesh-and-blood creatures should be controlled by extinguishing their life energies altogether or, less drastically, by transforming these creatures into something resembling life—in the instance of Primo, silicon-based life.

Even Brooks, an ardent spokesman for silicon-based robotic technology, is worried about the belief system of some technologists, known as transhumanism, or the extropianism of Vita-More's Extropy Institute

> Humans will go to great lengths to avoid an acceptance of death, of our personal mechanism grinding to a halt. So I am careful to try to separate the beliefs of extropians into those that are driven by ethnological imperatives and those that are driven by the fear of the unknown.
>
> We are a long way from being able to download ourselves into computers or robots.[49]

Silicon products can pretend to be human, but they do not share the personal, cultural, and historical processes that go into the creation of an actual human being. Introducing silicon-based life as a substitute for human experience is dangerous not only to individual human beings but to the entire human species.

The element closest to carbon and, to some extent, also showing its capacity to form multiple bonds, is silicon. This has led (mostly science-fiction authors) to speculate that, in other solar systems, silicon-based life forms have already developed. However, silicon, the only element situated in the same column (IV A) as carbon on the Periodic Chart of the Elements because of their extensive similarities, has one major difference. And, it is this difference that will make it impossible for silicon-based life to supplant carbon-based life. Silicon-based life cannot produce fantasies. And, it is the human fantasy life that transmits erotic vitality to the carbon-based human body. Without erotic vitality, there is only the steady march to nothingness—even with a fully functioning silicon body encased within a sensitized silicon skin, and filled up with fully functioning mechanical body parts including genital organs. Silicon-based "creatures" might be capable of sexual behaviors, perhaps even a kind of reproductive capacity achieved through a hook-up with a computer program. However, since they cannot fantasize, they are eternally deprived of erotic experience. These bodies would be consigned, for all eternity, to a deathlike form of aliveness.

Finally, in order to fully appreciate the crucial differences between the artificial intelligence of robots and the natural intelligence of humans, we have to examine the meaning of the word "artificial." Aside from the fact that artificial always implies something that is consciously fabricated to seem natural, artificial can have two distinct meanings. For example, there is "artificial" as in silk, paper, or plastic flowers, which have been fabricated to look like natural flowers, and perhaps even to look more lifelike than some real flowers that sometimes begin to droop and die within a day. Artificial flowers give an illusion of life, but they are not really what they look like. If we touch them we don't sense any life in them. When, however, we think about something like "artificial" light—a substitute for the natural force of sunlight—these electric bulbs, candles, gas-lights, and hurricane lamps do not look at all like sunlight, yet they give off the same effect as natural light and in that sense are more natural than artificial flowers.[50]

There are those purists who say that "artificial" should only be used in the first sense, to mean something illusory or merely apparent. They claim that robots are made up of mechanical processes that give the illusion of life. Therefore, they are only apparently alive. There are others, like Brooks, who would claim that although robots are fabricated artifacts constructed and controlled by human beings or computers designed by human beings, once they are set in motion they are capable of thought. Robots do have a real form of intelligence. Robotic intelligence has its own special vitalities and energies.

But we don't have to settle for one or the other stark alternative, artificial vs. natural. We do not have to set the human brain and nervous system against the computer or the robot. We don't have to think of natural intelligence as something carried on in the brain and artificial intelligence as something carried on by the computer. In other words, rather than yield to the fetishism strategy and deprive the artificial/natural dilemma of its vitality, we can keep the motion going and in the process learn some new things about the meaning of the term "intelligence." It is not how much AI can produce in terms of practical, tangible results but how much it can "illuminate" our understanding of the human mind.

Nearly two decades ago, when the artificial intelligence debate was gathering steam, Robert Sokolowski, a professor of philosophy at the Catholic University of America, argued against establishing firm distinctions between artificial and natural intelligence. The approach of defining intelligence according to the medium in which it takes place puts our thinking about intelligence into a strait-jacket.[51]

> This approach is blunt and naïve because it neglects something that bridges natural and artificial intelligence: the written word. Artificial intelligence does not simply mimic the brain and nervous system; it transforms, codifies and manipulates written discourse. And natural intelligence is not just an organic activity that occurs in a functioning brain; it is also embodied in the words that are written on paper, inscribed in clay, painted on a billboard. *Writing comes between the brain and the computer* (*itals*. mine).[52]

If we are willing to acknowledge that writing is an activity that mediates between the brain and the computer (somewhat analogous to the way skin mediates between the inner body and the outer world), we will be in a position to open our minds to some alternative visions of human intelligence.

For me, the major problem with the way some robot engineers and scientists settle this dilemma of natural vs. artificial intelligence is that they do away entirely with the distinctions between human flesh and blood and robotic metal parts. In *Flesh and Machines*, Brooks has stated again and again in many different ways that the human body is nothing but a machine. For example: "The human body is a machine with billions and billions of parts, parts that are well ordered in the way they operate and interact. We are machines, as are our spouses, children and dogs."[53] He concludes by arguing that these machines are nothing but, "a big bag of skin full of biomolecules interacting according to describable and knowable rules."[54]

Robots and androids are not our enemies. Nor are they "creatures" who are turning out to be better and more humane than human beings, as they are so often depicted in science-fiction literature and films. It would be senseless and meaningless to do what Jeremiah and Ben Sira did. We need not destroy these marvelous creations of the human mind. But it is vitally important that we try to understand how silicon-based machines with their unique and peculiar forms of intelligence might enlighten us about human intelligence and the fantasies that emerge from our carbon-based human minds.

Essentially, I am agreeing with Sokolowski's view that we put ourselves in an intellectual strait-jacket when we pose firm and absolute boundaries between the natural intelligence of humans and the artificial intelligence of computers and computerized robots. It is true that an understanding of the intelligence of computers can teach us important new things about human intelligence. Moreover, I am particularly impressed with his highly original sentiment that we humans and our computers share a common affinity for the written word. *Writing comes between the brain and the computer.*

Nevertheless, I am not willing to do away with *all* distinctions between silicon-based creatures like robots and androids and carbon-based creatures like us. One of these crucial distinctions, which I called attention to earlier, is the fantasy life of humans. "Silicon-based life cannot produce fantasies The human fantasy life transmits erotic vitality to the carbon-based body." And this body is not just "a bag of skin," as Brooks would have it. The skin twists around like a Mobius strip to include the brain and nervous system. The skin suffuses the brain and the nervous system with erotic vitality. Analogously, when a human being writes, her words are imbued with erotic vitality, even when she is writing about death and the deathlike grip of the fetishism strategy.

Primo[*] Levi concluded *The Periodic Table*, a series of short stories on twenty one of the elements that appear on the Periodic Chart of the Elements, with an extended reverie on carbon. Essentially he made up little tales about the possible origins of carbon-based life. In doing so, he inadvertently created a powerful argument for maintaining some distinctions between silicon-based "creatures" and carbon-based "creatures" Robots, the creations of humans, and humans, the creations of Nature, have many affinities. But they are not and can never be interchangeable.

Levi, the chemist who might have been struck mute by his experiences as a starved and abused prisoner in Auschwitz, instead decided to write about them. His meditation "Carbon" is not directly about those holocaust

---

[*] It is coincidental and ironic that Levi's first name, Primo, and the name of Vita-More's full body transplant, "Primo," are the same. Everything else about them is different. The writer is emblematic of carbon-based life. The body transplant is emblematic of silicon-based life.

experiences, but it is about the crucial importance of writing as a way of preserving and salvaging the human spirit. It is also, at the same time, a parable
about the way that carbon comes to make up the cells of the human body.

> It [Carbon] is again among us, in a glass of milk. . . . It is swallowed; and since
> every living structure harbors a savage distrust toward every contribution of
> any material of living origin, the chain is meticulously broken apart and the
> fragments, one by one, are accepted or rejected. One, the one that concerns
> us, crosses the intestinal threshold and enters the bloodstream; it migrates,
> knocks at the door of a nerve cell, enters, and supplants the carbon which was
> part of it. This cell belongs to a brain, and it is my brain, the brain of the *me*
> who is writing; and the cell in question, and within it the atom in question, is
> in charge of my writing, in a gigantic miniscule game which nobody has yet
> described. It is that which at this instant, issuing out of a labyrinthine tangle of
> yeses and nos, makes my hand run along a certain path on the paper, mark it
> with these volutes that are signs: a double snap, up and down, between two
> levels of energy guides this hand of mine to impress on the paper this dot,
> here, this one.[55]

And so with that dot (.), *The Periodic Table* ends.

Levi's intricately woven meditation on carbon is a vivid illustration of the
incommensurability of human intelligence with the intelligence of creatures
like robots; not because the human's intelligence is natural and the robot's is
artificial, but because, ultimately, carbon-based intelligence can accomplish
feats of writing that are beyond the most extraordinary perfections of a silicon-
based intelligence.

Although Levi is ostensibly writing a scientific description of the tangled
and convoluted journey of a chemical element as it moves through the body,
the essential humanity of his words is a testimony to the human spirit, "that
flamelike spirit which delights in defying order and neatness and logic."[56]
Levi's "Carbon," like most serious writing, is a model of the "delicate and
humane process" that Strachey attributed to biography.[57] And, as Edel,
despite his own partiality for biography, might have agreed, Levi's tale
"partakes of all the ambiguities and contradictions of life itself" and is a
record in words of something that is "mercurial and as flowing, as compact
of temperament and as the human spirit itself."[58] Finally, therefore, Levi's
"Carbon" is tantamount to an overcoming of the fetishism strategy.

Levi illuminates the life energies that reside in what might otherwise be
thought of as an inanimate substance. His words bridge the borders that
separate animate from inanimate. Levi does not proclaim that machines can
become human; or that humans can be transformed into machines. By demonstrating the differences between carbon-based life and silicon-based-life, he
counters Marx's prediction that if "we endow material forces with intellectual
life," we must necessarily "stultify human life with a material force."[59]

Silicon and carbon are cousins and share some fundamental characteristics.
But, in the end, there are also crucial differences between them. Silicon does
not journey through the bloodstream and knock at the door of a nerve cell,

enter and supplant the element in that cell. And even if "someday" silicon could be transplanted into a carbon-based human cell, that cell though it migrated to a transplanted silicon brain could not fire the imagination of a writer. It could never be part of "the brain of the *me* who is writing."

In the next and final chapter, we will be confronting the vast challenges of retaining our essential humanity in a technology-driven culture—a culture that breeds and nourishes all varieties of the fetishism strategy. Despite their basic differences, silicon, which belongs essentially to the world of technology and carbon, which belongs to the world of humans and other natural entities, nevertheless can, because of their similarities, eventually become amicable partners in the progress of human existence. For example, in the past few decades, I have come to depend on the neatness and orderliness that my computer imparts to my disorderly thoughts. Even though the hand that wrote the words of this chapter defied logic and neatness, my computer makes it all come out looking pure. But, at the same time, the ambiguities and contradictions that haunt my words defy purity. So let us see what mischief the partners can come up with. The brain who is the *me* who is writing has decided to let Levi have the last words. Therefore I will conclude "Robots and Humans," which I have transferred to my silicon-based computer from its original location on the sheaf of carbon-based papers that were written on with my carbon pencil, by impressing on the virtual paper before my eyes, "this dot, here, this one."

T E N

Cultures of Fetishism

The twenty-first century ushered in a technology-driven world where machines, not only supercomputers, but also those on the small-scale level of personal computers and iPods and cell-phones and TV sets, have begun to assume the place of human relationships.

One of the major differences between the earlier cultural activities that evoked the fetishism strategy and the later cultures of the twenty-first century, is the way human beings increasingly are substituting controllable, technological proficiencies for the uncontrollable "insufficiencies" of human biology. Something elemental about the human being is being tamed, subdued, distorted beyond all recognition. The repetitive monologues offered by machines are replacing the variegated dialogues of human beings.

Stephen Holden's review of the film *In My Skin*, which I called attention to in chapter four, "The Body of a Woman," bears repeating here.[1] Although Holden focuses exclusively on the skin-cutting that was the central motif of the film, his ideas could be applied to any variety of writing on the skin. He emphasized that skin-cutting, the compulsion to cut into one's own flesh, represented "a desperate attempt to re-establish a connection with the body that has been lost."[2] He also identified the culture that breeds and nurtures this disconnection with the physical body. "In a sterile corporate culture where human appetites are quantified, tamed and manipulated by market research and where people have been rewarded for functioning like automatons, it implies, uncontrollable tics are really the anxious protesting twitches of an oppressed animal spirit."[3]

Many of us, who on the surface seem to be happily and unquestioningly adapting to the technologies that are offered to us, are responding, unconsciously, with the tremblings of an animal possessed by a torment it does not comprehend. Writing on the skin is one way of expressing this torment. Writing on the skin can also be a sign of the protest and rebellion of the oppressed animal.

It would be all too easy to blame the machines, which, of course, have no needs, desires, or motives for transforming humans into a species just like themselves. Humans are inventing the machines and humans are here to receive them and also to determine the manner in which they will be received. In order to understand the transformations of human existence that are taking place at the beginning of the twenty first century, we have to examine the susceptibilities of human beings. Why are human beings so vulnerable to the allure of the machine? What makes us so accepting of dehumanization, alienation, and commodification? Have we begun to feel more comfortable in a monologue with a machine that simply mirrors whatever we need and desire, than in a relationship that requires the uncertain and ambiguous give-and-take of human dialogue?

The "sterile corporate culture," which manipulates human desires and appetites through its duplicitous marketing practices, is a variation of the commodity fetishism that alienates human beings from other human beings and from themselves. Corporate culture, these days personified by the omnipresence of Donald Trump and his TV show *The Apprentice*, is a powerful force not only on reality TV but in real, everyday life.

When interviewed by *The New York Times* about what kinds of new technologies they would wish to see invented, most people reported feeling overwhelmed by the number of gadgets they had to lug around with them on a daily basis. "I find myself toting two cellphones and a P.D.A. and a laptop and a Swiss Army Knife . . . and even with all these tools I find I am unable to make the kinds of connections I want at the times I want."[4] This frustrated human being, John Perry Barlow, a co-founder of the Electronic Frontier Foundation and former lyricist for the Grateful Dead, solves his problem by wishing for the invention of "the brain implant . . . Presumably that would be an ultimate interface between your nervous system and the larger accretive nervous system that you could switch on or off in different ways that would be constantly reconfigurable so that you wouldn't have to upgrade it by buying a new one every six months."[5]

Another frustrated interviewee, Donald Trump, echoed Barlow's wish for brain implants. "I would like a computer chip that I could attach to all the brains of my contractors so that they would know exactly what I wanted, when I wanted it and at what price I wanted it. This would save me a lot of time and a lot of yelling."[6]

If wishes like these could be granted, technically speaking, Barlow himself and Trump's contractors would be called cyborgs. Cyborgs are human beings that have had silicon-based machine parts introduced into their bodies, usually to enhance their own powers but sometimes to extend the powers of their master, who wants to make them more amenable to his wishes.

Kevin Warwick, a professor of cybernetics at the Universtity of Reading in England, made news when he became one of the world's first cyborgs by having an active computer chip implanted in his arm. "The computer in my building knew where I was at anytime, so my lab door opened for me, lights came on, and the computer welcomed me with a 'hello.' "[7]

Warwick, emboldened by the success of his first implant, attempted another experiment, which became the basis of his book *I, Cyborg*. Warwick had his nervous system linked to a computer. The computer and he sent signals to each other, back and forth. It gave him a kind of extra-sensory thought power. He could switch on lights. He "could manipulate a robotic hand directly from the neural signals" he emitted, and even feel how much force the arm was using.[8] Using his neural signals, Warwick could control technology on the other side of the world. He followed up with the "first direct nervous-system-to-nervous-system communication experiment."[9] Warwick could communicate with his wife (who also had electrodes inserted in her nervous system). When these implants were removed after three months, Warwick said that he and his wife felt "much closer, more intimate," than they had before they became a cyborg couple.[10]

The cultures that breed and nourish the fetishism strategy did not originate in the sterile corporate culture of the early-twenty-first century. They have been around for a long time. In the first chapter I called attention to Hal Foster's commentary on the fetishism strategy in seventeenth-century Dutch still-life, *Nature Morte*, Pronk paintings. He compared the Reaganomic culture of fundamentalism mixed with greed to the seventeenth-century Dutch religious and political structure that simultaneously encouraged the imperatives of moral restraint and economic expansion. The fetishism strategy displayed in the Pronk paintings were an expression of those inherently contradictory social imperatives. Foster observed: "Pronk still life was asked to represent these imperatives simultaneously—thus its negotiation between order and disorder, godliness and greed, a negotiation that helps to explain emotively conflicted tableaus such as a spilled chalice immaculately composed or a spoiled pie exquisitely glazed."[11]

When I described Foster's "The Art of Fetishism," I remarked that it reminded me of analogous trends in our contemporary Bushomics, where the interplay between spending and saving, luxury and frugality, acquisitiveness and asceticism is plainly evident. In chapter three, I also recalled Foster's ideas when I thought about the social contradictions of nineteenth-century Neo-Confucianism, with its oscillation between a moral restraint that was meant to eliminate desire, and a license for extravagant indulgences in sensual pleasures, especially food and sex. Nor should we forget footbinding, a writing on the skin that expressed the contradiction of keeping a woman bound to the hearth, while at the same time transforming her body into the very embodiment of lavish sensual pleasures. Nineteenth-century Neo-Confucianism, twenty first-century Bushomics, like twentieth-century Reaganomics and the economic acquisitiveness of the seventeenth-century Protestant Dutch government, encourage a moral climate that allows human beings to have it both ways: exquisite moral purity on the one hand and profligate economic indulgences for the already affluent, on the other.

Thus an entire culture can be pulled in two directions simultaneously. We can indulge in the moral scrupulosity of a pro-life, anti-abortion position, but also simultaneously be drawn to an anti–birth control platform that inadvertantly expresses cruelty toward the poor and misfortunate who end up contracting AIDS and giving birth to children who are likely to starve to death before they finally die of AIDS. This mingling of moral scrupulosity and cruelty was vividly displayed in Mel Gibson's blockbuster film *The Passion of The Christ*, where the blood and bloodied scraps of Christ's flogged skin were sopped up by a cloth given to his mother by a compassionate onlooker, who very likely assuaged her voyeuristic guilt by her act of charity, as did the thousands of moviegoers who "wept their eyes out" after indulging themselves in two hours of gazing intently at the unspeakable sufferings of Jesus Christ.

Having it both ways is not only an expression of the fetishism strategy, it is the sine qua non of sexual fetishism. As Freud described in "Fetishism," the man knows that the woman does not have a penis. But with fetish in hand or in mind, he obliterates the genital differences that are so threatening to him. He reassures himself that the woman's genitals are identical to his. "Yes, the woman does have a penis." *Disavowal*, the psychological defense of having it both ways, is now thought to be one of our basic and primary defense mechanisms, prior to and more fundamental than repression, originating in the earliest years of childhood, at a time of life when the blurring between what "is" and what "is not" is characteristic.

The relationships between the fetishism strategy and the moral and ethical contradictions in most political and social structures are also fundamental. The contradictions have been there for centuries—and possibly for all of human history, ever since the first human societies came into existence. The fetishism strategy is intrinsic to the human mind. It is a powerful defense that can be evoked, whenever there is a need to exercise control over what is experienced as an enigmatic and uncontrollable force—a force of nature, a force of human creativity, a force of human vitality, a force of violence and aggression.

The fetishism strategy is also activated by fears of death and destruction. Unfortunately, when the fetishism strategy is enlisted to regulate and control aggression, violence, or destruction, it is likely to fail. The fetishism strategy is habituated to partnering death and following its lead. Disavowal, having it both ways, seems to be built into the fetishism strategy. Therefore, as the fetishism strategy attempts to regulate the full strength of potentially murderous impulses, it simultaneously gives some expression to these impulses to flog the skin, chew it up, cut into it, tear it apart, hack it to pieces, burn it to ashes. Although the fetishism strategy cannot always tame aggression and violence, an understanding of the principles of the fetishism strategy can be a "weapon" against the forces of destruction.

In the chapter "Writing on the Skin," I alluded to some of the biological underpinnings of the psychology of the fetishism strategy. Its fundamental inspiration derives from our distrust and fear of the uncontrollable vitalities of the human body. Studies of self-mutilation identify the physiological substrate for the psychological need to control, tame, and subdue anything or anyone that represents an uncontrollable and dangerous aliveness. The delicate-self-cutter imagines that menstruation is her enemy. If menstrual blood, tears, feces cannot be controlled, they might leak out to cover and demolish the world. Analogously, if sparks of creativity are not controlled or extinguished, they might burst forth and set the world afire.

Unknowingly, though not guilelessly, the "sterile corporate culture" plays on these elemental fears by developing marketing techniques that seduce consumers to purchase more commodities than they could possibly need. The psychoanalyst Paul Wachtel observed that most human beings "are aware that something is awry in the kind of consumerism their societies spawn. . . . What is less likely to be clearly perceived is that the ways members of our society organize their lives in pursuit of these continually escalating consumption standards are not always beneficial to their children."[12]

Wachtel describes how a life spent in pursuit of commodities is a life spent alienated from our own selves and from those we love. Parents who purchase more and more consumer goods must work more and more hours to afford them. They assuage the guilt and shame they feel about their greed for material goods by repeating the mantra, "I am doing this for my family."[13] "The irony is that these very choices, which deprive children of the things that really matter in their lives, are likely to lead these children to turn to material goods for comfort, to define their needs not in interpersonal or experiential terms but in terms of status and the right material objects."[14]

In all times and in all places, the greed for material objects has been an intrinsic aspect of the human experience. The material objects that humans have lusted after may have been beads and canoes, or jewels and furs, or palaces and mansions, or automobiles and yachts, or Pronk paintings and steel sculpture. But, now the greed is for objects that alienate us from human dialogue.

At the start of the twenty-first century, we find parents buying more elaborate and interconnected computers for their homes. In this way they can just stay home after they return from a day of work and still have a fairly full life. Their kids can have fun and enjoy themselves and keep in contact with their friends without ever having to leave the house other than to go to school—and maybe soon they can have computers that enable them to go to school at home. It is said that the computer will soon become the "heart" of the information age.[15] It will make us feel as warm and cozy as those old-fashioned fireplaces once did. In fact, Intel, in collaboration with Microsoft, has designed a teenage bedroom "where the sleek all-in-one PC has become part television tuner, part video game machine, part stereo jukebox, part DVD player, part photo archive."[16] In the same spirit of insulating human beings from irritating and potentially humiliating human interactions, more and more consumers are reaching out to the touch-screens that have been installed at the checkout counters of supermarkets, automated ordering stations at McDonalds, airline and train ticketing booths, and movie ticket pickup stations, to name just a few of the machines that now offer consumers the opportunity to avoid "frustrating, hostile or guilt-inducing interactions with service workers,"[17] and employers the opportunity to reap the profit benefits of the "robotization of large chunks of the service sector."[18]

I do not wish to imply that technology is some evil spirit intent on mangling and destroying the human spirit. As with the telephone and email and the railways and airplanes, technology can foster intimacy by bringing people closer to one another. In a global economy, in fact, without technology, the physical distances between people would be an impediment to communication. Within a modern household, technology, *used appropriately*, increases efficiency, and thereby liberates family members from everyday tasks like shopping for food and balancing checkbooks, giving them time to sit and talk, read to their kids, and enjoy leisure time. The problem is the way technology is often being abused. Human beings are using technology as a substitute for human intimacy. We could say that any activity that *substitutes* material objects for human communication and personal interaction is a symptom of the fetishism strategy. In this age of globalization, most societies are dominated by commodity fetishism. Material objects are being imbued with life, while the personal, human life is being stultified and deadened.

I have written several books on "the human dialogue," a dialogue that originates in the intimacies of the parent-child relationship. Therefore, I am particularly disturbed by the insidious ways that the fetishism strategy is reaching down from the adult world to infants, children, and adolescents. When parents permit the fetishism strategy to intrude on this dialogue, they are, without knowing it, depriving their children of the emotional vitalities that make them human. Paradoxically, but not surprisingly, the fetishism strategy feeds off the parental anxiety of wanting their children to have the best of everything and the most that technology offers.

For example, there is the Baby Einstein phenomenon. In the late nineties, as we approached the turn of the twenty-first century, there was a flurry of publicity describing research that showed how the earliest years of life were the most important for the child's brain development. In a nanosecond, before we could catch our breath, the baby media blitz took off, creating an extravagant devotion to certain material objects where, once upon a time, parent-child dialogues had sufficed. Parents were induced, if not seduced, into purchasing videotapes featuring voices, music, and accompanying visual effects that were designed to capture the attention of babies and toddlers. Instead of playing with mommy and daddy, babies and toddlers could listen to and watch their personal TV sets, playing the "Baby Einstein" series, which now includes, "Baby Shakespeare," "Baby Galileo," "Baby Newton," and the flashcards and puppets that go with them. And then there is "Right Brain Baby," "Genius Baby," "Mozart and Friends," "Bach and Friends," and discs with popular nursery rhymes in English, French, German, Hebrew, and Russian.

Only a Grinch would want to outlaw the Baby Einstein series. For example, there is the enchanting Baby Galileo, which features background music adapted for baby's ears from Beethoven, Chopin, Schubert, Strauss and Tchaikovsky, and dazzling motion pictures of the sun, the moon, colorful planets, whirling galaxies and shimmering stars set their constellations. This would have been quite enough for an impressive DVD. But, to make sure they touched all the bases, the producers put in the requisite politically correct, multi-ethnic children playing with some planet-shaped toys as well as a cartoon mommy-baby animal couple and a cartoon mouse that gobbles up a chunk of a cartoon moon. In the end, despite the high-minded musical and artistic effects, Baby Galileo is predominantly a hodge- podge of conventionality.

The problem, however, is not with the contents of any particular Baby Einstein but with the way it will be used by parents. The series was meant to encourage interactions between parent and child. However, in my experience, all-too-often Baby Einsteins are used to baby-sit the baby, who sits alone staring at the images on the TV screen while the parent emails friends, surfs the web, takes a nap, chats on the cell phone—and all without a twinge of guilt. The parent can rationalize that the baby is developing her brain and becoming a genius who will soon be able to identify the heavenly bodies and say, "moon," "planet," "constellation," and "galaxy" when she points her finger at the nighttime sky.

Within a few years, the flourishing market for these DVDS generated another fetish, baby computer equipment. My neighbor's two-year-old daughter has a special computer table with all the latest technology for infants and toddlers. In addition to the "Baby Einstein" and "Brainy Baby" series that she has been watching and listening to since she was ten months old, she now has a bunch of special video-games designed for toddlers, a dozen or so book-marked web sites, and a television remote control designed especially for her tiny fingers and rapidly growing brain.

Technology is reaching into the cradle, with specially designed mobile phones that can be programmed to soothe a wailing toddler. As Doreen Carjaval reported in *The New York Times*, "The target customers are children who may be incapable of a coherent telephone conversation but will cuddle with a portable phone to watch *Sesame Street's* Ernie deliver an ode to his chubby rubber ducky."[19]

Efforts to get parents to resist the baby media-marketing blitz by returning to the good old, tried and true human dialogue, meet with considerable resistance. Unfortunately, when parents are told that child development experts are advising against the purchase of these mechanical gadgets— "Children do best with maximum free play, maximum personal interaction, and maximum face-to-face time with their parents,"[20] or, "We're programmed as human beings to learn through interpersonal relations"[21]— many of them shrug off these words of wisdom with a bit of the day-to-day practical wisdoms that the marketers of brainy baby gadgets have programmed them with. Mothers and fathers explain their hesitancy to give up the quest for brainy babies, "You want to make sure you're doing everything you can for your child and you know everyone else uses Baby Einstein so you feel guilty if you don't."[22]

What parents may not realize is that so-called smart toys with programmed music and programmed stories do not make a child smarter. They may, in fact, interfere with the development of intelligence. Toys and play help children learn. But the play that is best for children is the kind that encourages them to use their imaginations. Dr. Kathleen Kiely Gouley of the New York University Child Study Center questioned the smartness of "smart" toys. "You want the child to engage with the world. If the toy does everything, if it sings and beeps and shows pictures, what does the child do?"[23]

If things continue this way, Rodney Brooks' prophecy about the robot-human interchange might come true. After a few more decades of the already escalating collaboration between the robotic and biotechnology revolutions, machines will have become more like humans and, more disastrously for the survival of the human dialogue, humans will be more like machines, or more like mere attachments of those machines.

One of the additional symptoms of living in a social order that breeds so many varieties of the fetishism strategy is a side effect of this increasing robo-tization. Some of us suffer from a paralysis of the will. We are unable to take action against the cultures of fetishism that are infiltrating our everyday lives. There are many reasons and motives, both conscious and unconscious, that make all of us want to preserve the deceptive comforts of the social order in which we live. The fetishism strategy robs us of creativity and freedom of choice, but it also makes us feel safe and normal.

We crave to be the same as, if not better than, everyone in our immediate social order. We want and desire, sometimes more than any freedom offered to us, to be considered normal—which means to be just like everyone else. Even after we open our eyes and are able to see the symptoms of the fetishism strat-egy all around us, it is still immensely difficult to choose to be different. For those sorts of changes might make us seem weird—even weirder than the sex-ual fetishist who cannot perform sexually without his stiletto. The fears of being different and out-of-step with our neighbors are sometimes much greater than the desire to liberate ourselves from the shackles of the fetishism strategy.

Psychoanalysts can also be victims of the fetishism strategy, very much like the run-of-the-mill corporate executive and like most ordinary mothers and fathers. When I discussed the training of psychoanalysts, I called attention to the several ways that the fetishism strategy had infiltrated the psychoanalytic enterprise. I pointed out that one of the major impediments to psychoana-lytic creativity was the need for certainty. In that context I turned to the poet John Keats for some words of understanding. To preserve psychoanalytic creativity, and to transmit the benefits of that creativity to her patients, a psychoanalyst must be in possession of *negative capability*.

When Keats formulated the concept of *negative capability* he was referring to a flexible mind and a certain manner of negotiating the ineffable complex-ities of life. He said that a person who "is capable of being in uncertainties, Mysteries, doubts, without any irritable reaching after fact and reason," eventually arrives at truth.[24] However, "a man who cannot feel that he has a personal identity unless he has made up his mind about everything . . . will never come at truth so long as he lives; because he is always trying at it."[25] Certainty might be said to be the motto of the fetishism strategy. Uncertainty and a tolerance for ambiguity keeps life alive and in motion. They stand in opposition to the fetishism strategy.

Primo Levi intuited some of the principles of psychoanalysis when he wrote short stories and essays about the subject he loved and knew best,

"Chemistry." Two decades had elapsed since my first readings of *The Periodic Table*, when Levi's writings came to mind as I was trying to understand the fundamental differences between the silicon-based life of robots and the carbon-based life of humans and other animals and plants. I concluded the last chapter on robots and humans with his words about carbon's intimate affiliation with the activity of writing.

Now, as I am writing this last chapter, some other words of Levi come to mind. This time they are about zinc. How satisfying for me, that what I believe to be crucial to psychoanalytic wisdom should be given such apt expression by a chemist who used his extensive knowledge of the elements on the Periodic Chart to enrich our understandings of the elemental forces in human nature. Levi's words on zinc substantiate my belief that the "aliveness" of psychoanalysis or, for that matter, of any cultural activity, is synonymous with the aliveness of the unavoidable impurities of a human existence.

Levi describes how zinc, when it is tainted with the merest impurity, immediately yields its essence to an acid.[26] Zinc behaves very differently when it is pure and untainted. When zinc is pure, it resists the attack of acid, warding it off with great tenacity and determination.[27]

> One could draw from this two conflicting philosophical conclusions: the praise of purity, which protects from evil like a coat of mail; the praise of impurity, which gives rise to changes, in other words, to life. . . . In order for the wheel to turn, for life to be lived, impurities are needed. . . . Dissension, diversity, the grain of salt and mustard are needed. Fascism does not want them, forbids them and that is why you're not a Fascist; it wants everybody to be the same, and you are not. But immaculate virtue does not exist either, or if it exists it is detestable.[28]

Have I been asking you to be pure? Do you feel the message of *Cultures of Fetishism* to be that you must resist every inclination to arm yourself against sadness and depression by shopping and more shopping? ***Stop*** shopping; ***stop*** enlisting the fetishism strategy every time you sense that you are about to dare a creative move; ***stop*** dressing up in stilettos and fetish fashions; ***stop*** buying computers, iPods, Blackberry notepads, and fancy up-to-date electronic equipment for yourself and your teenage children; ***resist*** the lure of those Baby Einstein CD's and cuddling mobile phones that you want to buy for your infants and toddlers. ***Toss*** them into the trash.

But, such demands for purity would be detestable, as authoritarian as the fascism of the fetishism strategy, whose primary aim is to capture the errant vitalities of the human body and mind, bring them under its jurisdiction and control—and if necessary, stamp out every sign of remaining vitality.

The way I see it, resistance does not have to take the form of a sterile purity, which would turn out to be more damaging to the human spirit than the impurities it is trying to ward off. The resistance to impetuous techno-logical progress, the resistance to consumerism, the resistance to the surplus labor "rush to the bottom" of commodity fetishism, the resistance to endow-ing machines with life and depriving humans of their vitalities, does not have to come from a purity of motives. In fact, this entire volume could be regarded as "A Plea for a Measure of Impurity."

An understanding of how the fetishism strategy infiltrates our daily lives can be a powerful weapon in the battle against soul-crippling, social con-formities. And, as I have frequently re-iterated, we have another ally to assist us in this battle: human dialogue. The human dialogue is the heartbeat of human existence. Through the gestures and exchanges of everyday life, the parent transmits to the child the emotional language of his species and eventually the verbal language and symbolic communications that enable the child to participate in human culture.

It is this basic *reciprocal* dialogue between an infant and his caregiver that truly brings a newborn into human existence. The basic dialogue is a language of gesture and action. The basic dialogue is crucial to the learning of love, of hate, of joy, of play, and, in the human being, the acquisition of symbolic language.

I had thought that I would conclude this book with a few more pages on the reciprocities of human dialogue. During that process, I planned to remind my readers to do what they can, whenever they can, to foster the human dialogue not only between themselves and their children, but also between themselves and the other significant (and even insignificant) people they encounter in the course of a day. However, when I read over the last few paragraphs, I realized that I had been on the verge of creating an apocalyptic narrative. Just like the film directors I had criticized in "The Body of a Woman" and "Writing on the Skin," I was attempting to resolve the vast human dilemmas I have been posing throughout *Cultures of Fetishism*, by taking recourse to the intimacies of mother-infant dialogue.

"Always watch out for the return to the embrace of Mother Nature, a device of the fetishism strategy designed to deny the traumas implicitly displayed in the film."[29] Our long and complicated journey through the traumas and devastations I have been describing would have ended in the milky simplicity of the mother-infant embrace. True, the human dialogue, with all its potential for goodness, begins in that embrace. But almost at once, that basic dialogue goes on to acquire around it an array of human emotions: joy and love, sensuality and sexuality, desire and longing, loss and depression, rage and hatred, violence and destruction.

If I were to have let these matters stand as they were, it would have been tantamount to succumbing to the fetishism strategy. Of course, I might simply have deleted or amended the offending "Mother-Infant" passages and no one would have been the wiser—except myself.

I decided to leave my fetishism aberration as it was and proceed to write a more challenging ending; one that would encompass the vital importance of human dialogue but also, at the same time, be commensurate with the complex psychological dilemmas I have been posing in this book. In fact, as

I stressed in my earlier discussions of the apocalyptic narratives in films:

> It would constitute a symptomatic narrowing of vision to focus exclusively on
> the violence . . . and thereby overlook the themes of intimacy and emotional
> transformation. There is a discordance, however, between the violence and sex-
> ual violence of the first half of the film(s) and the journey toward a mystical
> reunion in the second half. In order to animate the full text of the film and
> bring it into full focus it is essential to discern and interpret the discordance.
> To attempt to mask the trauma of loss, by counterposing an experience of
> grandiosity and elation is a fetishism strategy that enhances and perpetuates the
> repression of trauma—which then will always return, perhaps the next time in a
> more devastating form.[30]

To conclude with a lullaby on the significance of the mother-infant
dialogue could be an invitation for a repetition of the traumas. On the other
hand, to delete all evidence of the mother-infant dialogue would not solve
the problem, either. The resolution resides in an understanding of the
discordance between the trauma of loss and the embracing lullabies.

I have, on several occasions, verged on becoming a victim of the fetishism
strategy. Immediately preceding my imposturous memoir, A-Hsui's *"My
Beloved and Terrible Lotus,"* I predicted that I might look back upon the
words I had given A-Hsui and detect in them elements of the fetishism
strategy.[31] I questioned briefly then, and now I question even further and
more deeply, some of the assumptions that guided the writing of that chapter. There is, for example, a whisper of magical thinking that hovers over both
my wish to write this imposturous memoir and the way in which I wrote it.

The most obvious magical thinking has to do with my belief that I could
attenuate the virulence of A-Hsui's body mutilations by offering her sexual
pleasure. As I was writing those conciliatory scenes of erotic pleasure,
I already questioned them, wondering if I was employing these "gifts" to disguise and cover over the traumas suffered by A-Hsui? At this point, after having reviewed the manifestations of the fetishism strategy in several cultural
endeavors, I would have to conclude that I was being deceptive, but mainly
because I had been deceiving myself. I was deceived by my therapeutic zeal,
my overpowering wish to effect a cure; as if the obscuring of trauma by an
offering of pleasure could ever amount to an amelioration of mental suffering.

My greatest self-deception was my belief in the power of the written word.
After recognizing that I couldn't bear to make A-Hsui's "entire life a litany
of unspeakable sufferings," I turned my attention to the transformative
power of writing.[32] I said that writing was comparable to the remembrances,
dreams, fantasies, and wishes that emerge in the course of psychotherapy.
This magical thinking about the power of writing became the servant of my
therapeutic zeal—a cure of suffering through writing.

Later on, as I was trying to reconcile the carbon-based vitalities of human
life with the silicon-based energies of robots, I again brought in the subject
of writing. I cited Robert Sokolowski, a pioneer in the artificial intelligence

community who depicted writing as the link between natural human intelligence and the artificial intelligence of computers and other machines. Though I did not agree entirely with Sokolowski's resolution, it led me, nevertheless, to conclude "Robots and Humans" with Primo Levi's meditation on carbon. Levi describes how within the nerve cell in his brain an atom of carbon is in charge of his writing. "It is that which at this instant, issuing out of a labyrinthine tangle of yesses and nos, makes my hand run along a certain path on the paper, mark it with these volutes that are signs."[33]

My compelling and irresistible attraction to Levi's "volutes that are signs," my magical belief in the transformative power of writing, had been given expression in an earlier chapter, "Writing on the Skin," when I called attention to some words of Peter Greenaway's heroine Nagiko. At one point, shortly after the first fiery destruction takes her out of Japan and immediately preceding her search for a calligraphy lover who possesses the talent to write on her skin, Nagiko says, "Writing is an ordinary thing but how precious. If writing did not exist what terrible depressions we would have."[34] And I, carried away by my passionate longing to believe in the magical powers of writing, follow up Nagiko's prescription by recommending writing as a form of therapy that protects the writer from succumbing to depression and anxiety.

But here we come upon a crucial irony. Writing, an expression of human vitality, writing, a source of transformative energy, can also be an avoidance of the trauma of loss. Writing can serve as a disavowal of death. "Yes, he is dead," but, "No he is really still alive." Writing, then, is a most ingenious and convoluted method of having it both ways. Insofar as writing is a disavowal, it is, to that extent, a servant of the fetishism strategy. Perhaps if I just keep on writing, I will have the illusion that I am creating a better ending for this book. At the same time I may also be attempting to assure that this book never comes to an ending. The analogy I am making between ending a book and ending a life has not escaped me.

As I contemplated the double-faced imago of the writing enterprise, I was reminded of the way I expressed, and to some extent tentatively resolved, these dilemmas in "Archive Fever: Writing Lives:" As I said, the biographer stands at the abyss between life and death:

> Writing a biography is an enterprise fraught with the dangers and duplicities of fetishism. There is a susceptibility in the biographical impulse that makes it one of the more telling illustrations of the insidious manner in which material force may be employed to stultify human life. Desiring only to bring to life the flesh-and-blood essence of another human being, the biographer all unknowingly stands at the abyss between Life and Death, always haunted by the prospect of drowning in the fathoms of facts she amasses, always verging on crushing her subject under the weight of the archival detritus she has marshaled in her earnest efforts to be true-to-life.[35]

Two of the most illustrious early-twentieth-century writers seemed hell-bent on exposing the death instinct as it worked silently and prodigiously to sabotage the biographical impulse. Lytton Strachey said of biography: "These two fat volumes, with which it is our custom to commemorate the dead—who does not know them, with their ill-digested masses of material, their slipshod style, their tone of tedious panegyric, their lamentable lack of selection, of detachment, of design? They are as familiar as the *cortege* of the undertaker, and wear the same air of slow, funereal barbarism."[36]

And then, of course, there was his comrade-in-arms, Virginia Wolff, who knew exactly how to express the loveliness of Strachey's allegiance to life and also their shared contempt for biographers afflicted with archive fever. She tells us that the first duty of a "true" biographer "is to plod without looking to right or left, in the indelible footprints of truth, unenticed by flowers; regardless of shade, on and on, methodically till we fall plump into the grave and *finis* with a tombstone over our head."[37]

> The *cortege* of the undertaker,
> the slow, funereal barbarism,
> the falling plump into the grave
> with a tombstone over our head.[38]

Could all this dirge and dread be the monstrous outcome of a desire to bring a subject to life? What could possibly be so sinful about the desire to write a biography? Why does it summon forth images of death? And then, here am I, wanting to convince you about the crucial importance of the written word for expressing and preserving the human spirit, and instead haranguing on the impulse to murder vitality with words, words, words, and more words. What am I doing? Why do I seem to be arguing against my most cherished beliefs?

I am not a very good devil's advocate. Of course, I do believe and will always believe in the transformative power of writing. However, in every creative human undertaking there seems to be a struggle between an impulse to bring out the vitalities of the human spirit and a contrary impulse to squelch and destroy that spirit. Biography, a particularly susceptible genre of writing, has a form that brings out the nature and consequences of that struggle.

When I started to conclude this book with an image of the mother-infant embrace, I was trying to forget about the forces of destruction and aggression which had been so much a central theme of this book. The fetishism strategy is not entirely a force of evil or entirely a foremost enemy of human life. It also protects us from the full force of destruction. Though I have on several occasions discussed the fifth principle of the fetishism strategy "destruction-tinting itself in erotic colorations," I did not take full account of the subtle interactions between the erotic elements and the destruction it was disguising. The erotic is not just a duplicitous tint. It is also a counterforce that tames, limits, and regulates destruction. If it were not for that "tint," we would be faced with the grinning mask of death in all its horror.

The discordance in an apocalyptic narrative has to do with glorifying idealizing the mother-infant dialogue, the hymns to Mother Nature, as though such regressive fantasies could counteract the traumas of loss, violence, and destruction also represented in those narratives. The promise of eternal life and eternal goodness is being used as a way of avoiding confrontation with the traumas. In many religions, as in many ordinary human fantasies, the promise of perpetual erotic bliss in an afterlife in a land of milk and honey is promulgated as a solution to trauma—and, even more dangerously—as an excuse for encouraging violence and destruction in the name of the Holiness of some God or other.

This fantasy of the land of milk and honey that awaits us after death does not originate in the mind of an infant. It is the outcome of a wish that can originate at any juncture in a human life when there is some aching sense of disappointment and loss. When the infant becomes a child who must reckon with the humiliation that he is forever excluded from the passionate excitements that cement his mother and father into a bond of oneness, he looks back at "the time that was"—the heavenly days when he was cradled in a milky embrace with mother, and there was no father, or work, or friends, or shopping to come between them. He creates a fantasy of "the time that was" retroactively to console himself for the humiliations and losses in the time that is now. When faced with the inevitablity of a separation from mother, a young child often tries to create a fantasy of oneness.[39]

Then, later, during adolescence, when a child on the brink of adulthood experiences the sense of all that she is leaving behind, once again there is that look backward, but this time the longed-for past is experienced in conjunction with the conviction that it will never come again.[40] We call this bittersweet emotion, "nostalgia." The infancy years were pure and innocent. No matter how frightening or humiliating infancy might sometimes have been, we fantasize it as the glorious time.

The heartbreak and grief of the adolescent years are often difficult to bear. By arousing memories of a delicious and joyous infantile past, the disappointments of the present are mitigated.[41] The family rivalries and jealousies revived by the adolescent passions are screened out by "memories" of having been an infant or child who was perfect and absolutely adored. In a nostalgic mood it is always the romance of infancy that is revived; never the frustrations and defeats. The adult romancers would have it that "Heaven lay about us in our infancy," or that infancy was "The happy highways where I went/and cannot come again." "Time it was and what a time it was. It was a time of innocence. A time of confidence and hope." "Where have you gone Joe DiMaggio?" What has once been is gone. It cannot be brought back—except in those fantasies we call memories and in longing for the time that was. Nostalgia softens grief. It takes the sting out of the sense of loss.[42]

This universal wish to envision infancy as the golden time, the time of perfection and bliss, is also a device for avoiding the challenge of trying to understand and possibly reconcile the contradictions and conflicts between erotic discourses and the discourses of aggression and destruction. The everlastingly entangled relationships between these two basic forms of human experience—the erotic and the destructive—are difficult to articulate, nearly impossible to fully grasp. So, more often than not, the search for understanding the complex relationships between the erotic and the destructive is short-circuited by evoking the fantasy of a mystical reunion with Mother Nature.

I shall speak, just for a moment, of these inevitable everyday conflicts in the abstract language of Eros and Thanatos. Abstractly, there is always this doubt, this eternal and everlasting doubt: Is it because the death drive tints itself in erotic colors that we become susceptible to the deceptions of the fetishism strategy? Or, do our susceptibilities to the deceptions of the fetishism strategy arise from the fantasy of Eros holding Thanatos—the death drive,—in abeyance? This uncertainty has been present in every chapter. Moreover, this very uncertainty and ambiguity has sustained the movement of this book.

I turn once more to Karl Marx, who sustained the movement of his theories by writing too many words for any one human being to read and absorb in one lifetime—unless she were to devote that entire life to Marxist scholarship. Yet, the prophetic vitality of so many of those words and phrases are particularly germane to the conclusion of this book. Because a central focus of *Cultures of Fetishism* has been on the various ways that the fetishism strategy leads to an undermining of human vitality and creativity, I want to return to Marx's ideas on the repetition compulsion, where the past "weighs like an incubus on the present."[43]

Sometimes when I am wondering why the peoples of this Earth do not rebel against the conditions that dehumanize them and alienate them from themselves and those they love, I recall Engels' comment, "It really seems as if Hegel in his grave were acting as a World Spirit and directing history, ordaining most conscientiously that it should all be unrolled twice over, once as a great tragedy and once as a wretched farce."[44] When Marx, a year later, went on to expand on Engels' memory of Hegel's wisdom, he described how human beings, as they make every effort to create a form of human existence that does not yet exist, continually repeat the slogans and spirits of dead generations. Just as human beings appear to be engaged in a revolutionary transformation of themselves and their material surroundings, "they anxiously summon up the spirits of the past to their aid, borrowing from them names, rallying cries, costumes, in order to stage the new world historical dream in a time-honored disguise and borrowed speech."[45]

As I re-read these words, for possibly the hundreth time, I saw how they relate to the principles of the fetishism strategy. It is safer to stick to what is known and certain, even if it means to suffer and re-suffer the traumas of the past, rather than attempt to create something new and uncertain, with all its tempting ambiguities and challenging possibilities. Creativity is a danger. "Where there is a spark, there may develop a fire. Extinguish it before it is too late."[46]

Where does hope lie? With so much weighing against the possibilities of altering the human condition, when so many cultural enterprises are vulnerable to the fetishism strategy, what might we do?

I find myself drawn once more to the biographers. I return to the conclusion of Leon Edel's elucidation of Lytton Strachey's tribute to biography as "the most delicate and humane of all the branches of the art of writing."[47] Because biography is a delicate and humane process, "it partakes of all the ambiguities and uncertainties of life itself. A biography is a record in words of *something that is mercurial and flowing, as compact of temperament and emotion as the human spirit itself.* The biographer must be neat and orderly and logical in describing this *flamelike human spirit which delights in defying order and neatness and logic.*"[48]

As I said earlier in this chapter, we might think of *Cultures of Fetishism* as "A Plea for a Measure of Impurity." Perhaps a defiance of order and neatness and logic keeps alive this flamelike human spirit? Perhaps, then, we should not be so frightened of this flamelike spirit that delights in defying law and order? Perhaps we might take the risk of defying the order of the world? Perhaps we might take the risk of being different from our friends and neighbors and begin to challenge the order and neatness of our own lives? Perhaps we should not be so afraid of creating something new? At the very least, we should be alert to the danger of repeating the traumas of the past each time we venture forth to create something different and new.

In order to create something new, we need to be willing to tolerate staying in "the knot of not-knowing."[49] We want to be friendly to uncertainty and ambiguity. We need to embrace Keats' negative capability. And even though it is difficult to sustain, it is certainly an advantage to brave "being in uncertainties, Mysteries, doubts, without any irritable reaching after fact and reason."[50] We needn't swaddle up all the uncertainties and mysteries into a tidy bundle of wisdom. We need to give them room to breathe and wriggle around and kick their feet.

I ask myself, "Am I afraid of ending the dialogue I have had with you?" The ending of a book, after all, is not the same as the ending of a life. Ending a book is not a wrapping up of all the loose ends and "falling plump into the grave, with a tombstone over our head." It is an opportunity to keep the motion going. Many of the words I have written here will probably reappear, materialize in some other form, in the essays and books that I write in the future. Ending a book is difficult because it entails the grief of separating from something precious we have been engaged with and become attached to. Finally, ending a book is simply one more acknowledgment that however free we sometimes imagine we are or might become, we are eternally bound by the unrelenting laws of time and space. Sometimes "house arrest" is a blessing.[51]

References and Notes

1 Fetishism and the Fetishism Strategy

References

Bloom, Harold (2002). *Genius: A Mosaic of One Hundred Exemplary Creative Minds.* New York: Warner Books, 2002.

Brooks, David (2003). "A Fetish of Candor," *The New York Times*, Op-Ed, December 13, 2003.

Cox, Caroline (2004). *Stiletto.* New York: Harper Design International.

Derrida, Jacques (1996). *Archive Fever: A Freudian Impression.* Trans. Eric Prenowitz. Chicago/London: The University of Chicago Press.

Foster, Hal (1993). "The Art of Fetishism: Notes on Dutch Still Life," *Fetishism as Cultural Discourse.* Eds. Emily Apter and William Pietz. Ithaca and London: Cornell University Press.

Kaplan, Louise (1991). *Female Perversions: The Temptations of Emma Bovary.* New York: Nan A.Talese/Doubleday.

Marx, Karl (1867) [1976]. *Capital Vol. I.* Eds. Ernest Mandel and New Left Review. Trans. Ben Fowles. London: Pelican Books. Reprinted in 1990 by Penguin Classics.

——— (1856). "Speech at the Anniversary of the *People's Paper*," in *Surveys from Exile.* Ed. David Feinbach. New York: Vintage Press.

Norwich, William (2003) "Rubber Maids," *The New York Times: Fashions of the Times*, August 17.

Ping, Wang (2000). *Aching for Beauty: Footbinding in China.* Minneapolis and London: University of Minnesota Press.

Smith, Dinitia (2004). "Real-Life Questions in an Upscale Fantasy," *Television, The New York Times.*

Thurman, Judith (2003). "Exposure Time," *The New Yorker*, April 13, 2003.

Webster, Merriam (1986). *Webster's Third New International Dictionary of the English Language, Unabridged.* Ed. Philip Babcock Gove. Springfield, MA. Merriam Webster, Inc.

Notes

1. Webster, 842, definition 2.
2. Kaplan, 35–6.
3. Norwich, 76–8.
4. Webster, 842.
5. Webster, 842.
6. Thurman, 108.

7. Bloom, 8.
8. Brooks.
9. Brooks.
10. Brooks.
11. Marx (1867), 342.
12. Marx (1867), 342.
13. Marx (1856), 300.
14. Kaplan, 33.
15. Derrida, 11.
16. Smith, 5.
17. Cox, *passim*, 82–3, 86.
18. Ping, 9.
19. Foster, 253.
20. Foster, 253–54.
21. Foster, 254.
22. Foster, 255.
23. Foster, 255.
24. Foster, 257.
25. Foster, 257.
26. Foster, 260.
27. Foster, 264.
28. Foster, 264.

2   UNRAVELING FREUD ON FETISHISM

References

Chernow, Barbara A. and Vallasi, George A., eds (1993). *The Columbia Encyclopedia* Fifth Edition. New York: Columbia University Press, Houghton Mifflin Company.

Freud, Sigmund (1905). "Three essays on the theory of sexuality," *Standard Edition*, Vll.

——— (1917). *Introductory Lectures*. Part III, *Standard Edition*, XVI.

——— (1924). "The dissolution of the Oedipus Complex," *Standard Edition*, XIX.

Freud, Sigmund (1925a). "Some psychical consequences of the anatomical distinction between the sexes," *Standard Edition*, XIX.

——— (1925b). "An autobiographical study," *Standard Edition*, XX. Postscript. (1935). *Standard Edition*, XX.

——— (1927). "Fetishism," *Standard Edtion*, XXI.

——— (1937). "Analysis terminable and interminable," *Standard Edition*, XXIII.

——— (1960). *Letters of Sigmund Freud*. Selected and edited, Ernest L. Freud; trans. by Tania and James Stern. New York: Basic Books.

——— and Andreas-Salome, Lou. *Letters*, Ed. Ernst Pfeiffer (1966), trans. Willaim and Elaine Robson Scott (1972). New York: Harcourt Brace Jovanovich, Inc. A Helen and Kurt Wolff Book.

Gay, Peter (1988). *Freud: A Life for our Time*. New York and London: W. W. Norton and Company.

Jones, Ernest (1957). *The Life and Work of Sigmund Freud: The Last Phase*, III. New York: Basic Books, Inc.

Kaplan, Louise J. (1991). *Female Perversions: The Temptations of Emma Bovary*. New York: Nan A Talese, Doubleday.

Nafasi, Azar (2000). *Reading Lolita in Tehran*. New York: Random House paperback, 2004.

Schur, Max (1972). *Freud: Living and Dying*. New York: International Universities Press, Inc.

Notes

1. Freud (1927), 154.
2. Freud (1927), 154.
3. Freud (1927), 154.
4. Freud (1927), 154.
5. Freud (1927), 157.
6. Freud (1927), 152.
7. Letter to Kata and Lajos Levy, June 11, 1923, Freud (1960).
8. Ibid.
9. Gay, 421, citing postcard to Sandor Ferenzi, Freud-Ferenzi Collection, Library of Congress.
10. Schur, 360, citing Freud's October 15, 1926 letter.
11. Ibid.
12. Gay, 422, citing Freud's August 13, 1923 letter.
13. Gay, 422, citing Freud's August 18, 1923 letter, Freud Museum, London.
14. Gay, 422, citing Freud's October 15, 1926 letter.
15. Schur, 365.
16. Jones, 94.
17. Jones, 94.
18. Jones, 95.
19. Jones, 95.
20. Jones, 95.
21. Jones, 95.
22. Schur, 396.
23. Schur, 364.
24. Schur, 379.
25. Freud and Salome, 154.
26. Freud and Salome, 154.
27. Freud (1925b) (1935), 71.
28. Freud (1925b) (1935),71.
29. Freud (1925b) (1935), 72.
30. Freud (1925b) (1935), 72.
31. Freud (1925a), 248.
32. Freud (1925a), 248.
33. Freud (1925a), 249.
34. Freud (1924), 178. Editors note that this paraphrase of Napoleon's epigram had already appeared in 1912, *SE*, 11, 189.
35. Freud (1925a), 252.
36. Freud (1925a), 252.
37. Freud (1925a), 252.
38. Gay, 515.
39. Gay, 515.
40. Gay, 515.
41. Gay, 515.
42. Freud (1925a), 252.

43. Freud (1925a), 252.
44. Freud (1925a), 253.
45. Freud (1925a), 253.
46. Freud and Salome, 154.
47. Schur, 384.
48. Freud (1927), 152.
49. Freud (1927), 152.
50. Freud (1927), 153.
51. Freud (1927), 155.
52. Freud (1927), 154.
53. Freud (1927), 154–55.
54. Freud (1937), 250–52.
55. Freud (1927), 157.
56. Freud (1927), 157.
57. Freud (1937), 250–52.
58. Chernow and Vallasi: Iran, 1355–6.
59. Nafasi, 26.
60. Nafasi, 27.
61. Nafasi, 72.
62. Nafasi, 73.
63. Nafasi, 73.
64. Nafasi, 73.
65. Freud (1927), 157.
66. Freud (1927), 157.
67. Freud (1927), 157.

3   Footbinding and the Cultures of Fetishism that Breed It

References

Levy, Howard S. (1966). *Chinese Footbinding: The History of a Curious Custom.* London: Neville Spearman Limited. New American edition: *Lotus Lovers: The Complete History of the Curious Erotic Custom of Footbinding in China.* Buffalo, NY: Prometheus (1992).

Ping, Wang (2000). *Aching for Beauty: Footbinding in China.* Minneapolis/London: University of Minnesota Press.

Tylim, Isaac (2004). "China: psychoanalysis' new frontier," *The Round Robin*, Spring.

Notes

1. Ping, 145.
2. Tylim, 5–6.
3. Tylim, 21.
4. Ping, 29–53, *passim.*
5. Ping, 29–30.
6. Ping, 33–4.
7. Ping, 145–73; 235–37.
8. Ping, 46–7.

9. Ping, 48.
10. Ping, 145–73.
11. Interviews: Levy, 203–85, *passim*.
12. Levy, 261–62.
13. Levy, 258.
14. Levy 225, 254, 263.
15. Levy, 24, 25.
16. Levy, 222–23 and 203–28, *passim*. Ping, 18–24.
17. Levy drawings 42, 43, 115, photographs 79, 94, 231.
18. Levy, 136–37.
19. Levy, 134–35.
20. Levy, 133.
21. Levy, 160–63.
22. Levy, 160–63.
23. Levy, 160–63.
24. Levy, 160–63.
25. Levy 78–92, 99–103.
26. Ping, 36–41.
27. Levy, 207.
28. Levy, 276–77.
29. Levy, 209–10.

4   THE BODY OF A WOMAN

References

Bourneville, D. M. and P. Regnard (1877, 1878, 1879–80). *Iconographique de las Salpetriere, Service de M. Charcot*. Vols I–III. Paris Delahaye (as cited in Evans).

Calef, Victor and Edward M. Weinshel (1972). "On certain neurotic equivalents of Necrophilia," *International Journal of Psychoanalysis* Vol. 55, Part 1, 67–75.

Denby, David (2003). "American Dreamers." Film review: "Open Range," "Thirteen." *The New Yorker*, September 1, 2003.

Dervin, Daniel (1992). "Foucault's preemption of Freud's sexual discourse," unpublished paper.

Dijkstra, Bram (1986). *Idols of Perversity: Fantasies of Feminine Evil in Fin-de Siecle Culture*. New York and Oxford: Oxford University Press.

Evans, Martha N. (1991). *Fits and Starts: A Geneology of Hysteria in Modern France*. Ithaca: Cornell University Press.

Holden, Stephen. "Desperately Trying to Relate To Her Body by Cutting It," *The New York Times*, November 7, 2003.

Isaak, Jo Anna (1991). "What's love got to do, got to do with it: woman as the glitch in the postmodern record," *American Imago* 48: 351–80.

Kaplan, Louise J. (1993). "Fits and misfits: The body of a woman," *American Imago* 50: 457–80.

Legrand du Saulle, Henri (1891). *Les Hysteriques: Etat physique et dal mental. Actes, insolites, delictueux, et criminels*. Paris: Bailliere (as cited by Evans).

Miller, Arthur (1971). *Collected Plays*. Vol. II. New York: Viking.

Oppenheimer, Joel (1981). *Marilyn Lives*. New York: Delilah.

Ostow, Mortimer (1986). "Archetypes of apocalypse in dreams and fantasies," *American Imago* 43: 301–33.

Richet, Charles (1980). "Les Demoniagues d'aujourd'hui et d'authrefois," *Le Revue des Deux Mondes* 37: 340–72 (as cited by Evans).

Rollyson, Carl (1986). *Marilyn Monroe: A Life of the Actress.* Ann Arbor: UMI Research Press (reprinted 1993). New York: De Capo Press.

Schnitzler, Arthur (2002). "Dream Story" in *Night Games*, trans. Margaret Schaefer. Chicago: Ivan R. Dee.

Simon, John (2002). Foreword: Schnitzler, *Night Games.*

Spoto, Donald (1993). *Marilyn Monroe: The Biography.* New York: Harper Collins.

Summers, Anthony (1985). *Goddess: The Secret Lives of Marilyn Monroe.* London: Victor Gollanz, Ltd.

Notes

1. Photographs, Isaak, 364, 365.
2. Dijkstra, 101.
3. Legrand du Saulle, 495.
4. Legrand du Saulle, 495.
5. Legrand du Saulle, 495–96.
6. Legrand du Saulle, 496.
7. Richert, 346.
8. Evans, 31–40.
9. Kaplan, 459.
10. Dervin, 7.
11. Kaplan, 460.
12. Dervin, 7.
13. Dervin, 7.
14. Kaplan, 461.
15. Rollyson, 59.
16. Summers, 190.
17. Spoto, 443.
18. Summers, 192.
19. Kaplan, 466.
20. Miller, 29.
21. Miller, 110.
22. Miller, 111.
23. Spoto, 435.
24. Spoto, 446.
25. Summers, 175. Spoto, 471.
26. Oppenheimer, 55.
27. Kaplan, 471–72.
28. Kaplan, 473.
29. Kaplan, 474.
30. Ostow, 301–33.
31. Ostow, 308.
32. Ostow, 321.
33. Ostow, 321.
34. Simon, ix.

35. Simon, viii.
36. Simon, ix.
37. Simon, xi.
38. Denby, 131.
39. Holden.
40. Holden.

5   WRITING ON THE SKIN

References

Anzieu, Didier (1989). *The Skin Ego*. London: Karnac.
——— (1990). *A Skin for Thought: Interviews with Gilbert Tarrab*. London: Karnac.
Asch, Stuart (1971). "Wrist scratching as a symptom of anhedonia: a pre-depressive state," *Psychoanalytic Quarterly* 40.
Bram, Christopher. Personal communication, October 15, 2005.
Crabtree, L. (1967). "A psychotherapeutic encounter with a self-mutilating patient," *Psychiatry* 30.
Doctors, Shelley (1979). "The Symptom of Delicate Self-Cutting in Adolescent Females: A Developmental View." Doctoral dissertation, Ferkauf Graduate School, Yeshiva University.
——— (1981). Abbreviated version of thesis. *Adolescent Psychiatry* 9.
Emerson, L. E. (1914). "The case of Miss A: a preliminary report of a psychoanalytic study of self mutilation," *Psychoanalytic Review* 1: 41–54.
Erikson, Erik (1950). *Childhood and Society*. New York: W.W. Norton and Company, Inc.
Green, Terisa (2005). *Ink: The Not-Just-Skin-Deep Guide to Getting a Tattoo*. New York: New American Library.
Grosz, Elizabeth (1994). *Volatile Bodies: Toward a Corporeal Feminism*. Bloomington and Indianapolis: Indiana University Press.
Grunebaum and Klerman G. (1967). "Wrist Slashing," *American Journal of Psychiatry* 124: 527–34.
Kafka, John S. (1969). "The body as transitional object: a psychoanalytic study of a mutilating patient," *British Journal of Medical Psychology* 42.
Kaplan, Louise J. (1977). *Oneness and Separateness: From Infant to Individual*. New York: Simon and Schuster.
Kaplan, Louise J. (1984). *Adolescence: The Farewell to Childhood*. New York: Simon and Schuster.
——— (1991). *Female Perversions: The Temptations of Emma Bovary*. New York: Nan A.Talese/Doubleday.
Kitamura, Takahiro and Katie M. Kitamura (2001). *Bushido:Lagacies of the Japanese Tattoo*. Atglen, PA: Schiffer Publishing Ltd.
Lincoln, Bruce (1981) *Emerging From the Chrysalis*. Cambridge, MA: Harvard University Press.
Lingis, Alphonso (1984). *Excesses: Eros and Culture*. New York: State University of New York.
Novotny, Peter (1972). "Self-Cutting," *Bulletin of the Menninger Foundation: Clinic* 36: 505–14.
Ping-Nei, Pao (1969). "The syndrome of delicate self-cutting," *British Journal of Medical Psychology* 42.

Podvoli, Edward M. (1969). "Self mutilation in a hospital setting: A study of identity and social compliance," *British Journal of Medical Psychology* 42.

Rosenthal, C. Rinzler, R. Wallsh, and E. Klausner (1972). "Wrist cutting syndrome: the meaning of a gesture," *American Journal of Psychiatry* 128.

Turner, Victor (1969). *The Ritual Process.* Chicago: Aldine Publishing Company.

van Gennep, Arnold (1960) [1908]. *The Rites of Passage.* Translated by Monika Vizedom and Gabrielle I. Caffee. Chicago: The University of Chicago Press.

Wakefield, P., Frank A., and Meyers R. (1977), "The hobbyist: A euphemism for self-mutilation and fetishism," *Bulletin of the Menninger Foundation Clinic* 41.

Notes

1. van Gennep, 72.
2. Lincoln, 1.
3. Lincoln, 98.
4. Turner, 53.
5. Erikson, 130.
6. Erikson, 130–32.
7. Erikson, 129.
8. Erikson, 129.
9. Erikson, 129.
10. Erikson, 129.
11. Composite, Anzieu (1989), 14 and *Columbia Encyclopedia*, "Epidermis."
12. Kaplan, Clinical experience.
13. Kaplan, Clinical experience.
14. Anzieu (1990), 63–64.
15. Composite, Grosz, *passim* and Kaplan, Clinical experience.
16. Grosz and Kaplan, Clinical experience.
17. Grosz.
18. Lingus, 140.
19. Kaplan (1991), 368.
20. This book: chapter one.
21. This book: chapter three.
22. Kaplan (1984), 106–07; Kaplan (1991), 373–74.
23. Kaplan (1991), *passim*.
24. Doctors (1979), 184.
25. Doctors (1979), 185.
26. Novotny, . . . 505.
27. Grunebaum and Klerman, 529.
28. Clinical experience of author.
29. Rosenthal et al., 1367.
30. Clinical experience of author.
31. Kafka, 210.
32. Kafka, 209.
33. Identification with mother: Asch, 614–17.
34. Author interpretation.
35. Asch, 613.
36. Asch, 613.
37. Wakefield et al., *passim*.
38. Wakefield et al., *passim*.

39. Wakefield et al., 547.
40. Wakefield, et al., 547–48.
41. Wakefield et al., 541.
42. Green, 82–3.
43. Green, 87.
44. Composite, Green 24–37 and author observations.
45. Green, 24–37.
46. Green, 24.
47. Kitamura and Kitamura, 4.
48. Kitamura and Kitamura, 7.
49. Kitamura and Kitamura, 9.
50. Kitamura and Kitamura, 19–20.
51. Kitamura and Kitamura, 20.
52. Kitamura and Kitamura, 30.
53. Kitamura and Kitamura, 147, 151.
54. Kitamura and Kitamura, 23.
55. Kitamura and Kitamura, 129.
56. Kitamura and Kitamura, 128.
57. Grosz, 138.
58. Grosz, 139–43.
59. Grosz, 142.
60. Grosz, 142.
61. Grosz, 142.
62. Grosz, 142.
63. Bram.
64. Kitamura and Kitamura, 115.

6 Archive Fever

References

Derrida, Jacques (1996). *Archive Fever: A Freudian Impression*, trans. Eric Prenowitz. Chicago: The University of Chicago Press.

Deresiewicz, William (1999). "His Cigar is Just a Cigar," *The New York Times Book Review*, November 14, 1999.

Edel, Leon (1984). *Writing Lives: Principia Biographica*. New York and London: W.W. Norton and Co.

——— (1962). "The Biographer and Psycho-analysis," read at the Edward Hitschmann Memorial Meeting at the Boston Psychoanalytic Society and Institute, March 23, 1961, *International Journal of Psychoanalysis* 42: 458–66.

Eder, Richard (1999). "The Long and the Short of an Author's Life," *The New York Times*, October 15, 1999.

Fish, Stanley (1999). "Just Published: Minutiae Without Meaning," *The New York Times*, Op-Ed, Tuesday, September 7, 1999.

Hoddeson, David (1997). Special editor, "Biography," in *American Imago* 54, No. 4. Introduction, 323–32.

Karl, Frederick R. (2001). "The Long and the Short of It," *Biography and Source Studies* VI, ed. Frederick R. Karl. New York: AMS Press, Inc., 115–38.

Marx, Karl (1844). "Speech at the Anniversary of the *People's Paper*," in *Surveys from Exile*, edited by David Feinbach. New York: Vintage, 1974.

Maurois, Andre (1929). "Biography as a Means of Expression," in *Aspects of Biography*. Trans. Sydney Castle Roberts. New York: Appleton, 1929.

Schorer, Mark (1968). "The Burdens of Biography," in *The World We Imagine*, selected essays. New York: Farrar, Strauss and Giroux.

Smith, Dinitia (2004). "Graham Greene Biography, Heavy on Sex, Draws some Outrage," *The New York Times*, Thursday, November 4, 2004.

Strachey, Lytton (1918). *Eminent Victorians*. London: Chatto & Windus, Penguin Books (1948/1986), Preface, 9–11.

Updike, John (1999). "One Cheer for Literary Biography," *The New York Review of Books*, Vol. 46, No. 2, February 4, 1999.

Willis, Ellen (1999). "Other People's Lives," *The New York Times Book Review*, November 21, 1999.

Wineapple, Brenda (1997). "Mourning Becomes Biography," in *American Imago* 54, No. 4, 437–49.

Woolf, Virginia (1928). *Orlando*. New York: Penguin Press.

——— (1933). *Flush*. New York and London: Harcourt, Inc.

Notes

1. Marx, 300.
2. Derrida, 91.
3. Strachey, 9.
4. Strachey, 10.
5. Woolf (1928), 65.
6. Woolf (1928).
7. Woolf (1933).
8. Edel (1962), 460–61.
9. Edel (1962), 461.
10. Edel (1962), 461.
11. Edel (1962), 460.
12. Edel (1962), 460.
13. Edel (1962), 460.
14. Edel (1962), 460.
15. Edel (1962), 460.
16. Strachey, 10.
17. Edel (1984), 33.
18. Edel (1984), 33.
19. Hoddeson, 324.
20. Maurois, 125.
21. Edel (1984), 68.
22. Maurois, 125.
23. Schorer, 238.
24. Schorer, 239.
25. Edel (1984), 74.
26. Edel (1984), 77.
27. Edel (1984), 78.
28. Edel (1984), 78.
29. Edel (1984), 78.
30. Strachey, 9.
31. Edel (1984), 98.

32. Edel (1984), 98.
33. Edel (1984), 101.
34. Edel (1984), 101.
35. Eder.
36. Marx, 300.
37. Smith.
38. Smith.
39. Smith.
40. Smith.
41. Smith.
42. Eder.
43. Eder.
44. Eder.
45. Eder.
46. Eder.
47. Eder.
48. Eder.
49. Eder.
50. Eder.
51. Eder.
52. Eder.
53. Deresciewicz, 42.
54. Deresciewicz, 42.
55. Deresciewicz, 42.
56. Fish.
57. Fish.
58. Willis.
59. Updike, 3.
60. Updike, 3.
61. Updike, 3.
62. Updike, 4.
63. Updike, 4.
64. Updike, 4.
65. Updike, 5.
66. Updike, 5.
67. Karl, 115.
68. Karl, 122.
69. Karl, 115.
70. Karl, 117–18.
71. Karl, 119–21.
72. Karl, 135.
73. Karl, 135–36.
74. Karl, 136.
75. Derrida, 11.
76. Wineapple, 446.
77. Wineapple, 440.
78. Wineapple, 438.
79. Wineapple, 441.
80. Wineapple, 444.
81. Edel (1962), 458.

82. Edel (1962), 458.
83. Edel (1962), 459.
84. Edel (1962), 459.
85. Edel (1962), 465.
86. Edel (1962), 465.
87. Edel (1962), 465.

7   UNFREE ASSOCIATIONS

References

Arlow, Jacob A. and Charles, Brenner (1963). *Psychoanalytic Concepts and the Structural Theory*. New York: International Universities Press.

Bergmann, Martin, ed. (2000). *The Hartmann Era* (transcripts from 1998 conference sponsored by Psychoanalytic Research and Development Fund). New York: Other Press.

Bion, Wilfred R. (1967). "Notes on memory and desire," *Psychoanalytic Forum*. 2:272–273: 279–80.

—— (1977). "On a quotation from Freud," in *Borderline Personality Disorders: The Concept, The Syndrome, The Patient*, ed. P. Hartocollis. New York: International Universities Press, 511–17.

Brenner, Charles (1976). *Psychoanalytic Technique and Psychic Conflict*. New York: International Universities Press.

—— (1982). *The Mind in Conflict*, Madison, CT: International Universities Press.

Derrida, Jacques (1996). *Archive Fever: A Freudian Impression*, trans. Erick Prenowitz. Chicago and London: The University of Chicago Press.

Dimen, Muriel (2003). *Sexuality, Intimacy, Power*. Hillsdale, NJ: Analytic Press.

Edel, Leon (1962). "The biographer and psycho-analysis," *International Journal of Psychoanalysis*, 42, 458–66.

—— (1984). *Writing Lives, Principia Biographia*. New York: W.W, Norton and Co.

Freud, Sigmund (1923). *Two encyclopedia articles: (A) psychoanalysis, Standard Edition* 18: 233–259. London: Hogarth Press.

Grossman, William (1992). "Comments on the concept of the analyzing instrument," in *The Analyzing Instrument of Otto Isakower, M.D.* (see below Wyman and Rittenberg).

—— (1995). "Psychological vicissitudes of theory in clinical work," *International Journal of Psychoanalysis*, 885–899.

Keats, John (1818). *Complete Letters of John Keats*, ed. Hyder Rollins, Cambridge, MA: 1988.

Kernberg, Otto (1996). "Thirty methods to destroy the creativity of psychoanalytic candidates," *International Journal of Psychoanalysis*, 31–1040.

Kirsner, Douglas (2000). *Unfree Associations: Inside Psychoanalytic Institutes*. London: Process Press.

Lear, Jonathan (1998). "Knowingness and abandonment: an Oedipus for our time," as reported by Christopher J. Allegra in *Bulletin* of The Association for Psychoanalytic Medicine 38, Spring, 2003.

Morganthaler, F. (1986). "Der Traum.Fragmente zur Theorie und Technik der Traumdeutung," *Edition Qumran*. Frankfurt, Germany and New York: Campus Verlag, as cited in Zweibel.

Schulman, Martin (2004). "*The Hartman Era*," a review in *Psychoanalytic Psychology*, Spring, 2004.

Wachtel, Paul (2003). "Full pockets, empty lives: a psychoanalytic exploration of the contemporary culture of greed." *American Journal of Psychoanalysis* 63. New York: Association for the Advancement of Psychoanalysis.

Waelder, Robert (1960). *Basic Theory of Psychoanalysis.* New York: International Universities Press.

Wyman, Herbert M. and Stephen M. Rittenberg, eds (1992). *The Analyzing Instrument of Otto Isakower, M.D.: Evolution of a Psychoanalytic Concept, Journal of Clinical Psychoanalysis* 1, No. 2. Madison, CT: International Universities Press, Inc.

Zweibel, Ralf (2004). "The third position: reflections about the internal analytic working process," *Psychoanalytic Quarterly* 73, No. 1.

Notes

1. Waelder, x.
2. Kirsner, 2.
3. Derrida, 1.
4. Derrida, 2.
5. Kernberg, 1039.
6. Edel (1984), 33.
7. Kernberg, 1032.
8. Kernberg, 1036.
9. Kernberg, 1036.
10. Kernberg, 1037.
11. Kernberg, 1038.
12. Kirsner, 24.
13. Kirsner, 31 (quoting Zvi Lothane).
14. Freud, 239.
15. Wyman and Rittenberg, 201.
16. Grossman (1992), 268.
17. Grossman (1995), 895.
18. Kirsner, 31 (quoting Jacob Arlow).
19. Bergman, 106 (quoting Andre Green).
20. Bergman, 248–49 (quoting Andre Green).
21. Schulman, paraphrasing Bergman, 60.
22. Bergmann, 5.
23. Bergmann, 161 (quoting Anton Kris).
24. Bergmann, 228–29 (quoting Otto Kernberg).
25. Bergmann, 232 (quoting Mortimer Ostow).
26. Bergmann, 233 (quoting Mortimer Ostow).
27. Arlow and Brenner, foreword, viii.
28. Author's paraphrasing of Brenner (1982), 252.
29. Brenner, 1976, 190–92
30. Bion (1967), 222.
31. Brenner (1982), 251–52.
32. Keats, December 21, 1818.
33. Keats, December 21, 1818.
34. Bion (1997), 511.
35. Bion (1997), 511.
36. Bion (1997), 512–13.

37. Bion (1977), 513.
38. Lear reported by Allegra, 5.
39. Lear, 5.
40. Dimen, 39.
41. Dimen, 40.
42. Dimen, 32.
43. Zweibel, 217.
44. Zweibel, 217, quoting Morgenthaler.
45. Zweibel, 217.
46. Wachtel, 110.
47. Wachtel, 110.
48. Wachtel, 112.
49. Wachtel, 113.
50. Edel, 465.
51. Wachtel, 113.
52. Wachtel, 118.

8   THE FETISHISM OF COMMODITIES

References

Amariglio, Jack and Antonio, Callari (1993). "Marxian Value Theory and the Problem of the Role of Commodity Fetishism," in Apter and Pietz.

Apter, Emily and Pietz William, eds. (1993). *Fetishism as Cultural Discourse*. Ithaca and London: Cornell University Press.

Bai, Matt, "The New Boss," *The New York Times Magazine*, January 30, 2005.

Barboza, David (2005). "Stream of Chinese Exports is Becoming a Flood," *The New York Times*, April 4.

——— (2005). "China, New Land of Shoppers, Builds Malls on Gigantic Scale," *The New York Times*, May 25.

——— (2005). "Ogre to Slay? Outsource It To the Chinese," *The New York Times*, December 9.

——— (2006). Sharp Labor Shortage in China May Lead to World Trade Shift, *The New York Times*, April 3.

——— (2005). and Altman, Daniel, "That Blur? It's China Moving Up the Pack," *The New York Times*, December 21.

Bradsher, Keith (2005). "Tycoons Extend Rivalry to Chinese Television," *The New York Times*, August 27.

——— (2005). "China Retreats Now, But It Will Be Back," *The New York Times*, August 3.

——— (2005). "Saying Goodbye to Mr. Greenspan," *The New York Times*, July 21.

Brottman, Mikita (2005). Reality TV: history and format. Personal communication, April.

Engels, Friederich (1845). *Conditions of the Working Class in England* (Liepsig: *Die Lage der arbietenden Klasse in England*) London: Blackwell, 1958.

Fenichel, Otto (1938). In *Collected Papers of Otto Fenichel*, Second Series. New York: W.W. Norton and Company, Inc., 1954.

Fernbach, David, ed. (1974). *Surveys from Exile* (Karl Marx, Political Writings Vol II). NewYork: Vintage Books.

Freud, Sigmund (1920). *Beyond the Pleasure Principle, Standard Edition*, XVIII. London: The Hogarth Press and the Institute of Psychoanalysis.

Human Rights Watch: Child Labor (2005). 1–4.

Kahn, Joseph (2004). "China's Elite Learn to Flaunt While the New Landless Weep," *The New York Times*, December 25.

Kamenka, Eugene, ed. (1983). *The Portable Karl Marx*. New York: Viking Penguin.

Kaplan, Ann E. (2005). *Survivor* format. Personal communication, April.

Keenan, Thomas (1993). "The Point is to (Ex)change it." In Apter and Pietz.

Klosterman, Chuck (2004). *Sex, Drugs and Cocoa Puffs: A Low Culture Manifesto*. New York: Scribner.

Lohr, Steve (2005). "Unocol Bid Denounced at Hearing," *The New York Times*, July 13.

Marx, Karl (1867), [1976]. *Capital Vol. I*. Eds. Ernest Mandel and New Left Review, trans. Ben Fowles. London: Pelican Books. Reprinted in 1990 by Penguin Classics.

—— (1856). "Speech at the Anniversary of the *People's Paper*." In Fernbach.

—— (1852) [1869]. "The Eighteenth Brumaire of Louis Bonaparte," In Fernbach, In Kamenka, In Wilson.

—— (1848). "Manifesto of the Communist Party." In Kamenka, in Wilson.

—— (1844). "Alienated Labour: First Manuscript." in Kamenka.

—— (1844). "On the Power of Money in Bourgeois Society." In McLellan.

—— (1842). "The Leading Article," as cited by Pietz.

McLellan, David, ed. (1977). *Karl Marx, Selected Writings*. Oxford: Oxford University Press.

Ollman, Bertell (1971). *Alienation*. Cambridge: Cambridge University Press.

—— (1993). *Dialectical Investigations*. New York and London: Routledge, Chapman and Hall.

Pietz, William (1993). "Fetishism and Materialism: The Limits of Theory in Marx." In Apter and Pietz.

Siddiqui, Farraaz and Harry Anthony, Patrinos (2005). "Child Labor: Issues, Causes and Interventions." Human Capital Development and Operations Policy.

Stein, Mark A. (2005). "China's Shot Heard Around the World," *The New York Times*, August, 3.

Thompson, Ginger (2005). "Fraying of a Latin Textile Industry," Made Elsewhere series. *The New York Times*, March 25.

Wheen, Francis (1999) (2001). *Karl Marx: A Life*. New York and London: W.W. Norton and Company.

Wilson, Edmund (1940) (2003). *To The Finland Station*. New York: The New York Review of Books.

Notes

1. Fernbach, 300.
2. Marx (1867) [1976], 163.
3. Fenichel, 91.
4. Vilfredo Pareto as cited by Ollman (1971), 3. Pareto was referring to the ambiguities in Marx's writings. I am saying that the ambiguities in Marx's language reflect the ambiguities of the world he was trying to understand.
5. Marx (1867) [1976], 342.
6. Described in Pietz, 135–36.
7. McLellan, 110—11.
8. Kamenka, 133.
9. Marx (1867) [1976], 163.

206   REFERENCES AND NOTES

10. Wilson, 140–41.
11. Wheen, 83.
12. Wheen, 83.
13. Wheen, 85.
14. Wheen, 87.
15. Wheen, 85.
16. Wilson, 131.
17. Wilson, 134.
18. Wilson, 147.
19. Wilson, 156–57.
20. Wilson, 158–59.
21. Kamenka, 287 footnote; Fernbach, 146 footnote.
22. Kamenka, 287 footnote; Fernbach, 146 footnote.
23. Freud (1920).
24. Marx translated by Wilson, 310.
25. Marx in Kamenka, 287.
26. Kamenka, 372.
27. Kamenka, 69.
28. Ollman, 11.
29. Wilson, 284.
30. Marx (1867) [1976], 163.
31. Wilson, 286; Wheen, 309.
32. Keenan, 183; Mandell, 163.
33. Marx (1867) [1976], 163
34. Wilson, 206.
35. Wheen, 184.
36. Wheen, 185.
37. Wilson, 207.
38. Wilson, 206.
39. Wilson, 206.
40. Wheen, 185.
41. Marx, in Kamenka, 132.
42. Marx, in Kamenka, 132.
43. Marx, in Kamenka, 132.
44. Marx, in Kamenka, 133.
45. Marx (1867) [1976], 353.
46. Marx (1867) [1976], 355.
47. Marx (1867) [1976], 356.
48. Marx (1867) [1976], 366–67.
49. Marx (1867) [1976], 367.
50. Marx (1867) [1976], 367.
51. Marx (1867) [1976], 535.
52. Marx (1867) [1976], 535.
53. Marx (1867) [1976], 611.
54. Bai, 40.
55. Bai, 40.
56. Thompson.
57. Thompson.
58. Barboza, April 4, 2005.

59. Barboza, December 9, 2005.
60. Barboza, December 9, 2005.
61. Barboza and Altman
62. Kahn.
63. Barboza, April 3, 2006.
64. Bradsher, August 3, 2005; Stein.
65. Bradsher, July 21, 2005; Stein; Lohr.
66. Barboza, May 25, 2005.
67. Bradsher, August 27, 2005.
68. Human Rights Watch: Child Labor, 1.
69. Siddiqui and Patrinos, 2
70. Human Rights Watch: Child Labor, 1.
71. Author observations, Kaplan A., and Brottman. (for *survivor* and *apprentice*)
72. Author observations.
73. Brottman.
74. Klosterman, 28.
75. Klosterman, 28.
76. Klosterman, 28
77. Klosterman, 29.
78. Klosterman, 29.
79. Klosterman, 31.
80. Klosterman, 31.
81. Klosterman, 32
82. Klosterman, 33.
83. Klosterman, 40.
84. Marx (1856), 300.

9 ROBOTS AND HUMANS

References

Breazeal, Cynthia (2002). *Designing Sociable Robots.* Cambridge, MA, and London: The MIT Press.

Brooks, Rodney A. (2003). *Flesh and Machines: How Robots Will Change Us.* New York: Vintage Books, division of Random House.

Chamberlain, Ted (2005). *National Geographic.com/news*, July 6.

Davis, Joseph (2005). Personal communication on Jeremiah parable. December 20, 2005.

Edel, Leon (1984). *Writing Lives: Principia Biographia.* New York and London: W.W. Norton and Company.

Ginzberg, Louis (1968) [1928]. *Legends of the Jews* Vol. IV (from Yalkut Reubeni). Philadelphia: The Jewish Publications Society.

Ichbiah, Daniel (2005). *Robots: From science fiction to technology revolution*, translated from the French, *Genese d'un peuple artificiel* by Ken Kincaid. New York: Harry N. Abrams, Inc.

Kaywin, Louis (1968). "The evocation of a genie: a study of an 'as-if' character type," *The Psychoanalytic Quarterly.* New York: The Psychoanalytic Quarterly, Inc.

Levi, Primo (1984). *The Periodic Table*, translated from the Italian by Raymond Rosenthal. New York: Shocken Books.

Marx, Karl (1856). "Speech at the Anniversary of the *"People's Paper,"* in *Surveys from Exile*. Ed David Fernbach. New York: Vintage Press.

Maturana, Humberto and Francisco, Varela (1973) [1980]. "Autopoiesis and Cognition: The Realization of the Living." Eds. Robert S. Cohen and Marx W. Wartofsky. *Boston Studies in the Philosophy of Science* 42. Dordrecht, Netherlands: D. Reidel Publishing Co.

MIT Robotic Life Group, personal communication, April 28, 2005.

Reich, Steve and Beryl, Korot (2001). "Three Tales," video-concert performance at Brooklyn Academy of Music.

Ross, Nathaniel (1967). "The 'as if' concept," *Journal of the American Psychoanalytic*, 15, No. 1. New York: International Universities Press, Inc.

Sokolowski, Robert (1988). "Natural and Artificial Intelligence," in *DAEDALUS* Journal of the American Academy of Arts and Sciences 117, No. 1. Cambridge, MA: Academy of Arts and Sciences.

Strachey, Lytton (1918). *Eminent Victorians*. London: Chatto & Windus, Penguin Books (1948/1986). Preface.

Turo, Joann, personal communication: as-if as the new hysteria, July 21, 2004.

Weiss, Joseph (1966). Reporter, Panel: "Clinical and Theoretical Aspects of 'As If' Characters," *Journal of American Psychoanalytic Association* 14, No. 3. New York: International Universities Press, Inc.

Wikipedia.com, "Autopoeisis," April 30, 2005.

Notes

1. Ginzberg, 402. Source, Prof. Davis.
2. Ichbiah, 114.
3. Ichbiah, 40–1.
4. Ichbiah, 40–1.
5. Ichbiah, 41.
6. Ichbiah, 41.
7. Ichbiah, 43.
8. Ichbiah, 50; Brooks, 72.
9. Brooks, 11.
10. Kaywin, Ross, Weiss, *passim*.
11. Kaywin, 22–4.
12. Turo.
13. Breazeal with Kismet in Reich and Korot.
14. Brooks, 93 (with photo).
15. Breazeal, 109.
16. Breazeal, 109.
17. Breazeal, 123.
18. Breazeal, 109–10
19. Breazeal, 157–68; photos, 166, 168.
20. Brooks, 54–5.
21. Brooks, 95.
22. Breazeal, 235.
23. Breazeal, 235, footnote.
24. Ichbiah, 121.
25. Ichbiah, 121.
26. Ichbiah, 121–22, photos, 122, 123; Brooks, 70–1.

27. Ichbiah, 122.
28. Ichbiah, 125.
29. Ichbiah, 125.
30. Ichbiah, 185.
31. Ichbiah, 185.
32. Ichbiah, 183.
33. Ichbiah, 128.
34. Ichbiah, 190–92.
35. Ichbiah, 150.
36. Chamberlain, 1.
37. Chamberlain, 1.
38. Ichbiah, 152.
39. Ichbiah, 152–53.
40. Ichbiah, 152.
41. Brooks, 73.
42. MIT Robotic Life Group; Wikipedia.com.
43. Varela and Maturana, 78.
44. Wikipedia.com.
45. Ichbiah, 516–19.
46. Ichbiah, 516.
47. Ichbiah, 518.
48. Ichbiah 519.
49. Brooks, 208.
50. Sokolowski, 45–8.
51. Sokolowski, 48.
52. Sokolowski, 48.
53. Brooks, 173.
54. Brooks, 174.
55. Levi, 232–33.
56. Edel, 33.
57. Strachey, 10.
58. Edel, 33.
59. Marx, 300.

10   CULTURES OF FETISHISM

References

Carey, Benedict (2004). "Babes in a Grown-up Toyland," *The New York Times*. November 28, 2004.

Carroll, Linda (2004). "The Problem with Some 'Smart' Toys: (Hint) Use Your Imagination," *The New York Times*, October 26.

Carvajal, Doreen (2005). "A Way to Calm Fussy Baby: 'Sesame Street' by Cellphone," *The New York Times*, April 18.

Derrida, Jacques (1996). *Archive Fever: A Freudian Impression*, trans. Erick Prenowitz. Chicago and London: The University of Chicago Press.

Dimen, Muriel (2003). *Sexuality, Intimacy and Power*. Hillsdale, NJ: Analytic Press.

Edel, Leon (1984). *Writing Lives: Principia Biographia*. New York and London: W.W. Norton and Co.

Foster, Hal (1993). "The Art of Fetishism: Notes on Dutch Still Life," in Emily, Apter and William, Pietz, *Fetishism as Cultural Discourse.* Cornell: Cornell University Press.

Harmon, Amy 2003, "More Consumers Reach Out to Touch the Screeen," *The New York Times*, November 17.

Holden, Stephen 2003, "Desperately Trying to Relate to Her Body by Cutting It," *The New York Times*, November 7.

Ichbiah, Daniel (2005). *Robots: From Science Fiction to Technological Revolution.* Trans. Ken Kincaid, *Genese d'un peuple artificiel.* New York: Harry N. Abrams, Inc.

Kamenka, Eugene (1983). *The Portable Karl Marx.* New York:Viking: Penguin.

Kaplan, Louise J. (1977). *Oneness and Separateness: From Infant to Individual.* New York: Simon and Schuster.

——— (1984). *Adolescence: The Farewell to Childhood.* New York: Simon and Schuster.

——— (1995). *No Voice is Ever Wholly Lost.* New York: Simon and Schuster.

Keats, John (1818). *Complete Letters of John Keats.* Ed. Hyder Rollins. Cambridge, MA: 1988.

Kernberg, Otto (1996). "Thirty methods to destroy the creativity of psychoanalytic candidates," *International Journal of Psychoanalysis* 30.

Levi, Primo (1984) [1975]. *The Periodic Table.* Translated from the Italian by Raymond Rosenthal. NewYork: Schocken Books.

Lewin, Tamar (2003). "A Growing Number of Viewers Watch From Crib," *The New York Times*, October 29.

Markoff, John (2003). "Vision of Personal Computers as Heart of Home Entertainment," *The New York Times*, November 17.

Marx, Karl (1852) (1869). "The 18th Brumaire of Louis Bonaparte." In Kamenka, in Wilson.

Schiesel, Seth (2003). "Ideas Unlimited, Built to Order," *The New York Times*, October 30.

Strachey, Lytton (1918). *Eminent Victorians.* London: Chatto & Windus, Penguin Books (1948/1986). Preface.

Wachtel, Paul (2003). "Full pockets, empty lives: a psychoanalytic exploration of the contemporary culture of greed," *The American Journal of Psychoanalysis* 63, No. 2.

Wilson, Edmund (1940) [2003]. *To The Finland Station.* New York: The New York Review of Books.

Woolf, Virginia (1928). *Orlando,* New York: Penguin Press.

Notes

1. Holden.
2. Holden.
3. Holden.
4. Schiesel.
5. Schiesel.
6. Schiesel.
7. Ichbiah, 522.
8. Ichbiah, 523.
9. Ichbiah, 523.
10. Ichbiah, 523.
11. Foster, 260.

12. Wachtel, 116.
13. Wachtel, 115.
14. Wachtel, 115.
15. Markoff.
16. Markoff.
17. Harmon.
18. Harmon.
19. Carvajal
20. Lewin.
21. Lewin.
22. Lewin.
23. Carroll.
24. Keats, December 21, 1818.
25. Keats, December 21, 1818.
26. Levi, 33.
27. Levi, 33.
28. Levi, 33.
29. This book, chapter four.
30. This book, chapter four.
31. This book, chapter three.
32. This book, chapter three
33. This book, chapter nine.
34. Greenaway's *The Pillow Book*. This book, chapter five.
35. This book, chapter six.
36. Strachey, 10
37. Woolf, 38.
38. Composite of Strachey and Woolf.
39. Kaplan (1977).
40. Kaplan (1984), 151.
41. Kaplan (1984), 151–52.
42. Kaplan (1984), 151.
43. Marx, in Wilson, 310
44. Marx, in Kamenka, 287 footnote.
45. Marx, in Kamenka, 288.
46. Kernberg, 1039.
47. Strachey, 10.
48. Edel, 33.
49. Dimen, 59.
50. Keats, December 21, 1818.
51. Derrida, 2.

INDEX